PENGUIN TRAVEL LIBRARY

THE COMING OF THE BARBARIANS

Pat Barr was born in Norwich and read English at Birmingham University and University College, London. She lived in Japan for three years before returning to Britain and now divides her time between Norwich and the Hebridean island of Coll. *The Coming of the Barbarians* was her first book. This was followed by *The Deer Cry Pavilion*, *A Curious Life for a Lady*, *To China with Love*, *The Memsahibs* and *Taming the Jungle*. She then turned her hand to fiction with the immensely successful *Chinese Alice*, *Uncut Jade* and *Kenjiro*, each set in nineteenth-century Japan.

The Coming
of the Barbarians

A STORY OF WESTERN SETTLEMENT
IN JAPAN 1853–1870

PAT BARR

PENGUIN BOOKS

For John

PENGUIN BOOKS

Published by the Penguin Group
27 Wrights Lane, London W8 5TZ, England
Viking Penguin Inc., 40 West 23rd Street, New York, New York 10010, USA
Penguin Books Australia Ltd, Ringwood, Victoria, Australia
Penguin Books Canada Ltd, 2801 John Street, Markham, Ontario, Canada L3R 1B4
Penguin Books (NZ) Ltd, 182–190 Wairau Road, Auckland 10, New Zealand

Penguin Books Ltd, Registered Offices: Harmondsworth, Middlesex, England

First published by Macmillan and Company Ltd 1967
Published in Penguin Books 1988

Made and printed in Great Britain by
Richard Clay Ltd, Bungay, Suffolk

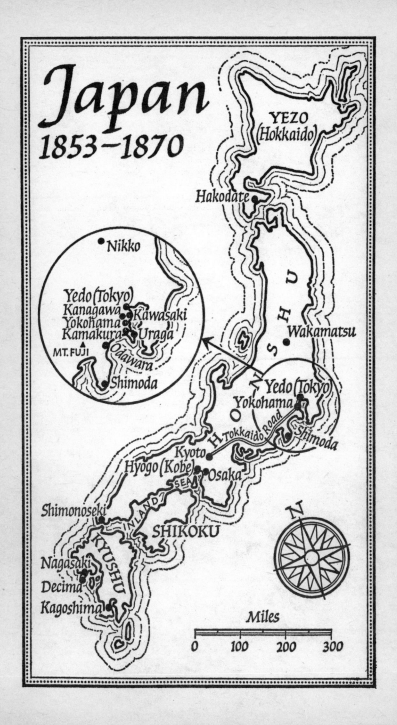

Japan
1853-1870

YEZO
(Hokkaido)

Hakodate

Nikko

Yedo (Tokyo)
Kanagawa   Kawasaki
Yokohama
Kamakura   Uraga
MT. FUJI   Odawara

Shimoda

H O N S H U

Wakamatsu

Yedo (Tokyo)

Yokohama

Tokkaido Road

Shimoda

Kyoto

Hyogo (Kobe)   Osaka

INLAND   SEA

Shimonoseki

SHIKOKU

KYUSHU

Nagasaki

Decima

Kagoshima

N

Miles

0   100   200   300

Contents

Illustrations

ACKNOWLEDGEMENTS FOR THE PLATES

Acknowledgements are due to Asahi Shimbun Publishing Company, publishers of *Yokohama Ukiyoe (Reflections of the Cultures of Yokohama in the days of the Port Opening)* by Tsuneo Tamba, for Plates 2, 3, 4, 5, 14, 15, 16, 17, 20 and the endpaper illustration; to the Bettmann Archive, New York, for Plate 1; to *The Illustrated London News* for Plates 8 and 19; to William Blackwood and Sons for Plates 9 and 10; to Longmans Green and Company for Plate 11; to the Mansell Collection for Plate 12; to the Radio Times Hulton Picture Library for Plate 13; to Chapman and Hall for Plate 18; to the Trustees of the British Museum for Plate 21; to Seeley, Service and Company for Plate 22; to the Trustees of the National Galleries of Scotland and Lord Bruce for Plate 7.

Author's Note

During my three-year stay in Japan I became interested – as most foreigners do – in the continuing process of Japanese 'westernisation'. Looking out over the bay from the house on Yokohama's 'Bluff' where I lived for two years, one could still trace the main outlines of the port as it used to be a hundred years ago. It was, I think, this magnificent view, allied to my already-established enthusiasm for the nineteenth century in general, which first encouraged me to explore the early development of Japan's contact with the outside world.

In writing this book I have been exceedingly fortunate in the variety and richness of the sources available to me. Because Japan was such a totally unknown land in the mid-nineteenth century, nearly every traveller who visited it felt an obligation to write about his experiences, and I have, therefore, been able to base virtually all my descriptions of scenery, events and personages on the accounts of eye-witnesses. I have listed my main sources in the bibliography at the end of the book but I wish to record my special debt to Sir Rutherford Alcock, Lord Redesdale, Laurence Oliphant and John Black for not only writing in detail about nineteenth-century Japan, but for doing it in such a vivid and valuable way. I am especially grateful also to Mrs J. Van der Corput and Professor R. A. Wilson, and the Rutgers University Press for permission to quote passages from their timely translation of Henry Heusken's *Japan Journal*, and to Mr Boleslaw Szeczesniak and the University of Oklahoma Press for permission to quote passages from their edition of George Henry Preble's *The Opening of Japan*.

For the illustrations I am chiefly indebted to the Asahi Shimbun Publishing Company of Tokyo who have most generously made available some of the plates from their enchanting pictorial history, *Yokohama Ukiyoe.*

In the early days of Japanese-western contact, no standard pattern had evolved for the English transliteration of Japanese words, and the reader will notice that they are often spelled differently by different writers. Although the older spellings of Tokyo, Kyoto and Osaka as Tokio, Kioto and Osaca were then in use, I have adopted the modern spellings to avoid confusion. However, it did not seem appropriate deliberately to change place-names used in the nineteenth century to their modern equivalent, so, for instance, I have preserved the name Yezo for the northern island now known as Hokkaido.

Lastly, I should like to express thanks to my friends in Japan – both Japanese and 'barbarian' – who made my stay there so pleasant, to my mother, who enjoyed her visit to the country so much and, above all, to my husband, without whose constant help and encouragement this book would never have been finished.

Pat Barr

August 1966

Introduction: What Went Before

There have been many historic western arrivals on the shores of Asia. Among them, one of the most celebrated is the arrival of Commodore Matthew Perry's small squadron in the Bay of Yedo (Tokyo) in 1853. This event, after all, exemplifies in the purest and most dramatic form one of history's hoariest clichés: new comes to wake up old, steam comes to make the horse redundant, guns come to defeat the finely-wrought sword, modern 'progressive' men pull out the roots of the static feudal society, and lords and ladies, castles and courts collapse into a picture-book past.

To appreciate just how dramatic Perry's arrival was, one must remember what had happened – or rather what had not happened – to Japan in the centuries before it. During the Middle Ages the Japanese, like their neighbours, traded with as much of the outside world as they could comfortably reach. Fleets of merchant ships sailed from the southern port of Nagasaki bearing sulphur, gold and ornamented swords for the mandarins of China and the noblemen of Siam and returned laden with nuts and spices from India, manuscripts, silks and porcelain from Pekin and Shanghai. Soon, inevitably, merchant-adventurers from Portugal, Holland, Spain and Britain arrived and tried to establish permanent trading-posts along the Japanese coasts.

However, along with trade the westerners brought Christianity and, by the end of the sixteenth century, Roman Catholic missionaries reckoned they had made almost a quarter of a million Japanese converts. At this period in Japan's history the Shoguns (generalissimos) of the new Tokugawa dynasty gained almost total mastery over the country and had reduced the Mikado (Emperor) himself to a strictly controlled and impotent puppet who was confined to his imperial city of Kyoto. The Shoguns saw Christianity, especially the uncompromising brand preached by zealous Spanish Franciscans and Portuguese Jesuits, as a dangerous and disruptive political menace which must be rooted out, and if this meant that foreign trade must go also – well, that was that; Japan was a very self-sufficient country. During the purge that followed, hundreds of native Christians and foreign missionaries were cruelly persecuted, beginning with the crucifixion of six Franciscan priests in 1597 and culminating in the slaughter of over 30,000 Christians in their last castle stronghold at Shimabara forty years later.

In 1623 the British had given up their attempt to live and trade in Japan and the following year the Spanish did likewise. In 1636, after a series of increasingly restrictive and reactionary measures against foreign intercourse of all kinds, the reigning Shogun decreed that henceforth no Japanese was allowed to go abroad, nor was any Japanese allowed to return from abroad, nor were citizens of any foreign nation, other than those still there, to be allowed inside the country. For good measure, the Shogun also forbade his people to construct any large, seaworthy vessel; only small fishing-boats were to be made, and even these had to conform to such a crazy and unwieldy design that it would have been extremely foolhardy to attempt an ocean voyage in them. The Portuguese suffered these restrictions for a while longer, mainly because of the proximity of Macao, but finally left Japan in 1638. And that left the Dutch who, three years after the Portuguese departure, were penned in leper-like seclusion on the small island of Decima in Nagasaki bay, from which they were allowed ashore, under heavy escort, once a year and where they conducted a limited but lucrative trade with the Shogun's government.

So began for Japan more than two hundred years of virtually total isolation from the rest of the world. Two hundred years. The situation has a Rip-Van-Winklish quality surely, for during this time London was stricken by plague and fire and rebuilt itself greater than before; George Washington gained America for the Americans; the French Revolution fractured the philosophies of civilised Europe; western trade with India, China, Africa and South-East Asia expanded, and sailors, explorers and missionaries carried their tales of the wondrous globe from land to land. The pyramids were common knowledge; the fabled temples of Bangkok were known to exist; Uttar Pradesh, Tahiti and Peru were put firmly on the map; but Japan was sealed, crystallised in the rigid patterns of a late medieval society.

During the whole of that two hundred-odd years no revolution or serious disturbance of any kind threatened the political supremacy of the Tokugawa Shogunate or the subtle hierarchies of its courts. There was an occasional rice riot, several earthquakes, the last great eruption of Mount Fuji, local feuds between one *daimyo* (baron) and his neighbour; but that was all. No one came and no one went; no one made a technical invention except in the fields of pottery and painting; commerce was a matter of silks, porcelain and rice; history was the study of national myths and legends; language was solely the tongue of the country – except for a few scholars and interpreters who were permitted to learn Dutch to communicate with the westerners of Decima; religion was a choice or a compromise between ancient classical Buddhism and local, chauvinistic Shintoism; life was a fairly untroubled rhythmic circle from one cherry-blossom season to the next. The rest of the world was a crude, rapacious place full of hairy barbarians.

Throughout most of this long period of isolation not more than a handful of foreigners – Will Adams, the English sailor, being the most notable example – managed to slip through this first Bamboo Curtain and live to tell the tale. It was not, however, that no one cared about Japan. From the late eighteenth century onwards there was a new wave of general western expansion in the Far East; the United States expanded its trade with China; in the north, Russian settlements crept ever closer to Japanese shores; in 1842 the British gained Hong Kong and the port of Shanghai, a mere five hundred miles from Nagasaki, was opened to foreign commerce. In short, the wealthy nations of the world were seeking new outlets for the goods which their new industrial skills could produce; Japan was known to be a relatively prosperous nation – a completely untapped market. The end of her seclusion was inevitable. It was mainly a question of who got there first.

As Doctor Francis Hawks, the official chronicler of the American expedition which did get there first, puts it in the opening sentence of his book, 'Viewed in any of its aspects, the Empire of Japan has long presented to the thoughtful mind an object of uncommon interest.' And he goes on to say that students of politics, geography, botany, navigation, science, commerce, ethnology, history, religion and literature would all look forward to 'the thorough exploration of a field at once so extensive and so inviting'. In addition to all these admirably disinterested people clamouring for access to mysterious Japan, the American government had a particularly strong motive for taking positive action: the recently formed Pacific Mail Steamship Company was planning a regular route between San Francisco and Shanghai, and Japan lay directly on it. But the Japanese were notorious for their policy of non-co-operation with passing ships – no fuel, provisions or water could be obtained from them, and sailors unfortunate enough to have been shipwrecked on their shores in the past had been very poorly treated.

It was a state of affairs which the curious, energetic, outward-looking Americans of the mid-nineteenth century could not tolerate. Early in 1852 it was announced that an American expedition was going to Japan. In November, Commodore Perry left Virginia on board the *Mississippi*, with his letters for the Japanese government from President Millard Fillmore of the United States all sealed and done up in a special gold-hinged rosewood box.

Part One

Ships and Bargainers

'Little did I dream that I should here, after crossing the salty path, gaze upon the snow-capped Fuji and this land.' – Japanese poet's idea of words used by Commodore Perry.

The hot, bright eastern day chosen for the end of Japan's two centuries of seclusion was 8 July 1853. The ships of Commodore Perry's command were black and tall; they were called the *Susquehanna* (the flagship), the *Mississippi*, the *Plymouth* and the *Saratoga*; they had come from China and established a base at Loo-Choo (Okinawa). Their Commodore, Matthew Calbraith Perry, was a big, dark, unsmiling man with a double chin that puffed over the gold braid of his high naval collar. He came from a famous family of hard-drinking, adventure-seeking successful naval officers. Matthew, who was born in 1794, followed in his father's and brothers' footsteps – except that he didn't much like drinking – by becoming a midshipman at the age of fifteen, getting his first taste of battle in the war of 1812 against the British and gaining experience of exotic lands and peoples during his voyages to West and South Africa, Tangiers and the Caribbean. At the age of forty-six he was made a Commodore and a commodore, wrote one of his biographers, 'was a titanic personage afloat or ashore' who occupied in solitary state the best quarters on the best ship of the squadron and who was surrounded by a retinue of secretaries, body-servants and aides. Perry was a man who gained the respect rather than the affection of those who worked under him and his most sympathetic characteristics were, perhaps, a great sense of fairness and a lively, inquiring mind which recorded all he saw and heard – stories of 'sailing fish', names (ancient and modern)

19

of prevailing winds, fishing techniques of the Malays, colours of rock, bird and native robe. On his expedition to the Far East, Perry's full title was 'Commander in Chief U.S. Naval Forces, East India, China and Japan Seas, and Special Ambassador to Japan'. For Perry had come to demand – not, he made it very clear, 'to solicit as a favour' – that the Japanese should make some kind of trading agreement with America and open at least two of their ports to foreign ships.

In the wood-and-paper village of Uraga, near Yedo, before the masts of Perry's squadron appeared on the horizon, life went on as usual. Old men were mending fishing-nets on the beach and women carried wooden buckets of water to the doorstep or clopped along in their high pattens to buy spinach, pickled radish and eels at the shops. In the bay before the village, broad-sailed fishing junks lolloped quietly over the waves.

But, as the strange ships came into view, the fishermen exhibited signs of great consternation. They furled the bellying sails which collapsed in wrinkled, tatty heaps on the decks, they shouted, pulled in their nets with tearing haste, grabbed oars and rowed madly towards the safe shore, 'like wild birds at a sudden intruder', wrote Francis Hawks, Perry's careful chronicler. Ashore too, however, the bright day was shattered and there was panic. Temple bells cried out a bewildered warning and ordinary citizens ran for cover indoors, while the local officials hurried down to the jetty and stared at the black, approaching hulks.

When the ships were within about a mile of Uraga a gun salute was fired and anchors were dropped. Twilight fell with summer suddenness. American sailors, leaning over the ships' rails, watched millions of jellyfish floating in the pale-grey sea, and, as night came, the shore shivered with agitated fires that had been lit on the headlands near the harbour. In Yedo itself every look-out tower was a-twitter with citizens craning their necks towards the dark ocean and every temple was filled with devout old women who clapped their wrinkled hands to call the gods' attention to this disaster and prayed for a tempest that would blow the intruders away. Inazo Nitobe, a contemporary Japanese commentator, wrote, 'The popular commotion in Yedo at the news of a "foreign invasion" was beyond description. The whole city was in an uproar. In all directions mothers were seen flying with children in their arms and men with mothers on their backs. Rumours of immediate action exaggerated each time they were communicated from mouth to mouth and added horror to the horror-stricken. The tramp of war-horses, the clatter of armed warriors, the noise of carts, the parades of firemen, the incessant tolling of bells, the shrieks of women, the cries of children dinning all the streets of a city of more than a million souls made confusion worse confounded.'

To add more terror to that sleepless night, a meteor with a scarlet wedge-shaped tail plummeted down the sky before dawn and the Japanese covered their eyes and bowed their heads with the fear of this baleful portent. But, as the meteor's incandescent light danced briefly over the steel of the foreign ships, Commodore Perry interpreted it quite differently and is recorded as saying that such a phenomenon 'may be so construed by us, as we pray to God, that our present attempt to bring a singular and isolated people into the family of civilised nations may succeed without resort to bloodshed'.

At any rate, in spite of the auguries, the Japanese discovered that the world did not end that night and, very rapidly, their naturally courageous curiosity reasserted itself. They decided to inspect the intruders. On the morning of the ninth, several high-prowed little boats bobbed at anchor near the steel sides of the *Mississippi* and the Americans were amazed to see that they were crammed full of artists who, equipped with slender-tipped brushes, inkstones and rolls of grainy rice-paper, were making hasty – and very lively – sketches of all that they saw. Within a week, Perry learned later, these first pictures of the 'hairy barbarians' and their strange ships had been sold to the owners of print-shops, coloured, copied, carved on wood-blocks and began to appear on banners, screens, scrolls, fans and even towels throughout the city of Yedo.

Later that same day, large, flat-bottomed barges put out from Uraga and these carried local government officials, called *yakunin*, garbed in stiff ceremonial robes with high lacquered hats tied on their heads. There then ensued a parley between the Japanese and the foreigners carried out in the cumbersome order of English to Dutch to Japanese and back again which was to impede and complicate all these East–West communications for quite a time – until, in fact, sufficient linguists were trained so that the intermediary of Dutch could be dispensed with. During the discussion, Perry let it be known that he would not speak to anyone lower than the Governor of Uraga, that he had letters from his President to the ruler of Japan which he wished to deliver personally and that – this last in response to a plea from the barge below – that he had no intention of retreating south to Nagasaki and there was nothing the Japanese could do to make him.

The Commodore himself did not appear. He had adopted the pose of a secluded, omnipotent leader whose face men did not look upon lightly and whose cabin was soon entitled by the Japanese 'The Abode of the High and Mighty Mysteriousness'. Accustomed to such imperious behaviour from their own rulers, the Japanese were suitably impressed; they sent the Governor of Uraga himself to speak with the strangers. The Governor was, by American standards, a very short man and, clad in baggy golden trousers, wide-sleeved brocade jacket and shining lacquer clogs, he looked, commented Hawks, 'like an unusually brilliant knave of trumps'. Nevertheless, the Governor behaved with amiability, elegance and dignity on board the flagship and entered with zest into a discussion of plans for Perry's visit to the shore. Whilst drinking champagne with great composure, he also made it plain to the Americans that he knew quite well where they had come from and what their deck-guns were for.

And, indeed, while these preliminary contacts were being made, it became evident that the Shogun and his government were reacting speedily to the presence of these weapons so unexpectedly and immovably trained on their innocent shore.

Survey crews sent out from the *Susquehanna* reported that the coastline was a warren of anxious activity: women and children carried baskets of stones slung from a pole over their shoulders to help strengthen the new earthworks; farmers turned grooms brought their horses and carts to aid the soldiers in the anticipated battle; *samurai* and their retainers from far and wide refurbished their war-dresses, feathered their arrows, polished their swords and hurried to the camps which were mushrooming on the plain behind Uraga.

But when the news was confirmed that His High and Mighty Mysteriousness would land to deliver the letters from the American President to his 'great and good friend' the ruler of Japan, preparations of a more conciliatory nature began on shore. A huge structure of wood and cloth was erected, the pyramid-shaped roof of which looked from a distance, said Hawks, like three grain-ricks. A raised path was built from this to the jetty, and the jetty itself was bolstered with rocks and sacks of straw and sand. To make sure that the barbarians did not see too much, the camps of the soldiers and the outskirts of the village were sheltered behind high screens of rough cloth stretched between bamboo poles, the cloths emblazoned with the crests of all the clans present.

First there was a lull while the foreigners celebrated their Sunday – Bibles in every sailor's hand, a band on deck and the martial Christian strains of a hundred manly voices proclaiming that *'Before Jehovah's awful Throne, Ye nations, bow with sacred joy'*. This scene, incidentally, which some might contemplate with misgiving nowadays, brought great satisfaction to a certain historian, Professor William Griffis, who arrived in Japan twenty years later and described it in his work *The Mikado's Empire*. He cites as an encouraging instance of the hymn's impact that 'Where cannon were cast to resist Perry, now stands the Imperial Females Normal College, an institution for young Christian converts.'

At last, on the fourteenth, the landing took place. American officers, marines and musicians from each ship, about three hundred in all, filled their small boats and headed shorewards, flags fluttering on every stern and a salute of guns behind them. To a certain Captain Buchanan fell the distinction of being the first westerner for over two hundred years to land in Japan with such uncompromising official pomp and, according to Griffis, the watching *samurai* growled in protest as Buchanan's foot crunched into the soil of their sacred country. With due decorum the whole western contingent formed into procession on the path leading to the Audience Hall: first two young ensigns carrying the box of letters; next Commodore Perry, martially erect even to the plume on his cocked hat; on either side of him, most amazing to Japanese eyes, an American Negro, 'two of the best-looking fellows of their colour that the squadron could furnish', Hawks recorded. Then came various officers, gilt buttons glinting in regular rows, epaulettes encrusted with gold stars; a few marines in correct, scarlet-slashed trousers and a band, its silver trumpets sounding, cymbals clashing, drums rolling. 'And all this parade', Hawks confesses, 'was but for effect.'

And then the foreigners, in their turn, saw strange sights. Along the beach, on either side of the path, stood rank upon rank of Japanese soldiers, encased in ribbed armour of leather and iron, bright banners of emerald, royal-blue or orange flying high above their heads. Behind them solid lines of cavalry were drawn up, the riders' horned helmets spiking at the sky, their jewelled swords sheathed, but handy, and on their flanks standard-bearers whose crimson swallow-tailed pennons swept ten fluttering feet to the ground.

The foreigners marched upon the path to the Audience Hall. Here the body of the procession waited while the coloured striped cloths guarding the entrance were held apart for Perry and a small group of officers, and they were ushered inside. The interior was warm, quiet and shaded. The walls were soft with hangings of violet silk divided by heavy tasselled skeins of white, blue and rose. At the far end of the thick-matted chamber was a dais with a red felt covering, and on the dais, patient

24

and still as china dolls, sat the official representatives of the Shogun's government in their padded, embroidered robes of ceremony. Perry and his men halted in silence. Then the westerners were motioned to sit in front of the dais – on chairs, incidentally, which had been hastily rounded up from the local temples, where they were normally used only by Buddhist priests during the conduct of a funeral service.

Finally the interpreters spoke. The box was delivered and the Commodore firmly explained its weighty contents: the President, he said, wanted peace with Japan and wanted to make a treaty so that trade could flourish across the Pacific between his great country and theirs, and then Japan too, would grow great and prosperous in her own right. Perry added that he would be back in the spring to receive the Japanese answer – bringing with him a larger squadron of ships. In twenty minutes it was all over. Blinking in the harsh sun outside the officers called their men to attention, the band clattered into action and the westerners returned safely to their black ships.

During the rest of the squadron's stay there was some fraternisation. Survey crews went out continually trying to map a little of the coast and dubbing each landmark with a suitably impressive name – Perry Island, Mississippi Bay, Treaty Point and so on. Some sailors were allowed on shore, though a very tight rein was kept on their activities. Local officials visited every American ship bearing gifts of eggs, fowls and *saké* (rice wine), and received in return bottles of liquor, puddings and bags of potato and sweet-corn seed, for the Commodore had issued strict orders that no sailor was to leave an unpaid debt of any kind behind. Yezaimon, the Uraga Governor, who had shed his earlier fears and was enjoying himself greatly, bombarded his western hosts with questions – about their trains, their printing-machines, their navigational instruments and, above all, how it was that their ships could move so quickly against the wind. Captain Buchanan promised him that when they returned in the spring, the westerners would bring presents for the Emperor including a locomotive on rails and a wire which would stretch from Uraga to Yedo and through which you could speak from one place to another in a single second. Yezaimon, recorded Hawks, was helpless with envy.

Three days after the audience ashore, Perry decided that no more could be accomplished for the moment; he had to wait, impatiently, for the spring. So, early on the morning of 17 July, just nine days after their arrival, whistles blew, anchor-chains rattled, bells rang on board, sailors leaning over the rails exchanged good-byes with fishermen bobbing in the junks below and the black ships puffed steadily away over the horizon, against the wind. And Commodore Perry recorded with satisfaction in his journal that 'to a maritime people, the contrast between their weak junks and slight shallops and our powerful vessels must have made a deep impression'. And that was indeed the case. The Americans left behind not only a deep impression of impregnable strength and vastly superior technical skill, but, even worse, an awful threat, an incalculable promise: their return in the spring.

I I

The country spent a very uneasy and fractious winter after Perry's departure. The Shogun's government, though they had received a few prior hints through the Dutch Embassy in Washington that this 'peaceful' western invasion was being contemplated, had kept the matter quiet and done nothing because they had not known what to do. Now they still didn't know what to do. The ruling council in Yedo split into the two factions which were to disrupt the political scene for twenty years: the conservatives who blindly advocated the total repulsion of the barbarians at no matter what cost; and the progressive realists, all of whom saw that Japan must bow to the inevitable and come to terms with the rest of the world, and some of whom positively welcomed this chance to break through the suffocating cocoon of the country's long, self-imposed withdrawal. Vacillating, the Shogun even asked the opinion of the Mikado in Kyoto and invited counsel from the *daimyo*. Naturally, the aristocracy of the court and landed gentry understood that, for them, the West would bring many unwelcome innovations, so they declared that, when the barbarians returned, Japan must expel them. But how? The Yedo government was at a loss, for the nation as a whole seemed to demand a course of action that it was impossible to carry out. As the Shogun realised, Commodore Perry had no intention – and no need – to go away empty-handed; he might speak softly, but, in the words of a later compatriot of his, he 'carried a big stick'.

And the 'stick' which Perry brought with him when he returned was, as had been feared, even bigger and more potent than his previous weapon. There were, in fact, nine ships approaching Yedo Bay in February 1854 to help the Japanese decide how to answer the American demands. These were two store ships, the sloop *Southampton* and three steamers, *Susquehanna*, *Powhatan* and *Mississippi* which each carried a sailing vessel – the *Macedonia*, *Vandalia* and *Lexington*. Between them they could muster about two hundred and fifty mounted guns and one thousand six hundred men – enough to make any unarmed nation they approached think twice before saying 'no'.

Among these men, serving as a lieutenant on the *Macedonian*, was a certain George Henry Preble. Preble was a serious, tough, kind, devout man from the rock-ribbed state of Maine. As had many of the forebears in his well-known old family, he combined a long and varied career as a naval officer with a scholarly interest in geography, botany and the naval sciences. Before joining Perry's expedition at the age of thirty-seven, Preble had been round the world several times – to the Mediterranean, to China, to the Caribbean. The sea was his chosen life; but he constantly wondered if he had made a wise choice. The trouble was that Preble's seafaring life meant constant and irksome separation from his wife – one Susan Zabiah Cox, daughter of John and Thankful Cox, Puritans – with whom he was deeply in love and to whom he wrote constantly during his absences. In addition to the purely personal content of his letters, Preble used them as the means of keeping a regular diary of his experiences during his voyage with Perry. He was forced to this expedient because the Commodore had forbidden all the members of his expedition to keep any journals or reports. Perry's stated reason for such a prohibition was to prevent any information leaking out to other nations which might 'imperil the success of our enterprise'; one also feels that Perry wanted to be sure that his official report came out well ahead of any others. At any rate, after searching his conscience in the matter, Preble decided that the Commodore's order was an unwarrantable restriction on his liberty and so circumvented it. It was a fortunate circumvention, for, as a result, we have a delightful collection of journal-letters which provide a far warmer, more immediate and unforced account of the whole episode than the official, dry and rather pompous report produced by Dr Francis Hawks.

Preble's first recorded letter was written in New York on a melancholy Sunday evening in April 1853, when he was about to sail half-way round the world to join Commodore Perry's second expedition to Japan. Sitting at his hotel window and looking down on the familiar streets below all bustling with stay-at-home citizens strolling or riding in the spring twilight, Preble tells his 'dear wife' that because of the suddenness of his departure he had no time to arrange financial matters: 'the navy agent had no money'; the 'Purser is not allowed an advance'; there was 'an enormous mess-bill' to pay. Nor has he had a chance to say good-bye to Aunt Harriet, 'a gifted and pretentious lady' and, oh dear, 'I am in such a turmoil and perplexity I don't know what to do, or which way to turn, but your love and love for you shines through it all and is my star of hope and promise. We do love each other, don't we, Susie?' he concludes pleadingly. The next day, in thick fog and heavy drizzle, the

Macedonian melted away out of New York harbour with her already homesick lieutenant dutifully aboard, his head weighed down with 'the sickening, saddening thought' of the two- or three-year separation before him, his sole consolation the memory of the promise he and Susan had made that they would each read one psalm and one chapter of Matthew every Sunday evening, 'counting the weeks of absence by the chapters'.

A week later poor George Henry was still miserable, still dreaming of home. 'Mine is a cruel life', he told Susan, 'and I wish I could loose myself from it.' He could have added that it was also a rather dangerous one – judging from the subsequent fates of the *Macedonian*'s officers. The Captain died of fever in Hong Kong in 1855, his son, acting as clerk, two years earlier, of consumption on the Indian Ocean, one lieutenant resigned, one shot himself, two deserted and were killed in the Civil War a few years later, the sailmaster and the assistant surgeon were 'lost in the Levant', one acting mate died at sea, another was taken off the ship at St Helena with tuberculosis and died there shortly afterwards. Preble, though he was of too melancholic a nature to believe it possible, was promoted to rear-admiral in 1876 and two years after retired to a happily land-bound old age with Susan and the family.

At any rate, after a while Lieutenant Preble recovered his spirits sufficiently to indulge in a little gossip about his companions: the marine officer who 'has been everything by turns and nothing long, except nine years married'; Fourth Lieutenant Winder who, 'though younger than I am has perfectly white hair'; and the Purser, who married the daughter of one Justice Taney to whom he wrote letters containing 'up to 12,296 words each'. Like Preble, the poor Purser 'takes his absence very hard . . . There is no rose in creation for him out here.'

The *Macedonian* sailed first to high green Madeira, then on towards Africa, entering the Tropic of Cancer where the temperature rose to ninety and 'the pitch melts in the seams of the decks'. They stopped at Princes Island and it was so wet that, when they let go headlines to release rain from the folds in the sails, the decks were a-swim with 'a deluging avalanche' of water. Here the crew wore flannel trousers, waterproof hats and little else, for, as Preble comments, 'The naked full-dress of the natives is sensible and healthy, however shocking to the good taste and ideas of civilisation and propriety.' The next port of call was St Helena, where the Master rated his chronometer by the Time Ball dropped from the Observatory each noon, the Surgeon bought some vaccine and Preble made a quick visit to the house where Napoleon died – the drawing-room now containing nothing but agricultural tools and corn-shellers, the bed-chamber now a stable for horses, the Emperor's own fishpond choked with weeds and slime.

The *Macedonian* continued east; scudded under close reefs round the Cape of Good Hope, was blown towards Java Head, the wind howling through the rigging, hailstones 'larger than buckshot' cutting like knives into the flesh; and on through the Straits of Sunda where Crakatoa Point rises, 'a smooth cone from the water', past two little islands called 'The Cap' and 'The Button' and one in the middle called 'Thwart-the-Way'; and on into the China Sea where, sitting writing in his sultry cabin one afternoon, Preble recalled that twelve years ago to the very day it was 'our Good Friday, dear Susie, when we happily became conscious of each other's love, though no words were spoken, in the woods at Gorham'.

At anchor off Cum-sing Moon, a large opium depot on the China coast, the *Macedonian* joined the rest of Perry's squadron and waited around there for a month while the Commodore himself 'lives in a fine house at Macao, fifteen miles away, little caring about the drear, monotonous anchorage here'. To everyone's relief on 9 October the ships received orders to carry on to Victoria Harbour, Hong Kong, where they remained for part of the winter. Preble, bored and restless with the enforced in-activity, meditated frequently on his sorry lot: 'What an artificial state of existence is mine', he complained to his wife, 'and how unsatisfactory that so much of my limited three score and ten must be passed in the same way – up late, turned out early, sleep irregularly interrupted, and drifted hither and thither by sudden summons, thousands of miles away from the home that is the haven of all my hopes and fears.'

Just before Christmas they finally sailed for Loo Choo and struggled heavily through the China Sea in gales so rough that there was no way of keeping the chess-pieces on the board long enough to finish the daily contest between Preble and the Purser. The Lieutenant and his friends went ashore often while anchored at 'Napa' (Naha) and paid several visits to a certain Doctor Bettelheim, a Jew turned Protestant missionary who spent years living in an abandoned temple of the island with his wife and children and preaching his own particular moral discipline to the easy-going natives. Up to that time Bettelheim had made but one real convert – a young rebel who was subsequently murdered by his own people when his heresy became known. The Loo-Chooans, Preble felt, were not ready for the imponderable aspirations of Christianity.

I I I

At long last, on 31 January 1854, Perry's squadron, stored brimful to the hatches with provisions and water enough for eight months, left Napa and got under way for the unknown Japan. Whales blew and blustered round their bows, porpoises rolled across the horizon and, one afternoon, Preble noted 'a solitary chocolate albatross and a piece of squid such as the sperm whale feeds on that floated by us, at least six feet square, looking like a piece of fat pork streaked with red meat'. The sea became icy and treacherous again. 'I was reefing, furling and tacking throughout the watches and have hallooed myself hoarse,' the lieutenant grumbled. The sole reward came on 7 February: a first wide-eyed glimpse of Mount Fuji outlined smooth white and magnificent against the sky, and 'Talk to me of the grandeur of the pyramids after seeing *this* creation of Almighty Power' was George Henry's devout comment. For three more tiresome days the *Macedonian* laboured northwards towards Yedo Bay, buffeted by freezing gales of hail and snow, each night so thick, dark and squally that the crew were in constant fear of crashing on the rocks. And indeed, on the 11th, the hull thumped over some coral patches and stuck fast on a reef. Rather ignominiously the vessel was pulled off by some helpful Japanese and the *Mississippi*'s tow-line and finally Preble's ship joined the rest of the squadron in the bay before the waiting city of Yedo on St Valentine's Day.

While Commodore Perry and his staff began thorny and devious negotiations aboard, other ships' officers took to small boats and started to survey the nearby coast with spy-glass and sextant. Preble's boat often lay within thirty feet of a projecting cliff which was crowded with curious Japanese who called to them, clapped their hands, waved scarves and ornaments and threw down branches of pink and white Japonica. Several local fishing boats arrived and there was much merry unofficial bartering of rice and eggs on the one hand for ship's biscuit and salt pork on the other. Potential business of another kind was also promised by the customs officials who explained, through interpreters, that once a treaty was signed the sailors could have plenty of 'wives'; but, as their women did not like hairy faces, the barbarians must first shave clean. 'We have decided', Preble remarked, 'that henceforth in Japan the morality of an officer is to be known by the length of his moustache.'

Though these informal relations were amiable enough on both sides, the government was much agitated by the squadron's proximity to Yedo, and all the first delegations went aboard with presents galore – sweetmeats, oysters, beancurd cakes and oranges – and entreaties that the foreigners would retire at least as far as Uraga. Perry was as adamant as always and his ships kept pressing closer to the capital until the Japanese were forced to accept his demands and it was agreed that there should be a

Grand Landing at the little fishing village of Yokohama for a conference and ratification of the Trade Treaty of the previous year.

An even more imposing Audience Building than the one used during Perry's first visit was erected even more hastily by a battalion of Japanese carpenters. It had a sixty-foot-long reception hall and various side apartments. Long banners of white and red cloth hung at the sides of its entrance and on the peaked, pine-wood roof was a tall staff surmounted by a circular ornament which looked, wrote Hawks, 'like the upper part of a chandelier'. Preble, taking the less official view, thought that the whole structure 'looks as if it would answer admirably for a coal-shed'.

Waiting around for a treaty to be negotiated was a weary business for officers and men alike. For one thing, they were all thoroughly disgruntled with the ships' food. On board the *Macedonian*, the Fourth Lieutenant – whose white hair had grown whiter during his spell of duty as Caterer – resigned and the Purser became 'monarch of our empty store-room'. They had a few hams, two kits of salmon, ship's biscuits and bully beef. The biggest treat of the month was the curried goat which was sent down to the wardroom one lunchtime from the Captain's own table. The abiding hope was that the Japanese could be prevailed upon to supply fowls, eggs and vegetables for all, and there was great excitement every time a likely-looking junk approached the ships. Some skinny hens did arrive, but, alas, Preble grumbled, 'Every succeeding one seems tougher than its predecessor. We know Japan to be a very ancient country and certainly the one we tried our teeth on today must have walked out of the Ark before Noah. By boiling them over in a stew with gravy, rice, pepper and other condiments they are made tolerably palatable and are an improvement on Salt Horse.' Much more rewarding, at first, than the fowls themselves seemed to be particles of 'gold' which were embedded in the gizzards of a quantity of ducks killed on board. Some sailors were preparing to jump ship and rush off to make a fortune in this rich new land where gold was left lying around for ducks to eat, when some kill-joy on the *Saratoga* submitted the metal to a test and found that it was copper after all.

Because of the monotonous and restricted existence aboard the anchored ships every man wanted to be included in the Commodore's escort when the landing was at last arranged. A quota of officers from each vessel was to attend and it was left to the luck of the draw to decide who should go. 'As it was Sunday I would not throw dice, so I cut for chance in a book with Garathney', Preble tells his wife, and then, remembering, perhaps, her serene but vigilant face, adds, 'a distinction without a difference you will say, but it satisfied my conscience'. Anyway, the Lieutenant's heedful God apparently appreciated the difference – he won the cut and formed one of the escort when Perry, on Wednesday, 8 March, staged his second landing in the country.

On the American side it was all very much as at Uraga – parading marines, gun salutes, flags – only bigger; on the Japanese side it was also much as before, only smaller. The comparatively slight contingent of the Shogun's troops mustered along the shore 'conveyed no idea of splendour or force', Preble remarked and he soon reached the conclusion that 'the Japanese have been a greatly over-rated people. I doubt whether they will, on the whole as a nation, compare to the Chinese.' In fact, it was all rather an anti-climax, 'Everyone was disappointed and tired with the pageant before it was over', and, from what Preble heard, the main topic of a lengthy discussion between the Commodore and the Japanese simply involved the fixing of a burial ground for a marine who had died aboard ship.

Nevertheless, the negotiations were going rather well. Five days after the first landing at Yokohama and as part of the softening-up process the Americans went ashore again bearing presents for the Shogun and the Emperor. There were stoves, a box of zinc plates, three Maynard's muskets, whisky (a barrel for the Shogun and ten gallons for each Great Councillor), lifeboats, some gutta-percha wires, potatoes and, above all, the promised locomotive and telegraph line. The locomotive was really a miniature, designed to run 350 feet round an eighteen-inch track. Nevertheless the Japanese were determined to ride it somehow.

'It was a spectacle not a little ludicrous', wrote Hawks, 'to behold a dignified mandarin [*sic*] whirling around a circular road at the rate of twenty miles per hour with his loose robes flying in the wind. As he clung with a desperate hold to the edge of the roof, grinning with intense interest and his huddled-up body shaking convulsively with a kind of laughing timidity while the car spun rapidly round the circle, you might have supposed that the movement somehow or other was dependent rather upon the enormous exertion of the uneasy mandarin than upon the power of the little puffing locomotive which was easily performing its work.' The telegraph, fixed up from Yokohama to a nearby village, was also a great success and, after the official opening words had been transmitted in Dutch, the Japanese queued for hours to send each other messages.

There was, incidentally, one further 'present' from the Americans, but a present that did not want to be presented: a certain Japanese fisherman, nicknamed Sam Patch. Sam's junk, floundering too far from land one windy night, had capsized and he had been picked up by a passing American merchant vessel and taken to San Francisco, where he had begged to be allowed to return to Japan as a seaman on the *Susquehanna*. However, as the beloved and sacred soil of his homeland drew nearer, Sam began to change his mind, and by the time he was brought on deck and presented to the august Governor of Yokohama he was terrified about what his countrymen might do to him if he left the ship. So Sam fell on his knees and, according to one spectator, 'turned a ghastly green i' the face, crouched down with his forehead on the deck, trembled all over and would not speak a word'. Amused by his *volte-face*, the crew kept Sam on as a kind of harmless and useful mascot. Later, Sam was befriended by a religious member of the crew, one Jonathan Goble, who taught him Christianity, English and how to live in New York. Later still, Mr Goble became a Baptist missionary and returned to Japan, bringing faithful Sam with him to help in his conversion of the 'Japanese heathen'.

In return for the Americans' liberality the Japanese, in their turn, displayed an array of gifts for their uninvited guests – ink-stones and scrolls, lacquer stands, one 'odd-shaped thing with an elephant on its top' Preble notes, ornaments sprinkled with gold dust, silk-rolls of crimson, primrose and watered blue, shells, soy sauce, umbrellas, tea-sets – but of all these the only thing the Lieutenant coveted was 'a doll with a Japanese face, hair done up à la Japanese and dressed to match' which he wanted for his daughter, 'dear little Lily'. 'A poor display, not worth over a thousand dollars some thought' he concluded and certainly 'our railroad engine and car cost several times their total value'.

After inspecting the presents in the Hall, Preble and his companions were taken outside and shown other gifts – great sacks of rice each weighing over a hundred pounds. While Preble was looking at them and wondering how on earth to transport them to the ship, a procession of fifty huge *sumo* wrestlers appeared, their bulging fleshy bodies naked except for 'a stout silken girdle concealing what modesty should not expose'. At a signal these giants heaved on a couple of sacks apiece and carried them, with apparent ease, to the edge of the water, one or two swinging an extra sack between their teeth for good measure. Later, the wrestlers staged a *sumo* display for the Commodore, who refused to be impressed. To him the men 'were like bulls, pawing the earth, flinging dirt, grunting, their faces swollen with blood in their efforts to force their opponents out of the ring'. After this spectacle the Commodore, a skilled practitioner of 'one-upmanship', ordered his marines to execute a drilled manoeuvre on the beach 'to match an exhibition of order and discipline against one of mere brute force'.

To rub in the lesson of the barbarians' disciplined and sophisticated strength several senior Japanese officials were invited to look round the *Macedonian* where, says Preble, 'we amused them with an exercise of our Great Guns and small arms, showing them how we boarded an enemy and how we repulsed one attempting to board and sent axemen into the rigging to chop it away when requisite. Then rang the Fire Bell and exercised at fire quarters, drawing water in buckets and throwing it and streams from our force pumps upon the imaginary conflagration.'

The presumably awestruck Japanese were then transported to the *Powhatan* (which Perry had made his new flagship) under a salute of seventeen guns and were set before an abundant feast on deck. The attending ships' officers were told, 'in accordance with the old adage', Preble remarked, 'that if they eat hearty they give us a good name', to keep their guests' glasses and plates full. 'Doing my duty therefore, in obedience to orders, I plied the Japanese in my neighbourhood well, and when clean work had been made of champagne, Madeira, cherry cordial, punch and whisky I resorted to the castors and gave them a mixture of catsup and vinegar which they seemed to relish with equal gusto.' It was all highly convivial. There were toasts to the President of the United States and to the absent Japanese ladies – which last was considered a great joke by the present Japanese gentlemen; the band played, and balding Pursers shuffled round to the music with princes in silken jackets on their arms; midshipmen danced the polka on the hurricane deck; one of the Japanese Commissioners was so far carried away as to throw his arms round the Commodore's neck and embrace him, and Preble reports that the officer who asked Perry if he would stand for such treatment received the reply, 'Oh, if he will only sign the Treaty he may kiss me.' Lastly, there was a minstrel show put on by 'The Ethiopian Band' of the *Powhatan* and, according to Hawks, Caucasoid and Mongoloid alike roared with delighted laughter at the clever and impudent imitations of the Negro.

Possibly it was the champagne and the minstrelsy, more likely
it was the persistence of Commodore Perry allied to the resigned wisdom of the Shogun's ministers, but at any rate, four
days later, on 31 March, Lieutenant Preble wrote triumphantly
in his journal, 'Eureka! It is finished. The great agony is over!
In vulgar parlance the egg has hatched its chicken today. The
Treaty of Amity and Friendship between Japan and the United
States was signed today to everybody's satisfaction. Even Old
Bruin (the Commodore) would smile if he only knew how to
smile.'

The Treaty contained twelve Articles: regulations governing
the exchange of currency and the supply of water, fuel and
provisions were fixed; arrangements were made for the shelter-
ing of any shipwrecked American seamen; it was agreed that
the ports of Shimoda and Hakodate should be opened to American ships in a year's time and that, in due course, consuls
appointed by the United States government should be allowed
to reside at Shimoda. These articles were, of course, the end
result of hours of tiresome, bickering discussion between the
representatives of the two nations – as a short excerpt recorded
by Hawks suggests:

> *Japanese:* 'We will not confine Americans or prevent them
> from walking around, but we would like to place a limit to
> the distance they may walk [from Shimoda harbour].'
> *Perry:* 'I am prepared to settle that matter now, but they
> must not be confined to any particular house or street.
> Suppose we make a distance they may walk the same
> distance that a man can go and come in a day? Or, if you
> choose, a certain number of *ri*? [A *ri* measures just over two
> miles].'

Japanese: 'We are willing that they shall walk as far as they can go and come in a day.'

Perry: 'There is no probability that sailors would want to go ashore more than once from curiosity. Besides, they will have daily duties to attend to on ship . . .'

Japanese: 'When you come back we would like you to settle the distance Americans are to walk. It is difficult for us to settle distance.'

Perry: 'Say the distance of seven Japanese "miles" [*ri*] in any direction from the centre of the city of Shimoda.'

Japanese: 'Very well.'

And so on, and on, and on.

Once the Treaty of Friendship was signed everyone was anxious to be on the move, but most of the squadron, including the *Macedonian*, hung about in Yedo Bay for another fortnight. Preble was as depressed as usual by the enforced idleness. He hadn't heard from Susan for the last two mail-deliveries, though he kept writing faithfully. 'It is literally casting my bread upon the waters hoping for a return after many days,' he told her and added bitterly, 'I wonder that Job was not sent to sea and deprived of all knowledge of his home and family for a twelve-month as I am like to be. It would have been a greater trial for his patience than any he was made to endure and he would have cursed and swore sooner than I did, I'm sure!' He was also 'dyspeptic again', and in the next of his pontifical homilies fears that their continual salt diet might turn him and the crew to pillars of that tough and indigestible substance.

At last, on 11 April, came orders to move. The *Macedonian* cruised across to the Bonin Islands to get supplies of fresh food, while most of the squadron went down to have a look at Shimoda. The Commodore was very pleased with the pretty little place: 'When its contiguity to the sea, its easy and safe approach, its convenience of ingress and egress are considered, I do not see how a more desirable port could have been selected to answer all purposes for which it was wanted.' Perry landed on the third day, partook of the customary official tea – sweet-meats and beancurd cakes – and, after that, the Americans strolled easily about the town and were fêted by the inhabitants who examined their jackets, buttons, weapons and hats 'with almost childish eagerness and delight'.

Two educated Japanese gentlemen of the district, however, were unsatisfied with this cursory and maddeningly restricted contact with the wide world. One dark night they rowed quietly out to the *Powhatan* and begged to be allowed to board – not only board, it turned out, but to remain aboard and return to the States with the Americans in order to learn more of the West. The men's urgent plea put Perry in a dilemma: it was obviously a deliberate violation of the government's official policy; on the other hand, the would-be adventurers assured Perry that they would be tortured and executed if they were returned to shore. Nevertheless Perry had them sent back, though he did his best to conceal from the local officials the object of the couple's foolhardy visit. In this he did not suc-ceed; Japanese officials are difficult to elude. A few days later, a group of Americans strolling through a Shimoda back street saw the two unfortunate gentlemen penned in a stiflingly small and barred prison cage. One of them managed to get a written message out to the foreigners and this deserves quotation as an illustration of the chafing, protesting restlessness – not unmixed with reproach – that assailed many an educated, liberal Japan-ese at the time:

'When a hero fails in his purpose, his acts are then regarded as those of a villain and robber. In public we have been seized and pinioned and caged for many days. The village elders and officials treat us disdainfully, their oppressiveness being grievous indeed . . . Regarding the liberty of going through the sixty states [of Japan] as not enough for our desires, we wished to make a circuit of the five great continents. This was our hearts' wish for a long time. Suddenly our plans are defeated and we find ourselves in a half-sized house where eating, resting, sitting and sleeping are difficult. How can we find our exit from this place? Weeping we seem as fools; laughing as rogues; silent only can we be.'

And silent they were from then on, though Perry heard later that their punishment had not been as drastic as they had feared.

On 2 May the *Macedonian* arrived from the Bonin Islands carrying supplies of yams, potatoes, onions and a hundred or so giant turtles which, wrote Preble, 'sprawling upon their backs between the guns and made comfortable with wet swabs under their heads by way of pillows, present an unusual spectacle'. After gladly devouring the fresh supplies, the sailors were told that they had one other call to make – at Hakodate, the port to be opened on the north island of Yezo (Hokkaido). They had a calm voyage up the coast, escorted by spouting sperm whales and guillemots until, coming nearer to land, they 'passed through rushing tide rips breaking boiling and scathing from the friction of counteracting winds and tides'. It was 'as cold as Greenland' again, everyone 'blue and shivering' and the *Macedonian* looked 'cheerless as a winter barn'. But if the climate was worse than Shimoda's, the 'vitals' were better. The local inhabitants positively inundated the ship's kitchens with large salmon trout, mullet and flounder, bags of spinach, buckets of glistening mottled clams and bamboo baskets full of angry red crabs.

For the Lieutenant there was more painstaking survey work – making soundings, measuring distances ashore with pikes and chains and, in the process, getting several 'wettings' from the sudden rain on land and the sudden squalls at sea which almost swamped the little survey boats on to the rocks. For the Commodore there were more negotiations with the Governor of Hakodate, who made things very difficult by protesting that he knew nothing whatsoever about the Treaty that had recently been signed at Yokohama! And there was more haggling over the question of how far Americans could walk – this time in

Hakodate. The commissioners, wrote Hawks, 'at first wished to confine them to one street, then to the whole town, then to the projecting promontory extending towards the sea, next to three Japanese *ri* and then to three and a half. Like a brave retreating army they thus contested the ground, inch by inch.' However, in due season, this dispute too was settled and Perry's mission was at a successful conclusion. He had got the preliminary treaty in his pocket; now it was time for the military to leave and for the diplomats to arrive so that detailed regulations for organising trade could be drawn up.

On 28 June the black ships heaved anchors for the last time and got under way – some bound for Manila, one direct to Hong Kong, others back to Loo Choo, and the *Macedonian* to Keelung in North Formosa to begin surveying all over again. It had been just about six months since they left Hong Kong 'to engage in opening this Japanese Oyster' as Preble puts it and adds, uncharitably, 'long, tedious, monotonous and disagreeable has been the interval. We have perforce been restricted to the abstemiousness of an anchorite (I mean no pun) drinking our tea-slops, improved with brown sugar because we could get no other, and discussing the merits of various kinds of bean soups and Japanese and American rice and mess pork and salt Junk.'

Nevertheless, in spite of the difficulties, the frustrating delays and the unpalatable food, there was also a certain sense of triumph as the ships headed away west and south towards the wide-open communicating world. They had challenged Japan and prised her two centuries of barricades apart without firing a shot or losing a man. As the Purser of the *Macedonian* put it to Preble – the two men leaning over the rail and watching the quiet wooded hills behind Shimoda blurring on the horizon – 'the military and warlike strength of the Japanese had long been to Europe like the ghost in a village churchyard, a bugbear and a terror which it only required some bolder fellow than the rest – like we Yankees – to walk up to and discover the ghost to be nothing but moonshine on the gravestones, or a poor old white horse. Our nation has unclothed the ghost and all the rest of the world will cry "bah" and take advantage of the discovery.' The Purser may have got rather carried away by his metaphor; but his forecast was right enough.

The first people who came hurrying to take advantage of rediscovered Japan were, in fact, more 'bold Yankees', by name Mr and Mrs Reed and family, Mr and Mrs H. H. Doty and Messrs E. Edgerton, T. Dougherty, William E. Bidleman and Horace W. Peabody. This enterprising group, who styled themselves 'American Pioneers in Japan', had chartered a schooner, the *Caroline E. Foote*, in Honolulu and set sail for Shimoda with a cargo of ships' chandlery which they intended to sell to whalers arriving at Hakodate – when that port was opened.

They were, unfortunately, premature. They landed at Shimoda in March of 1855 before the treaty rights could be fully invoked and more than a year before the American Consul himself arrived there. However, the Japanese, after wringing their hands and pleading with the barbarians to go away, allowed them to land 'temporarily'. They were still there in June when an American survey ship under the command of Captain John Rodgers happened on the scene. Rodgers, who shared his compatriots' belief that 'being Americans they should be as free as in other countries', supported the merchants' right to commence trading; and there ensued a long and, in retrospect, rather comic correspondence between the Captain and the Governors of both Shimoda and Hakodate as to the meaning of the phrase used in Perry's Treaty 'to live temporarily' on shore. To the Japanese, this meant, in the case of anyone shipwrecked, only until another foreign vessel came along, or, in the case of traders, for a week or two. Rodgers argued that the Japanese *had* granted Americans the right to live at these two ports and that, 'If the permission has any meaning, it intends protections and permission to reside in houses and buy food'; in other words, to set up a home there. The deadlock was absolute and, finally, from sheer exhaustion and lack of time, Rodgers and the pioneers had to admit defeat. At the end of June the gallant

Caroline E. Foote set sail again for San Francisco, its cargo unsold, its passengers quite disillusioned with the 'new world' of Japan.

But the next Americans to arrive at the little port would not be so easy to dislodge. For they came with the full backing of the United States government and according to the terms of the American-Japanese Friendship Treaty and their names were Consul-General Townsend Harris and Mr Henricus Conradus Joannes Heusken, commonly called Henry.

Townsend Harris was, as he told President Pierce in a letter written in August 1855, 'a single man, without any ties to cause me to look anxiously to my old home, or to become impatient in my new one'. Moreover, he added, 'I have a perfect knowledge of the social banishment I must endure while in Japan and the mental banishment in which I must live and I am prepared to meet it.' Harris, like George Preble, came from Puritan New England stock and his grandmother, called Thankful Townsend, had always impressed upon him that he must 'tell the truth, fear God and hate the British' – this latter injunction being Grandmother's revenge for the firing of her home by British troops during the Revolutionary War. To date, Harris had more or less followed this advice: his truthfulness was dogged and painful; his fear of the Almighty was genuine – though not un-mixed with slight scepticism and reproach at the hardness of his lot; his hatred of the British was expressed in a lifelong refusal to wear a suit cut from British cloth.

Six years before his appointment as the first American Consul to Japan, Harris had given up his post as President of the Board of Trade in New York and had begun a series of wandering trade expeditions to the East. He had voyaged to New Zealand and the South Sea Islands, to Singapore and the Philippines, to Ceylon and Siam. He had traded and lived in Canton, Penang, Macao and Hong Kong; the 'smell of Asia' was always in his nostrils; the indolent, resigned warmth of the East had per-meated his bones.

But in the year 1855 Townsend Harris, in common with

nearly all his countrymen, had not been to Japan. And he badly wanted to go there. When Perry called in at Shanghai on his way to Yedo in 1853, Harris, who happened to be there at the time, begged to be allowed to accompany that first expedition, but the Commodore refused him. And so the concept of Japan as the most sealed, mysterious, self-sufficient and civilised country in all Asia continued to tantalise Harris; were he 'offered the choice between Commissioner to China or Consul to Japan, I should instantly take the latter', he affirmed in the course of the same letter to the President. The President, who had also received several letters from influential New York business men supporting Harris's nomination, did not resist such apparently dauntless enthusiasm, and indeed, on the same day that Harris wrote to the President, the Assistant Secretary of State was writing to Harris confirming his appointment.

V

Just over a year later, on 21 August 1856, Townsend Harris arrived at Shimoda aboard the frigate *San Jacinto* (a vessel, incidentally, which nearly caused war between the United States and Britain a few years later when its crew – perhaps still indoctrinated by Harris's anglophobia – arrested on the high seas two Confederate agents escaping to Europe in a British ship). As the *San Jacinto* approached the quiet, isolated little harbour, Harris paced its deck in a mood of excitement and pleasure. 'I like the appearance of the Japanese,' he wrote in his diary, 'clean, well-clad, cheerful-looking, pretty fishing-boats.'

Harris's companion, Heusken, was a twenty-four-year-old Dutchman who had emigrated to the United States three years previously and had, apparently, been rather down on his luck when he was suddenly given the opportunity to become Harris's secretary-interpreter – an appointment which he owed, of course, to the fact that Dutch was still the communicating language between the Japanese and the Americans. The first exchanges which Heusken helped to translate between the Governor of Shimoda and Harris were not particularly encouraging from the latter's point of view. The Governor was extremely honoured to see the American Consul-General so soon, but, alas, the Governor had to explain that affairs were in a sorry state in his province. There had recently been a severe typhoon and an earthquake, the harvests were bad, the peasants were even poorer than usual. Wouldn't Mr Harris consider returning in a year or two when things were more settled? The Consul politely but firmly said he would stay. The Governor hopefully reiterated his request to 'their dear dear friend the Consul-General', wrote Heusken, 'whom they are so glad to see and whom they would be so glad to see returning to the United States'.

At length, realising that the Americans were quite unshakeable, the Governor capitulated and allowed them ashore to have a look at their new home – an abandoned Shinto temple located in the hamlet of 'Oyster Point' adjoining Shimoda. And so Harris and Heusken became the first, but by no means the last, of the early foreign diplomats to be given quarters in a place of native worship. The temples were not ideal residences by western standards. They were infested with rats, bats, spiders and even snakes; they were draughty and damp in winter and airless and insect-filled in summer. But they were, at least, secluded, and spacious enough to accommodate all the impedimenta of furniture, bedding, clothes and provisions with which the foreigners felt it essential to surround themselves.

The Consul and his interpreter landed permanently on 3 September 1856. As they left the *San Jacinto* for the last time the crew sent up three hearty cheers, the band on the quarter-deck struck up *Hail, Columbia!* – and one can imagine each cheering sailor turning to his mate and thanking Providence that *he* was not expected to remain at such a god-forsaken place in such an unknown land. Early the next day carpenters from the ship arrived at the new Consulate to set up the flag-staff on the bare open courtyard immediately in front of the low-roofed temple building. At two-thirty that afternoon, under a blazing sun and with no sound louder than that of the cicadas rattling and rasping in the nearby bushes, Harris hoisted the Stars and Stripes – the first ever to be flown in that secluded empire. He records the event in his journal with pride, but adds, with terse perspicacity, 'Grim reflections – ominous of change – undoubted beginning of the end. Query: if for the real good of Japan?'

Considering its proud start in life, incidentally, that particular flag came to a sorry end. Three days after it was hoisted it began to fray at the edges – a further example, Harris notes bitterly, of the bad workmanship done for government contracts! Later in the month the flagstaff was blown to an angle of sixty-five degrees in a typhoon and the flag almost ripped to shreds. So Harris, taking advantage of the Japanese ability to copy practically anything, had a new flag made by some needle-women in Shimoda. And it was this 'made in Japan' flag which was borne before the Consul on his triumphal hundred-mile journey to Yedo the following year and which finally came to rest in a glass frame on the north wall of the Director's office at the Townsend Harris Hall High School, New York, in June 1921.

For the first week or two there seemed so much to do that the two foreigners did not stop to think about the totality of their exile now that the *San Jacinto* had gone. There were shelves and cupboards to be fitted to frail temple walls, house-servants to find and train, and a constant bevy of officials to provide with glasses of whisky, brandy and wine – for the Japanese of Shimoda were as fond of western spirits as their compatriots in Uraga. In return, the Governor asked the Americans to dine, but this, in Heusken's view, turned out to be a pretty glum affair owing to the lack of female company. 'This absence of man's angel of mercy gives a sort of emptiness, a certain sadness to the Governor's dinner. Had some noble Japanese matron been hostess at table, had we been able to dance a polka with the Governor's daughters, what a good time we would have had!' But no. Important government officials were forced to leave their wives and children as hostages in Yedo while they did duty in the provinces and so lived in a state of celibacy which touched the young Dutchman's sensibilities: 'What a dismal life the poor Japanese officers must lead, forced as they are, by a suspicious and cruel law, to forsake that which makes the charm of existence!'

In the early days too, there were all kinds of odd crises to solve: the accommodation of Harris's four pairs of pigeons, for instance; trouble with the lock of his biggest iron chest which, at first, could not be opened and, once opened, could not be re-locked; and disputes with the Chinese tailor and cook who both turned out to be 'desperate characters' who would not work and were quickly in trouble with the police for making the rounds of all the chemist shops in the town and buying up every scrap of opium.

Then there were explorations to make of the surrounding countryside. The weather that September was glorious, the sky 'blue as sapphire' day after day, Harris remarked, fresh breezes whipping up whitecaps on the sea, each afternoon long and warm and golden. The rich land was heavy with ripe produce – rice, maize, millet and buckwheat crowded the small fields, pears the colour of russet, grapes, apples and the orange globes of persimmon were to be had for picking. Harris was amazed to find tea shrubs and cherry trees still with some late blossom and in the woods he came across the humble yellow bachelor's button whose sweet drifting fragrance induced 'so many home associations' that, he confessed, 'I was inclined to be homesick – i.e. miserable for the space of an hour'. Several other plants – Canterbury bells, Scotch thistles and heartsease – were familiar to him, but there were many he did not know and he repeatedly wished that he was more of a botanist.

While Harris walked, Heusken rode – on a thoroughbred horse which cost him twenty-seven dollars and forty-one cents.

'What an enormous amount for a thoroughbred horse!' young Henry exclaimed. 'It looks as though my affairs are not going too badly. I started off in Japan by taking a valet. Here I am now, owner of a horse! If I go on this way why shouldn't I maintain my own carriage and ask in marriage the Emperor's only daughter? Satrap that I am. Oh New York! Oh days spent without dinner and the fine chances I missed to sleep in the open air. Oh black clothes, shining with old age. Oh beloved shoes in which my heels and toes enjoyed perfect ventilation! Oh trousers with holes worn in them! Where are you old friends? Come and see his Very Serene Highness, Lord Heus-ken, parading on a horse!'

As the Japanese became more friendly with the strangers in their midst they brought them all manner of presents, some of which delighted, some of which quite embarrassed their recipients. Once the Consul was given the whole carcass of a wild hog, its flesh delicate as veal and subtle as the tenderloins of pork. Chestnuts, golden pheasants and a pair of canaries all came his way and – most prized of all – two spaniel-type dogs with bulging eyes and eager sturdy little bodies. Harris called them Yedo and Miako (the old name for Kyoto) in honour of Japan's two capitals and grew very attached to them. The canaries, however, gave him nothing but trouble. He fed the female a yolk of egg every day; in spite of that she deserted her nest. Later he tried again, but the eggs would not hatch and, on breaking one, he found that it was unfertilised. Judging from his journal, Harris seems to have fretted considerably over the marital problems of his canaries, but they never repaid his concern by producing a family.

Of course, all these affairs were side-issues, punctuation-marks in what soon became the blank and tiresome monotony of the days. For, after two months or so, Harris's journal is less and less a record of his joy and delight in this strange country and more and more a vent for his three principal worries: his health, the treaty negotiations with the Japanese and the isola-tion caused by the absence of any western ships. On Christmas

Day, about four months after his enthusiastic arrival, Harris writes: 'Merry Christmas! How happy are those who live in lands where these joyous greetings can be exchanged! As for me, I am sick and solitary, living as one may say in a prison – a large one it is true – but still a prison.' But come now, one feels inclined to protest, what about that 'perfect knowledge of social banishment' about which he spoke so confidently in his letter to the American President?

It must, however, be remembered that when Harris sought this remote post he did not foresee that his health would so deteriorate, and it is this deterioration which clouded his early zest for Japan and for the job he had come to do. The Consul seems to have suffered practically every minor ailment while in Shimoda. He trod on a nail and injured his foot, he had three attacks of 'cholera morbus', he had a bout of St Anthony's Fire' and recurrent indigestion which ruined his appetite; he lost so much weight that, at one point, he says, 'I am so shrunk away that I look as though a "Vice-Consul had been cut out of me"'; he had headaches and fever and, in the winter, colds and sore throats – this latter indisposition, incidentally, he blamed rather uncharitably on Heusken who never remembered to put coal on the fire. 'I believe', he adds testily, 'that Mr Heusken only remembers when to eat, drink and sleep – any other affairs rest very lightly on his memory.'

But, well or ill, Harris continued to have regular meetings with the Japanese to hammer out the framework for a workable treaty. What other ports were to be opened for foreign trade and when? How were American ships to be supplied at these ports? What rate of currency exchange was to be fixed? This latter was a particularly knotty issue as the Japanese had scant experience of dealing with foreign currencies and little idea of prices in the world's markets. The only solution at first seemed to be to judge the relative value of the coinage by weight – so many Japanese silver *itzibu* equalling so many silver dollars. Even then, the foreign traders would have to make tedious and detailed calculations because of the small worth of the little

Japanese *sen.* That the *sen* was worth something less than a quarter of a light-weight stiver is illustrated by Harris's amused admission that, between the time of his arrival and May of the following year, he had run up a bill with local shopkeepers for 3,476,594 *sen.* However, he was able to settle the whole account with 699 American dollars!

A further hindrance to ratification of a detailed treaty was that the authorities were still determined to limit as much as possible the number of westerners who could reside in Japan and to restrict their movements. Townsend Harris won the right for foreign diplomats to travel freely, but foreign merchants and sailors were still to be confined within the narrow areas negotiated by Commodore Perry. As it transpired later, the Japanese' principal concern was to keep all barbarians away from the Mikado's capital of Kyoto and even from Osaka, the port twenty-seven miles from it. The Japanese Minister insisted that a foreign merchant should be allowed to trade at Osaka only on condition that he would return to Sakkai – seven miles farther north – to eat and sleep. Angered at this, Harris suggested a hypothetical case to the Minister: an American merchant is taken suddenly ill in Osaka and the local authorities, acting under stringent orders, have him sent back to Sakkai. On the way the sick man dies. The American government, furious at such inhospitable and inhuman treatment of one of its citizens, demands instant retribution... The Japanese went away to ponder this affecting tale for a few days and then returned to Harris with the happy solution that they would build a lazaretto outside the walls of Osaka for the use of any Americans who happened to become ill there. Harris was angrier than ever; that, he said emphatically, was *not* the point.

For the time being, at any rate, this particular question was left open, and during the soft bright days of the Shimoda spring, the Consul gradually pinned the Japanese down on many other vital points. It was an irksome business. Sometimes the Americans went to see the officials and sometimes the officials came to see them. Always, inevitably, there would be much drinking of cordials and tea and smoking of tiny pipes and eating of beancurd cakes and fruit to interrupt the leisurely discussions. Then there would be much procrastination on the part of the Japanese, considerable shifting of ground and a good deal of hopeless reiteration. 'Travelled over the debates of yesterday like a horse in a mill,' Harris grumbled on 4 March 1857 and, two days later, 'I am really ill, yet I am forced day after day to listen to useless debates on points that have been exhausted and only varied by some new phase of falsehood.' A Russian Admiral, who had earlier experience of the Shimoda officials, recorded that the only way to get things moving was to play on their fear of central authority. He would gain his points by getting up during a conference and saying firmly, 'Well gentlemen, we will talk of this matter no longer, I am going to Yedo.' He would then make as if to leave and the Japanese would hurry after him with conciliatory suggestions.

In the end the American Consul's dry, unruffled pertinacity won the day and on 8 June he recorded that he had carried every major point with the Japanese: Nagasaki was to be opened to American ships, the currency valuation was fixed, Americans, exclusively under the control of their own Consuls, were to be allowed to reside at Shimoda and Hakodate and the Consuls themselves could travel where they pleased. After setting out these hard-won terms in triumphant order, however, Harris asks himself with bitter perception, 'Am I elated by this success? Not a whit. I know my dear countrymen but too well to expect any praise for what I have done, and I shall esteem myself lucky if I am not removed from office, not for what I have done, but because I have not made a commercial treaty that would open Japan as freely as England is open to us.'

As a pleasurable relaxation from his grinding task, Harris had had a small belvedere erected on the top of a hill near the Consulate in which he could sit and enjoy the cooler breezes from the sea and survey the wide clean sweep of the coast. Pure white skeins of sand lined the water's edge as far as he could see; junks pottered over the waves; the air hummed with the summer sounds of birds, crackling crickets and bees burrowing into foxglove and peony. But no foreign ships. 'Where oh where', cries the disconsolate Consul, 'is Commodore Armstrong?' By 18 April he was already recording in his journal that a ship was overdue; and by the end of the month he had all his correspondence ready to send to the State Department and his numerous friends. All through May and June he waited, yearning for news from the outside world, for the opportunity to publish the success of his convention-making, for medical advice and comfort, for some sustenance other than the interminable diet of rice, fish and stringy chickens and for some western face other than that of the good-natured, but too familiar, Heusken.

On 3 July a cannon sounded from the look-out point and Heusken dropped everything and 'ran like a deer to the top of the signal hill'. As the young man himself put it, 'This shot makes me thrill with joy; finally, after four months we shall see again the inhabitants of the civilised world. After two years without letters, I imagine an immense packet. I shall soon see my mother's handwriting. I shall know how she is, whether or not she is happy — if she can ever be happy in this world, poor dear soul! I shall hear from my friends. I shall soon know what is happening in the world. I leap from my chair; I dance and I sing; in spite of the heat of the vertical sun I climb at a gallop a neighbouring mountain; I run to a promontory that juts into the sea and that can afford an unlimited vantage point... I discover far, far away, the triple masts of a large ship!' Henry rushed back, breathless and sweating, to report the news, and then, after getting his wind back and having a drink, he returned to the look-out to watch the vessel's approach. Harris wrote a few last-minute letters and ate lunch briskly, joyously anticipating the meals of ham and fresh bread and butter the approaching ship would provide. At four o'clock Heusken came shambling back to the Consulate weary and low-spirited. The ship had gone, sailed carelessly past from south to north, quite oblivious of the anxious eyes of the westerners on the lovely, lonely shore. 'I never had anything to try my philosophy so hardly as this,' Harris complained.

The summer heaved heavily on. Heusken had ridden his own horse so much that he had laid it up with a sore back. The Consul kindly lent him his horse, but very soon, Harris noted, 'a difference of opinion arose between Mr Heusken and the horse – the latter wishing to return and Mr Heusken to go on. Then ensued a trial of force versus obstinacy which ended in the horse slipping his shoulder and thus disqualifying himself from ever being mounted again.' So there they were; without horses, without news, without letters, without company. As the Consul sat in his belvedere day after hot day and watched the sea he must have begun to wonder if the western world still existed at all, if there had not been some mighty cataclysm which had destroyed everything beyond the horizon – his friends in New York and Hong Kong, the Secretary of State to whom he kept writing dispatches that he could not send and the extremely tardy Commodore Armstrong, who was, by Harris's reckoning, more than five months overdue.

At long last, on 7 September 1857, the westerners' forlorn isolation ended. During the afternoon the signal cannon boomed again across the horizon; Heusken, in a paroxysm of joy, hired a boat and ten oarsmen and rowed towards the distant vessel. 'This time,' he exclaimed, 'I want to be sure of my ship and should I row all night, I just have to catch up with it, this ship will not escape us!' As the little boat bobbed out into the open sea from the bay the last light faded and even Heusken's anxious, questing eyes could not descry the longed-for vessel. He pleaded with the men to row harder, offered them outrageous tips, until, after two more desperate hours of effort, at last – a light, the triple masts of a frigate rearing above them and the strains of *Yankee Doodle* floating down from an open porthole! A few minutes later Heusken was aboard the corvette *Portsmouth* and being questioned by and rapidly questioning the captain and his officers. It was, Henry confessed, the pleasantest time he'd spent for the last five months.

About midnight he left, clutching a large packet of letters and newspapers at which he squinted by the light of a paper lantern as he was rowed back to the Consulate – where Harris, in his turn, stayed up until dawn eagerly poring over these coveted trophies from 'the civilised world beyond'. On the Wednesday of that suddenly hectic week the Consul went aboard the *Portsmouth* and, he notes with quiet relish, 'had my salute of thirteen guns from the heavy sixty-eight pounders, which were loaded with full charges and not with the reduced charge which is usual for saluting'. Things improved generally. The ship's captain wined and dined the two thin castaways and supplied them with lard, hominy grits, pork and hams from his own ship's stores. In return Harris gave the captain 'Yedo', one of his precious dogs and also a couple of pigs and a Japanese sword.

Although the *Portsmouth* sailed away in less than a week, its arrival had marked the end of the worst period of the westerners' exile. Soon after that more newspapers and letters arrived from Nagasaki and Hakodate and then, on the twenty-second of the month, the Japanese governors told Harris that the Shogun was willing to see him and that he should 'go to Yedo in the most honourable manner', there to present the new American President's batch of letters to the Shogun and his ministers.

VI

From then on, the preparations for the visit to Yedo dominated the Consul's days. His journey was to be a ceremony, a portent, a demonstration to the Japanese of the strength, dignity and potential amity of the huge land on the other side of the Pacific. Harris, who had a clear understanding of the oriental mind, fully appreciated the importance of the occasion. He was the first accredited representative of any foreign government to be granted such an unconditional, equitable audience on such an equal footing with the country's ruler; the American flag was to be carried into the Shogun's capital and on into his very palace. There must be no mistake on such an occasion; the Japanese had to realise that this 'barbarian' in their midst was no suppliant, no greedy merchant ready to jig to the Shogun's tune in return for a few trade concessions, but a Representative invested with what President Pierce termed 'full and all manner of power and authority', who came in peace – and yet one whom it would be foolhardy to slight.

With these considerations in mind, Harris turned his immediate attention to the formation of his retinue, which was to be a formidable one. The first estimate he made for his own personal train included about forty porters to carry luggage, cooking utensils and so on, and twelve guardsmen, two standard bearers, two shoe and fan bearers and two grooms – all but the porters to wear silk dresses bearing the American coat of arms. There would also be twenty bearers to carry his *norimon*. The *norimon* was the Japanese form of palanquin and was, for long and rather inflexible western bodies, a fiendishly uncomfortable means of transport. It resembled a kind of lacquer cage about four feet square with closed sides, and was suspended above the ground from a stout horizontal pole which was carried upon the shoulders of four bearers, two before and two behind. The hapless passenger, folded up inside like a jack-in-the-box, was jolted remorselessly up and down and could hardly move an inch except occasionally to poke his head out of the aperture which could be opened on one side. In summer, the sun beat down on the lacquered roof and the *norimon* was like a portable oven; in winter, wind blasted through the cracks in the wood bringing rain and snow with it; in short, all the early westerners who travelled in Japan were extremely glad when the *norimon* fell into disuse.

However, at this period, the *norimon* was still *de rigueur* for all official persons of rank, and Harris, though he longed to ride on horseback into Yedo so that he could see everything, realised that the shrouded respectability of the *norimon* was, in the eyes of the watching citizens, more consistent with the impression of dignified power that he intended to create. Even Harris, however, made one concession to his personal comfort and had a special six-and-a-half-feet long *norimon* made so that he could stretch his legs and avoid the rather inglorious affliction of pins and needles.

Of course, there was no reason why Harris should not ride on horseback for the first part of the journey, and on 5 October he tells us that he had acquired a new horse and constructed a makeshift saddle and bridle, but, 'alas Shimoda is no place for equestrian exercises. It is all up and down.' Both he and Heusken had been dismayed to find that the Japanese had no knowledge of horse-shoeing but were accustomed instead to fitting a horse with a straw sandal over each hoof. These flimsy and inadequate little shoes wore out in about an hour and it was the groom's job to follow his master at a jog-trot carrying fresh supplies – indeed, one of the Japanese measurements was 'the - distance - it - takes - between - one - straw - sandal - and - the-next'. Heusken had been far-sighted enough to get his horse shod by a crew-member of the *Portsmouth* and, as Harris notes, 'this proceeding caused a great sensation among the Japanese. They never saw anything of the kind before.' Heusken's foresight had far-reaching consequences, for, later, when he and Harris were living in Yedo, an officer came to them one day and asked to borrow the iron-shod horse for a few hours, and to refrain from asking why it was wanted. The officer took the horse and duly returned it unharmed. But it soon appeared that the Shogun's Regent himself had wanted to examine its footwear and that, as a result, the Regent's horses and those of all the other ministers were now being shod in the same way – an early example of the rapid adoption of new ideas so characteristic of the Japanese.

At length preparations for the journey were completed and on Monday, 23 November, at eight in the morning the first American Plenipotentiary to Japan left Shimoda for the capital in what even he termed 'a fine flow of spirits'. In the very front of the cavalcade were three agile boys each bearing a stick of bamboo with strips of paper attached to the top. Their job was to cry out in constant unison '*shita-ni-iro, shita-ni-iro*' which means 'sit down', 'sit down'; on hearing the call every ordinary citizen was expected to kneel on the ground and avert his eyes from the grandeur that was passing. The boys apparently continued their cries even along the remote mountain passes where there was no one to hear them, 'as if', Heusken remarked, 'the trees and plants should pay homage to the Embassy of the Republic Par Excellence'.

Next in the procession rode a captain of the Japanese army with his retainers and behind him the American flag was borne aloft by two robed guards. Then followed Townsend Harris himself with his train – made up of a standard bearer in a long gown of brown and white calico, open at the sides like a herald's tabard, and his private escorts each carrying two swords with the arms of the United States emblazoned on their jackets. Then came 'His Excellency, the Most Serene Mr Heusken on his steed', as he styles himself, with guards and bearers, and then a straggling line of porters who had to carry, in addition to bedding, clothing and provisions, all the presents which the Consul was taking to the Shogun – and these included cases of champagne, a barometer, books of natural history and an astral lamp. After all this, coiling away far behind the westerners' own entourage, came the Vice-Governor of Shimoda, the Mayor of the adjoining hamlet and the governor's secretary and by the time these local dignitaries had each added his quota of bearers and porters and guards and grooms and servants and servants' servants, there was a grand total of about 350 persons all going to Yedo with President Pierce's letters.

Heusken, who was temperamentally a more casual and spontaneous man than Harris, soon found the constant proximity of his numerous attendants very annoying. His umbrella-bearer and shoe-bearer followed him like two diminutive shadows.

'Why do I have that person with the umbrellas always by my side,' he asks complainingly. 'I'm sure that umbrella will bring me bad luck.' And oh, what wouldn't he give 'to be an ordinary traveller and go through these mountains leisurely, stopping at attractive spots, or stretching myself out on the grass according to my fancy'. The Consul, on the other hand, took great pleasure in discovering how elaborately and considerately everything had been prepared for him. The roads had been repaired and swept clean, bridges had been built over every stream, undergrowth had been cut away to make the narrow passes more accommodating and, at the temples in which they often spent the night, special bathrooms had been built for their private use.

On the second day of their journey the westerners had their first good view of Mount Fuji which was already snow-covered and, wrote Harris, 'in the bright sun it appeared like frosted silver'. Heusken's reaction was more intense and exuberant: 'Rounding a mountain I sight through the foliage of a few pine trees a white peak that gleams in the sun. In an instant I realise I'm looking at Fujiyama. Never in my life will I forget the sight of that mountain as I saw it today for the first time, and I don't think anything in the world will ever equal its beauty.' He reined his horse, took off his hat and shouted at the mountain for sheer joy, he wanted to celebrate its beauty in movement and sound: 'Ah, why don't I have about twenty of my friends of my younger days around me! The surrounding hills would soon repeat the echo of thrice repeated hip, hip, hip, hurrah, to the honour of the sublime Fujiyama.' That evening, from his hotel window, Henry tried to draw the sacred eminence, but the result was 'a detestable sketch, one that resembles anything but Fujiyama'.

Two days farther on they reached the famous Tokkaido, the main highway of Japan, a spacious avenue shaded with tough pine and fir, giant cypress and camphor, which, for centuries, had linked ancient royal Kyoto, the capital of the Mikados, with bustling bureaucratic Yedo, the capital of the Shoguns.

Pedlars of silk, ink and almanacs, gnarled beggars, saucer-hatted pilgrims had tottered along its weary length during many a dusty summer; princes of the realm had passed that way every year with such entourages of stewards and footmen and gentlemen-of-the-bedchamber and hat-bearers and pike, bow-and-arrow and chest-bearers as would have made the American Consul's 350 persons seem a very provincial display; and ordinary quiet citizens – anxious tea-merchants, long-haired mountain priests and sad old women selling sweetmeats, string and souvenirs – had trotted to and fro down the ages and rested in the shadow of the ancient trees. Unfortunately, the foreigners saw little of this bustling life, for the government had issued orders that the road must be kept clear of traffic. In the towns and villages, all shops were shut, blinds closed, and the inhabitants, in their holiday best, knelt silently, or, if they were of sufficient rank, bowed in salutation as the Great American Plenipotentiary passed on his honourable way. So much undeserved deference soon made Heusken uneasy and embarrassed. 'The sight of all these human beings as good as I am, or even better, on their knees began to disgust me,' he recorded. 'Here a white-haired old man bent his trembling knees and lowered his venerable brow; there a young girl turned her lovely face towards the ground and remained in a humiliating posture. It is certainly an excessive honour to see all the beauties of Japan on their knees before oneself; but this honour did not please me; if I had been allowed at least to kneel with her, this thing would have had a different complexion.'

The Tokkaido led them to the ascent of the mountain pass at Hakone, where the Consul had a battle royal with the authorities whose custom it was to search every traveller before permitting him to pass into the district of Yedo. Harris, affirming that he was a free diplomatic representative of the United States, claimed immunity and stalwartly refused to allow either himself to be searched or his *norimon* to be opened. After a deal of exclaiming and worry-hissing and hand-wringing on the part of the Japanese, he was finally allowed to go through un-molested but, because of the delay, it was after nightfall before the whole party reached Odawara on the other side of the pass. The loss of time was, however, almost a gain in the end, because, owing to the darkness, a vast quantity of bamboo flambeaux were lit along the whole length of the procession which, wrote Harris, 'wound and turned in the descents of the mountain, making a figure like the tail of an imaginary dragon'. As they approached Odawara they were met by a party of officials all carrying lanterns – red, orange, yellow, green and rice-paper white – and all decorated with the black-outlined crests of their owners. The total effect was both lovely and strange, as if the central region of this unknown land was a place filled with colour and harmony, where light blossomed like flowers.

The next day they reached Kanagawa, where Harris was interested to see the spot where Perry had negotiated with the Japanese. Looking across the bay towards Yokohama he was amazed to recognise three European ships in the harbour – vessels, he learned, which the Japanese had already bought from the Dutch to form the nucleus of their first navy. After Kanagawa the number of people and of houses increased and now, in every village, the local dignitaries who escorted the procession through were preceded by a number of policemen each carrying an iron rod six feet long. Four rings were attached to the top of the rod and these made a loud jingling noise as its bearer struck the base on the ground every two or three steps. This weird, rhythmical rattle was an oddly dis-quieting and compelling sound and, on hearing it, the people became quiet and still, though fewer people knelt, and, as he came towards Yedo itself, Harris noticed that the citizens no longer knelt at all, nor did they avert their eyes.

They spent the Sunday of that eventful week at Kawasaki, for Harris refused, as always, to conduct any business or even receive any message from the Japanese on the Holy Sabbath. Resting at an inn, the Consul read the service for the day, 'with

Mr Heusken as my clerk and congregation'. He was proud to realise that it must have been the first time that the Christian service had been audibly read in that place for many centuries – and that, too, while the law punishing such an act with death was still in force!

On Monday, 30 November 1857, Townsend Harris began his journal entry with these words: 'Today I am to enter Yedo. It will form an important epoch in my life, and a still more important one in the history of Japan.' Entering the dignified seclusion of his *norimon*, Harris was borne from Kanagawa to Shinagawa, where he was shown the execution ground on the banks of the river (a rather dispiriting and foreboding introduction) and then forward, 'with slow and stately step' into the centre of the capital itself. The streets were unpaved and bordered with shabby, unpainted, low wooden houses, and in front of every house, filling every window, blocking every door, cramming every space between houses and jamming the openings of the crossroads stood the citizens of Yedo watching the barbarians ride by. The people were quite motionless and quite mute, withdrawn, expressionless people, restrained, powerful and incalculable. 'Not a cry or a shout was heard,' Harris recorded uneasily. 'The silence of such a vast multitude had something appalling in it. Lord Byron called a silent woman "sleeping thunder".'

In front of the lines of spectators stood marshals dressed in uniforms of green, blue-grey or scarlet and each armed with a long white stave to control the crowds, though such a disciplinary check was seldom required as everyone was so perfectly, so disconcertingly orderly. At that time Yedo was divided into hundreds of small separate districts, each with its captain, each with its own internal regulations and its own policemen to enforce them. The divisions between one district and the next were unmistakably defined by strong high wooden stockades erected at 120-yard intervals along every main thoroughfare. These stockades were pierced by guarded gates which were closed at sunset every evening and only those citizens with passes were allowed through a narrow side-wicket after that time. It was a very effective – and very restrictive – system which allowed the authorities to keep a close check on all the people's activities and to split up the city into self-contained, almost impregnable little forts at any sign of trouble. At each one of these stockades, Harris's procession halted and there was a considerable 'knocking-of-heads', that is prostration until the forehead touched the ground, as the officials of each district formally permitted the cavalcade to proceed into the adjoining district. In this slow and burdensome manner the Consul was borne along, watched by thousands of dark, curious eyes, escorted by hundreds of policemen with evil-looking iron truncheons, swung up over seven bridges – including the famous Nihonbashi, the Bridge of Japan from which all distances were reckoned. At long last the procession turned north-west to follow a high stone wall and then, suddenly, Harris's bearers broke into a run and carried him at an uncomfortable jog-trot through a gateway, across a courtyard and deposited him carefully in front of his future temporary residence. The American Plenipotentiary had most honourably arrived in the Shogun's capital.

VII

To the foreigners' surprise and pleasure they found that the rooms in which they were to live while in Yedo were furnished with chairs, tables and bedsteads; for the Japanese – with that gracious desire to please which so charms most visitors to the country – had sent secretly to Shimoda to have exact copies made of the Consulate furniture, so that their guests would be surrounded by familiar things. The house itself was an imposing one, situated in Kanda, an area of the city which, at that time, lay within the remotest of the four walled circles that surrounded the Shogun's castle. From his sitting-room Harris could see one of these irregular, but very solid walls as it snaked along beside the broad moat and made its firm distinction between rulers and ruled. How long would it be, the Consul wondered, before he should pass through, not only that wall, but the inner ones as well, until he should at last come face to face with the man he had come thousands of miles and waited many weary months to see – the Shogun himself?

It was, in the event, only a week later; a busy week during which the Consul met the chief ministers (who, incidentally, brought him a gift, 'a box, my dears,' wrote Heusken irreverently, 'which contained a great quantity of bonbons. There was enough to fill the shop of a confectioner and make ill an infinite number of children!). There were also some tiresome interviews with eight princes of the realm who had been appointed 'Commissioners of the Voyage of the American Ambassador to Yedo' and who therefore felt it their duty to provide Harris with constant supplies of green tea, beancurd cakes and polite conversation.

As the hour of his audience with the Shogun approached, Harris carefully prepared his correct uniform – a coat embroidered with gold, 'after the pattern furnished by the State Department,' he adds, in case this should sound extravagant, and 'blue pantaloons with a broad gold band running down each leg, cocked hat with gold tassels and a pearl-handled dress-sword'. Such an outfit, though quite august to western eyes, must have seemed stark and unimaginative beside the costumes of the three or four hundred *daimyo* who sat in grim, silent rows as Harris strode past them on the way to the Audience Chamber in the Shogun's palace. Court dress for *daimyo* consisted of floppy-sleeved jackets made of various subtly-coloured watered silks and over which stiff, wide-shouldered outer garments were worn, bearing the nobleman's personal crest. The trousers were also wide, made of lemon-yellow silk and with legs each six feet long, so that they streamed out far behind their wearer when he waddled, giving

*Commodore Matthew
Calbraith Perry as
seen through American
eyes . . .*

*. . . and through
Japanese eyes*

A Japanese artist's view of a western ship

*The events of Commodore Perry's visit were recorded in
pictorial form on scrolls*

Here the artist has drawn the minstrel show presented for the Shogun's
ministers by some of the American sailors, an iron stove, and the tombstone of
a marine who died and was buried on shore.

Among the Japanese gifts to Perry's men were great sacks of rice

'. . . a procession of fifty huge *sumo* wrestlers appeared . . . and carried them with apparent ease to the edge of the water, one or two swinging an extra sack between their teeth for good measure.'

The American Consulate at Shimoda, drawn by Henry Heusken in 1856

The Eighth Earl of Elgin

Sir Rutherford Alcock, K.C.B., 'Her Majesty's Minister Plenipotentiary at the Court of the Tycoon'

The residence of the Earl of Elgin's mission in Yedo

From the first, foreign diplomats were frequently lodged in temple buildings which, while often draughty and vermin-infested, were at least secluded and commodious.

Lord Elgin's mission confronts the Shogun's Ministers

This plate and the preceding one were specially drawn to illustrate *The Narrative of the Earl of Elgin's Mission*.

Western travellers by the wayside

In June 1861, Alcock and a retinue travelled from Nagasaki to Yedo—a distance of 800 miles. With him went Charles Wirgman, an artist attached to *The Illustrated London News*, who drew and painted many scenes along their route.

an irresistibly comic impression of a man walking on his knees. The costume was topped with a hat which, as Harris says, 'defies description', though he tries to describe it as a 'Scotch Kilmarnock cap made of a black varnished material, which has been opened only some three inches wide and is fantastically perched on the very apex of the head ... This extraordinary affair is kept in place by a coloured silk cord which passes down over the temples and is tied under the chin.' Although the court coronets were certainly odd, it would never have occurred to Harris that their wearers might well have considered his own 'cocked hat with gold tassels' an equally 'extraordinary affair'.

However, no one, neither Great American Ambassador nor straight-facing *daimyo*, moved a muscle in a smile as Harris was ushered into the Audience Chamber. Here he was very disconcerted to find that he had been brought an hour early so that he could rehearse the part he should play in the actual meeting with the Shogun. This Harris gently refused to do, explaining that he was used to court procedure and that he should, at any rate, behave in an appropriate western fashion. He was not, he implied, prepared to learn how to 'knock heads' at this juncture. So the two foreigners were led back to the room they had first entered and given more refreshments and at the end of an hour were again conducted past the rows of *daimyo* – who had, presumably, been sitting like gaudy and improbable statues the whole while – and paused at the entrance of the Chamber. At a given signal, the Prince of Shinano, one of the commissioners who was responsible for presenting Harris, threw himself on his hands and knees and began to crawl forward into the August Presence. The Consul walked forward after him and, as he did so, a loud voice called out 'Embassador Merrican!'

Making suitable, but not too profound, bows, Harris walked to within ten feet of the Shogun who was seated in a chair on a raised platform. Having seen the splendid dresses of the courtiers, Harris was rather disappointed that the ruler wore a simple silk robe – no rich jewels, no elaborate embroidery, no ornamented weapon, indeed, as he disparagingly noted, 'my dress was far more costly than his'. With an effort, Harris broke the immeasurable silence with a formal little speech, bowed again and waited. After a pause, the Shogun first 'began to jerk his head backward over his left shoulder, at the same time stamping with his right foot' – actions which must have startled Harris not a little – and then replied with a short statement which was translated as follows: 'Pleased with the letter sent with the Ambassador from a far distant country, and likewise pleased with his discourse. Intercourse shall be continued for-ever.'

These quaint and rather touching words, the first ever uttered by a reigning Shogun to an accredited representative of a foreign power, set the official seal on Harris's whole mission. The Shogun may have been a puppet in the hands of his ministers, the ministers may have been in violent disagreement among themselves as to what policy should be adopted to-wards foreigners, the absent, silent Mikado in Kyoto may have had more actual sway in the country than Harris or even the Shogun himself realised; nevertheless, by actually seeing the Consul, by actually speaking to a barbarian who stood – not kneeled or crawled – before him, the Shogun had opened the doors of his nation a little wider. 'Intercourse shall be con-tinued forever' – it was, after all, a kind of promise.

Following the Shogun's speech Henry Heusken presented the silk-covered box which contained President Pierce's latest correspondence, and the audience was at an end. The American Consul 'retreated backward, bowed, halted, bowed, again retreated, again halted and bowed again and for the last time', and, this tricky manoeuvre successfully performed, walked back past the line of statuesque *daimyo* and returned by *norimon* to his residence.

While relaxing after this ceremonial ordeal Harris realised that he had caught a violent cold and spent the next few days in bed drinking hot rice gruel and swallowing cathartic medicines. But soon he was back at work and, during the first two months of 1858, while the north winds blew icy chill as steel straight from Kamchatka and the citizens of Yedo huddled muffled to the noses in front of their tiny charcoal stoves, he hammered out details of the Trading Treaty which, in July of that year, was finally concluded between the United States and Japan. On 27 February, however, soon after what Heusken calls 'one of the most alarming, boring, tiring, erratic, ignorant and childish conferences we have had so far with the sages of Japan', Harris was taken seriously ill; and on that day the meticulous and patient journal that the Consul had kept for just under three years was abruptly broken off.

For the next three weeks Harris wasted to the shadow of a life that was almost death. That he did not die was mainly due to the devoted attention of Henry Heusken who got him back to the fresher, healthier air of Shimoda by literally carrying him from shore to ship and from ship to *norimon*, who summoned several doctors and made sure that his chief obeyed their instructions. On 11 March Heusken records that brown spots began to appear on Harris's legs and 'they say it is the rot! His body is also covered with purple spots from rot and they say again it is impossible to save him.' Heusken pleads with the Consul to pray, pray for time is short; but Harris cannot understand and falls into a coma-like sleep. 'What am I to do?' Henry cries in agony. 'I am entirely alone here. My God! This is a terrible thing.' On the following day, during a brief period of lucidity, Harris repeats his prayers after Heusken and says, firmly, that he has no message for anyone at all, but is quite ready 'to see my God (or something to the kind)'. Poor Henry could not restrain his tears at this juncture, upon which the Consul said, 'Heusken, wipe your nose not so near my face. Heusken, you are a good boy and a true friend. I leave the care of my soul to you.' However, in spite of the affecting finality of this scene, it seemed that the crisis was over and, but two days later, Townsend Harris was sitting up in a chair drinking broth and asking for a shave.

After a period of convalescence, Harris was able to resume his negotiations with the Japanese ministers, the writing of dispatches to the State Department and, perhaps, the keeping of his journal. But if he did continue such a journal the document has, unfortunately, been lost. Townsend Harris spent three more years in the country, first in Shimoda, again as Consul-General, later in Yedo as the American Minister Resident, and he was respected by Japanese and westerner alike for the qualities of perspicacious tact and dry doggedness which had enabled him to conclude the Trade Treaty so successfully. But for first-hand accounts of these next years, one must turn to those written by other barbarians from Britain and America who came pressing, as it were, through the cracks in the tight shell of Japan which Commodore Matthew Perry and Consul Townsend Harris had made.

Part Two

Ports and Optimists

'... at least a terrestrial paradise where "all but the spirit of man was divine".' – John Black, author and journalist.

One of the first missions to come prising open the Japanese oyster was headed by His Excellency the Earl of Elgin and Kincardine. Elgin, who landed in the country in the summer of 1858, less than a month after the United States-Japan Treaty that Townsend Harris negotiated was ratified, had been instructed by the Foreign Secretary to take a fortnight or so away from his more important duties in China, slip up to Japan and arrange a similar treaty with Britain. Lord Elgin was a skilled colonial administrator who had already served an apparently honourable apprenticeship as Governor of Jamaica and had made his name as Governor of Canada during the stormy period when the French Canadians rioted in Montreal and pelted with rotten eggs, bottles and stones any British official who dared to approach the Government House. From his writings Elgin emerges as an enlightened and able man who hated the gunboat diplomacy in which he was sometimes expected to indulge. 'This abominable East,' he wrote on the way to China in 1857, 'abominable not so much in itself as because it is strewed all over with the records of our violence and fraud and disregard of right.' He disliked India and the way in which the whites turned their servants into 'salaaming machines', and he was keenly aware that the colonial situation frequently permitted westerners to adopt contemptuous, vicious attitudes towards the natives: 'I have seldom from man or woman since I came to the East, heard a sentence which was reconcilable with the hypothesis that Christianity had ever come into the world,' he wrote.

Elgin's personal secretary was Laurence Oliphant, who had secured the post more through his connections with his master's family than for any specifically secretarial talents. Oliphant had made his name also — as a sophisticated traveller, a wit, essayist and journalist, a man who, as he said of himself, constantly needed to go 'to some out of the way place and do something nobody else had done'. To assuage his need he had already been to Katmandu, across the Crimea in a farm cart, to Ubooch in the Western Caucasus, and from Lake Superior to the headwaters of the Mississippi in a bark canoe. He had been in Calcutta during part of the Indian Mutiny and watched the bombardment of Canton from the maintop of HMS *Furious*, and, there not being too much of the world left, Japan was a logical next step.

In order to sugar the pill of a treaty which Lord Elgin intended that the Japanese should digest, he brought, from Queen Victoria herself, a present of a yacht for the Shogun. The present was not an apt one. In the first place, the Shogun had died just about the time that Elgin's mission reached Japan, although, of course, Elgin was not to know this, and, in any case, the fact was kept a dead secret from nearly every Japanese and from the British during their short stay in the country. In the second place, the Shogun, even when alive, was of so exalted a rank that he was virtually a kind of state prisoner and, as Oliphant wrote, 'It was a cruel satire upon this unhappy potentate to present him with a yacht; one might as well request the Pope's acceptance of a wife.'

Happily unaware of these factors, Elgin and his party, towing the 318-ton yacht with them, steamed first into Nagasaki harbour for a day or two and then on to Shimoda, where they paid their brief respects to Consul Harris and Mr Heusken. Harris had, by this time, recovered from his illness and concluded the treaty in Yedo and the two Americans were again alone together in the Shimoda consulate which, wrote Oliphant, neither of them 'seemed altogether to appreciate... A well-stored library and a few rooms comfortably fitted up, gave an agreeable air of civilisation to the establishment; but what can compensate for two years of almost entire isolation and banishment from communion with one's fellow-men? Except upon the rare occasions of Shimoda being visited by some foreign vessel, these two gentlemen had not seen a creature with whom they could exchange an idea. They had been for eighteen months without receiving a letter or a newspaper, and two years without tasting mutton.' The hardship of his isolation was, undoubtedly, still one of Harris's recurrent obsessions.

The Americans, glad of the diversion, showed the British the limited sights of Shimoda – a temple or two, fine views of the coast and the recently established bazaar for foreigners, where Oliphant bought, for reasons he does not explain, a 'quantity of paper raincoats'. Harris also gave the visitors a feast to which the 'perpetually chuckling' Governor of Shimoda and his entourage were invited. In common with all westerners sharing a first meal with the Japanese, Oliphant was startled to observe their custom of taking the remains of the food away with them when they left. One sweet-toothed fellow apparently tried to carry strawberry jam away in the sleeve of his coat which, Oliphant suggests, 'was made full and baggy for the purpose'. Though the surmise might not bear investigation, it is pleasant to imagine that the commodious Japanese sleeve was first intended as a vehicle for strawberry jam.

The next day Elgin determined to press on, regardless of Japanese wishes, to the capital, and Harris kindly lent Mr Heusken to the British delegation so that they might have less difficulty in communication. Heusken proved invaluable and, indeed, one fails to see how a treaty could have been drawn up without him, as none of the British knew enough Dutch and none of the Japanese knew enough English. The mission steamed safely into the Bay of Yedo and on 17 August was staged another of those official landings on the sacred soil of the Empire to which the Japanese had, perhaps, by that time, become more or less resigned. The flags, the uniforms and the tunes were a little different, but otherwise the ceremony proceeded much as Perry's landing had done and much as that of the French which came soon afterwards. Rows of white-ducked ensigns lined the decks of the British ship and the band of the *Retribution*, crowded in a paddle-boat, dutifully blew out the strains of *Rule Britannia* as Elgin's barge, pennants flying, floated up to the landing-stage and the first British Representative to arrive in Yedo since the days of James I stepped ashore.

Once ashore, the British crammed as many experiences as they could into a hectic fortnight and enjoyed every minute of it. 'The Japanese', decided Elgin, 'are the nicest people possible.' They took several rides around Yedo, on horses which, Oliphant notes, were equipped with muslin reins and stirrups 'shaped like something between a catamaran and a Turkish slipper' and 'almost big enough to go to sea in'. They went as far afield as the outlying districts of Shinagawa and Kawasaki – hot, slow rides with crowds pressing to get a glimpse of them and mounted guards in escort to ensure that the foreigners did not see too much. This constant attention became very galling and the British had a nasty inkling that even the priests who lived in part of the temple where the delegation was lodged were 'selling peeps' through convenient wall-holes to Japanese with enough money and temerity to look at the funny barbarians sleeping or dressing. But at least this curiosity was innocent; much more oppressive was the continuous surveillance of the *ometsuke*, the 'eyes in attendance', that is, government spies who reported every movement of the westerners back to higher quarters. 'We are never for a moment unwatched,' Oliphant complained. 'If my servant runs after a butterfly, a two-sworded *samurai* runs after him.' As every Japanese official always had an *ometsuke* watching *him*, the native commissioners could not believe that Lord Elgin was without an *ometsuke* – a most imprudent omission on Queen Victoria's part, they felt. After a day or two, however, the

Japanese noticed that Lord Elgin always signed his correspondence 'Elgin and Kincardine' – so that was it: Kincardine was the 'eye in attendance' secretly watching Elgin, and Kincardine was such an efficient eye that no one ever saw him at all. Oliphant spent three hours explaining the niceties of British titles to the still-bewildered commissioners.

But, as Oliphant was the first to admit, on most matters the Japanese representatives were far from obtuse. And once Lord Elgin and the ministers gathered round the conference table and, as Oliphant quaintly puts it, 'mutually exhibited their full powers', the outline of a treaty was sketched very rapidly and Elgin was soon convinced that he had won another easy market for his dear nation of shopkeepers. So much so, that back in Scotland two years later, he informed his cheering Dunfermline neighbours of how he had been to Japan and of how he had managed to 'perform the whole business' of the treaty in a couple of weeks and of how, as a result of his efforts on their behalf, there would be new opportunities opening up in the East, for the Japanese, Elgin concluded, 'are a very changeable sort of people and will soon be fascinated by Dunfermline linens'.

Whether the Japanese ever succumbed to such fascination is not recorded; but certainly the British were fascinated by the products of Japan. They bought toy-size models of *norimons,* straw animals, jack-in-the-boxes, dolls whose tongues stuck out, tortoises whose tails moved, swords, masks and dogs. At least, nearly every member of the delegation bought dogs; Laurence Oliphant, however, was one who had no difficulty in resisting their charms and explains why: 'They used to demolish their paper kennels with their teeth, quarrel with each other, howl dismally during the still hours of night, or have spasms. They were subject to weakness and violent cramp in the loins and hind legs and then their owners used to devote the small hours of the morning to fomenting them with hot water and wrapping them in warm flannels. In spite of all their efforts some of these delicate little creatures died, to the inexpressible grief of those who had listened so often to their nocturnal whinings.'

As no exchange rate for foreign currency had yet been fixed, the British ordered and signed for all their purchases and then, on their last day in Japan, settled to the business of paying their accounts. It was a chaotic exercise. The foreigners' lodgings that morning were crowded with Japanese shopkeepers who had brought the goods ordered and sought payment and with the members of the mission who were rushing from one to another trying to remember what they had rashly bought in the enthusiasm of a moment ten days earlier. To restore order, a couple of reckoners were employed, 'two old Japanese, senior wranglers, probably, of their year', Oliphant wrote, 'with corrugated foreheads and countenances betokening unlimited sagacity, who stalked gravely in with attendants carrying balances, scales, weights, pens, ink and paper'. These dignitaries seated themselves in the centre of the room and 'then approached tremblingly the shopkeeper and the victim who was to pay him'.

In a surprisingly short time everything was settled. The British were relieved of their foreign money which went into the Japanese treasury, while the shopkeepers were paid in local *itzibu*; each man, except Oliphant, had his dog; Lord Elgin had a pair of green pigeons; and they all went for a final banquet at which the two countries toasted each other in hot *saké* and cold champagne. After the meal the delegation members were treated to an exhibition of the famous Japanese butterfly trick. The conjurer took a piece of white paper and twisted it skilfully into the shape of a butterfly; he then drew an ornamental fan from his kimono sleeve and opened it. 'He threw the paper butterfly up into the air', Elgin explained, 'and gradually it seemed to acquire a life from the action of the fan – now wheeling and dipping towards it, now tripping along its edge, then hovering over it, as we may see a butterfly do over a flower on a fine summer's day, then in wantonness wheeling away and again returning to alight, the wings quivering with a nervous restlessness! One could have sworn it was a live creature!'

As the conjurer brought the paper butterfly delicately to rest on the straw-matted stage, there was a general sigh of regret from the spectators; it was time to go; time, all too soon, for most of them, to leave this lovely secret land. At sunset on 28 August the British mission steamed out of Yedo Bay after receiving a salute of Japanese guns. 'It was', Oliphant noted, 'a lively and beautiful scene. The shores of the bay were lined with people; in places, green wooded banks came down to the water and the smoke from the guns still rested upon the island forts. Many-coloured flags fluttered in the breeze, hundreds of boats flitted to and fro on the still waters of the bay; while, rearing its conical summit far into the blue sky, old Fusi-yama [sic] formed a noble background.'

Elgin's mission had, of course, accomplished something; but its success was deceptively easy. All the preliminary spadework for it had been done by Townsend Harris and all the further difficulties which arose during the actual establishment of Anglo-Japanese trade relations were to be faced later. Elgin was there just long enough to present the yacht, agree to much the same terms as Harris had made, buy his pigeons and his porcelain and then he was off – back to China where, he considered, the situation was more urgent. Clearly, however, there were still many diplomatic jousts to be settled between the westerners and the Japanese and, realising this, the Foreign Office decided to send out one of their most valued 'Far East experts', Sir Rutherford Alcock.

II

Sir Rutherford had spent most of his early career as an army surgeon attached to the British Legion in Spain, where he had gained a reputation for skill and courage. A picture of him at about that time shows a curly-haired, intelligent young man with an aggressive chin, a sensitive soft mouth and large lonely eyes hinting at self-conscious moods of Byronic melancholy. Then, in 1844, Alcock had set off to the East as Consul to the newly-opened port of Fu Chou and was soon promoted to Shanghai where he was successful in establishing a form of municipal government. A picture of him at that time shows a firm, solid man whose curly hair was smooth and grey, whose mouth was firm and disciplined and whose eyes retained a certain withdrawn sadness. It was this middle-aged Sir Rutherford who landed in Japan in the summer of 1859, a man of determination and authority whose approach was thoroughly conditioned by his formidably extensive knowledge of China – from which celestial power, he felt, Japan was basically a rather wayward offshoot. Alcock never really liked the Japanese, never understood the Shogun-Emperor dichotomy which split the country and never trusted the Yedo government in any particular.

Compared to Townsend Harris's mercilessly circumspect journal, Alcock's book about his Japanese experiences, *The Capital of the Tycoon*, is individual, rhetorical, frank and, often, wrong-headed and intemperate. Algernon Mitford, who later served under Alcock in China and went to Japan after Alcock had left, felt that 'the Chief's' writings about the latter country were misguided. He would, Mitford comments, 'have been a greater man if he had never written a book about a country which he did not understand, or a grammar of a language which he could neither read nor write'. But, as Mitford goes on to explain, Alcock's weakness was that he considered himself a writer – a weakness which could be hard on his subordinates as mail-day approached each month. Though Alcock's dispatches, particularly those from China, contained excellent material, they were frequently spoiled – as his book on Japan is spoiled – by interminable lengths of ponderous verbiage. And, says Mitford, 'to copy these effusions with the thermometer at 108 in the shade, with a double sheet of blotting paper between my hand and the foolscap and a basin of water to dip my fingers in from time to time, was like being private secretary to Satan in the nethermost regions'.

Less tolerant, pertinacious and resigned than Harris, Alcock saw his work in Japan as being more of a struggle than a conciliation and he did not believe that any true sense of fellowship and fusion could result from this new East-West contact. On the other hand, because he lacked Harris's single-mindedness, Alcock was more aware of the wider issues, the philosophical and moral implications of the westerners' peaceful invasion of Japan. Again and again his writing veers off into broader concepts, into the broodings and castings-about of a cultured but diffuse mind. He believed in the efficacy of firm military action more than Harris did and, in the political crises which lay ahead, he occasionally yearned for the simple certainties of gunboat diplomacy. Nevertheless, he feared and deplored violence and there are occasional glimpses, in his more impassioned passages, of a suppressed, hysterical terror of swift and bloody assassination.

Though Sir Rutherford was obliquely critical of several of Townsend Harris's decisions, he admired the American's tenacity and his emphasis on formality, for both he and Harris understood the need for a dignified and punctilious bearing in their official dealings with the Japanese. Perhaps the quality which Harris and Alcock had most in common was the one which, of its very nature, precluded fellowship – their loneliness. For they were lonely men, and they hated and pitied themselves for it. Both, at times, felt shut away at the ends of the earth, neglected by their governments, forgotten by their friends, stranded like castaways on an alien and insignificant little island. The pious melancholy of their temperaments was nurtured by this sense of undeserved isolation and soon, as Harris had yearned for the vigour of New York, so Alcock yearned for the companionship of London. 'As a man never feels more alone than when the sense of loneliness comes upon him in a crowd,' Alcock wrote about two months after his arrival, 'in this wilderness of living men the foreigner is too entirely a stranger and too absolutely repudiated as having anything in common with the natives, to feel otherwise than banished and exiled from all social intercourse'.

On 6 July 1859 Alcock officially landed in Japan and the British flag was unfurled in the grounds of the Tozenji temple. This temple, part of which had been vacated by disgruntled priests so that the small British Legation could be accommodated, was one of the most lovely in Yedo. Its approach lay along a green-shade avenue of aloof cryptomerias, past imposing lichen-covered gateways, round waxen lotus-ponds and across an undulating lawn. A grainy-wood bridge spanned a still lake. A garden path led zigzag up a crumbling flight of steps which widened at the top to a 'viewing platform' from which one could see the wide blue spread of the bay and the soft, brown-grey jumbles of the wooden city – the distant view enclosed in a foreground frame of pine and bamboo foliage. The temple itself was low and wide, a sprawling conglomeration of passages, rooms, courtyards and outbuildings which provided a commodious and adaptable shelter but which, as Alcock had reason to discover later, was also a flimsy and vulnerable place to defend.

To this secluded and beautiful shrine the barbarians came. Six of them at first: Alcock himself, his secretary, a doctor and three student interpreters. They brought chairs and tables and sofas and saucers and knives and forks, though the latter implements were so completely lost in the confusion that all meals during the first week had to be shovelled up with chopsticks anyhow. They set up beds, kitchen stoves and dressing-tables; they tramped over the clean lemon-yellow mats in their heavy boots; their rough, hasty fingers fumbled clumsily with paper screens and dainty feather-light lanterns; their voices sounded harsh and deep in the fragile rooms and they kept knocking their heads on the low roof-supports. It was little wonder that some of the hired servants slipped away as quickly as they could and that the Tozenji priests scowled sullenly through the cracks in the walls.

Forced back on his own resources, Alcock, like Harris, found that time sagged. For work, there was the bickering with the Japanese authorities over the promised opening of Yokohama, the writing of dispatches, the supervision of his staff and his tenacious, exhausting attempts to learn Japanese and produce an English-Japanese grammar. The grammar, as Alcock confessed, turned out to be a Herculean exercise, part fact and part speculation. He was dismayed to find that Japanese had no genders for nouns, no precise definite articles, but a multiplicity of forms for addressing people of different rank, for numbering objects of different sorts ('There is one class of numerals for all animals – except the flying and swimming species, and insects. Another for birds, in which, however, hare and rabbits are included! – he exclaimed in horror) and a plethora of verbs. The verbs almost defeated him: 'my despair', he wrote, 'may be conceived when, as a mere tyro and foreigner, I came to the task of unravelling their intricacies, and digging beneath the surface, overlaid with distinctions, for the simple elements and the roots. Many times I was more than half disposed to give up the undertaking in utter hopelessness of ever seeing my way to any useful end.' An end was reached at long last, however, and interpreters and staff congratulated themselves when the last page of the book was sent to the printer. Unfortunately, apparently, Alcock's grammar was exceedingly inaccurate in spite of all effort that went into it and subsequent toilers among Japanese verbs and numerals speak very slightingly of its value.

When Sir Rutherford did take time off from these various labours, he could find little to please him beyond a quiet contemplation of local scenery and an occasional foray into the crowded streets of the city. The lax, gentle rhythms of oriental time marked only by slow seasonal changes did nothing to quiet Alcock's tensions. There were no church-bells to herald the habitual day of worship; no newspapers to bring tidings of a busy week; he woke up on Wednesday and thought it was Friday; indeed, he wrote fretfully, 'all days were Sundays here' – and who could enjoy a week of Sundays? Nevertheless, any disturbance that occurred was almost bound to be unpleasant: the first jolting shock of earthquake when the Legation joggled like a house of cards, the first bout of cholera which left the body spongy and flaccid for weeks and, worst of all, the first 'deed of blood' when three Russian sailors were literally hacked to pieces in a Yokohama street by a group of reactionary Japanese swordsmen, a taste of what was to follow.

To fill the hours more constructively, Sir Rutherford set himself two additional tasks. The first was to make some kind of accurate, honest record of the customs and culture of Japan in order to dispel a few of the weird and wildly inaccurate stories about the country which were still current in the West. Alcock's wide-ranging and haphazard curiosity was an asset here and he chats happily away on a quantity of odd subjects. He writes about the *moxa* for example, 'a pleasant ingenious device for burning a hole in a man's skin'. A *moxa* was a neat little parcel of dried leaves and bark which was placed on the body and burned there, either to relieve a particular malady or 'to expel all manner of winds and vapours'. Every Japanese housewife had her formidable supply of *moxa* ready for any emergency, and perhaps they were efficacious in so far as the application of one was painful enough for the patient to forget his original ailment. He describes the performances of jugglers, masked shrine-dancers, street-musicians and, most remarkable of all, top-spinners. These last could spin a heavy iron top on the edge of a fan, on the point of a sword, on the back of a neck, on the bowl of a pipe and, finally, send the toy spinning up a rope to the head of a mast where it continued to gyrate quite unexhausted. He gives too a pleasing account of a visit to a relaxed, old-fashioned draper's shop, where one sat on the clean-matted, raised floor, sipped tea and examined the sumptuous rolls of materials – snow-pale gauze, luxurious thick brocades, quiet, practical blue cottons, silks delicate as flower petals and dappled with designs of butterflies, dragonflies and birds.

Sir Rutherford's second self-imposed task was to make full use of the diplomatic right which officially allowed him to travel freely within the country. He considered it his duty to exercise this right frequently so that the Japanese would become accustomed to the foreigners' presence and so that the foreigners themselves would have more chance to break through the cordon of constant surveillance which impeded their movements within the capital.

During his stay in Japan, Alcock travelled north to Hakodate, went through the southern provinces between Nagasaki and Yedo and made a pilgrimage to the summit of Mount Fuji. This latter journey was, perhaps, the most enjoyable and successful of them. In those days, the peerless mountain was clearly visible all the way from Yedo, so that, from the first sparkle of white dawn on its crest to the last flicker of sun setting golden behind it, the foreigners could see their goal ahead as soon as they left the Legation. However, as many a later traveller was to discover, the actual ascent of Fuji was not the easy stroll up a beautiful hill which a distant view of it might suggest. Alcock's party had to leave their horses on the lower slopes and begin what was no less than a hard scramble over increasingly harsh and steep terrain. Trees became thinner and more stunted; grass gave way to scrubby patches of weed and then to fragmented, loose stones for the foot to slip on and jutting boulders for the shins to crack against. There were no animals, no birds and very little oxygen. The men panted in the rarefied air, their hearts drumming as they sprawled out on the floors of the cramped little huts which had been built at two-mile intervals to give overnight shelter for climbers. These huts specialised then – and for years afterwards – in two particular discomforts: they were icy cold and they were infested with fleas. And many a traveller, as he huddled his aching limbs under a thin blanket and scratched and gasped through the chill hours of darkness, wondered if he would have been wiser to keep the 'matchless mountain' at a picturesque distance.

As soon as the first clean light spread above the mountain's cone the party rose, swallowed coffee and biscuits and stumbled painfully upwards for three or four hours until, at last, they reached the gaping lip of the crater itself. Thankful to have accomplished the ascent without incident, Alcock rested against a rock and looked round – first into the yawning hole of the volcano, then away to where the country lay 13,000 feet below, swaddled in a canopy of cloud. Mysterious, unpredictable country; fair and unspoiled and strangely innocent; cruel and rigid and very old. Alcock rubbed his eyes and tried, unsuccessfully, to pierce the thick swathes of the mist. What was it really like, this secret land? What did its people think of them, a small, unprotected band of foreigners perched on their sacred mountain? They were questions to which he, for one, never found answers.

III

On the way back to Yedo Alcock and his party made a short detour to have a look at the progress of Yokohama, a port which was already growing at a prodigious rate and which, more than any other place in the country, offered clear evidence that the West had arrived – and not only arrived but come to stay.

For four years after Commodore Perry's Grand Landing, Yokohama had remained a collection of unpainted, shabby fishermen's huts straggling along a desolate shore, its limits roughly bounded on the west by a salty swamp, on the south by a tidal creek, on the north by a river estuary and by the uncharted Pacific on the east. But in the year 1858, in high summer when the sun slamming down on the land day after day made even the rough straw mats (*tatami*) in the fishermen's homes gleam like gold, eighty-four men affixed their eighty-four signatures to the Treaty Concerning the Ports, and the closed and torpid mussel of Yokohama was prised open to the world. Carpenters and labourers and masons arrived, dragging loads of grainy wood, of rope and bamboo canes and lumps of granite; tucking their scanty blue aprons high above their thighs, and winding a band of cloth round their foreheads to keep the sweat from their eyes, they began to build.

They built a few houses, one storey high with paper windows; they built jetties faced with granite thrusting seawards and backed by a solid, magisterial Custom House; they built a stone pier that ran out firmly into the soft bay; they built the first godowns – easily inflammable tarred wood-and-stone storehouses to hold the merchants' booty; they built a bridge across the creek, another across the river and a causeway across the swamp; and on each side of the bridges they built little guard-huts, and at the end of each bridge they built sturdy gates which were shut at sunset, and two large barricades at each end of the causeway.

Yokohama looked like a prison settlement, a Dartmoor of the marshes within which the undesirable foreigners could be isolated as utterly as the Dutch had been on the island of Decima during the seventeenth and eighteenth centuries. It was hardly surprising that when Sir Rutherford Alcock and Townsend Harris first saw Yokohama they argued vehemently with the Japanese authorities that Kanagawa, a small town on the main Tokkaido road, was a much more suitable and accessible site for a settlement and that this circumscribed enclave would not do at all.

But the Japanese officials were equally determined that it could and would do. They conducted Alcock and Harris through the new Main Street, where, says the former, 'out of a marsh by the edge of a deserted bay, a wave of the conjurer's wand had created a considerable and bustling settlement of Japanese merchants' whose mushroom-rapid appearance

Alcock could compare only to a similar phenomenon in eighteenth-century Russia when, 'at the order of Potemkin, villages appeared as if by magic to greet the Empress Catherine'. As everyone knows, Alcock and Harris were defeated on this issue – by the energetic ingenuity of the Japanese (some of whom were still unpacking their belongings, for they had been precipitated into their new homes that very morning in order to give a promise of permanence to the place) and by the foreign merchants themselves, who cared little whether they were isolated from the natives or not. The merchants came to trade; they wanted jetties on which to unload, storehouses to fill, land to rent. Yokohama had these things and they little heeded the croakings of their Consuls who warned them how easy it was for the Japanese to regulate their trade and restrict their movements and how limited was the amount of land available for development. Hardly had the Foreign Representatives turned their backs than the first arrivals, adventurers of all nations, from Nagasaki, Shanghai and Hong Kong, took possession of every rickety hut, every flimsy godown and every yard of swamp they could afford. Yokohama was ready for business.

But, at first, business did not prosper. The Japanese, extemporising with their usual skill, had made solid-looking silver coins which were to be exchanged, weight for weight, with foreign dollars. But when the first sailors and merchants threw their dollars into the scales at the Yokohama Custom House, they found that the coins they received in exchange, though glittering fresh and pretty with promise, were worth only one-third of what they had expected. Currency fluctuated alarmingly, and the problem of making these tempting *itzibu* a meaningful and fair unit of exchange in the trading marts of Asia where the price of rice in Siam, copper in Constantinople and tea in China had to be taken into account, was one which worried consular and commercial minds for several years.

Soon, however, the foreign merchants discovered that, because the Japanese had put all their trust in silver, they could put theirs in gold. Four pretty *itzibu* – equivalent to about six shillings – would buy a whole *cobang* of gold – and a *cobang* of gold was worth about eighteen shillings and fourpence outside Japan. Realising that they were on to a very good thing, the merchants ceased to bother about such cumbersome items as tea and silk and bought as much gold as they could lay their hands on and exported it as fast as they could find a ship to take it away. For a few glittering months there was a miniature gold rush as the foreigners poured Japanese gold out of the country and turned up neat little profits of two hundred per cent on every *cobang* sold in the Chinese markets. Every foreigner wanted *itzibu* to convert into gold; the customs men sitting behind their scales in the Custom House on the jetty were bribed and besieged by clamouring merchants; at least two American officers who happened to call in on their way to San Francisco resigned their commissions on the spot, chartered ships and started export firms; and the Japanese, bewildered to find all their gold being sent to China, began to understand that the pegging of an artificially high value on their silver had not been such a good idea after all.

The mad bonanza was, inevitably, a short one, and Alcock was instrumental in finally persuading the Japanese government to adjust the relative value of their gold and silver to the established world prices. Nevertheless, a few wily early birds among the foreign merchants had time to make their fortunes without so much as filling a warehouse; more seriously, the Japanese had become so highly suspicious of foreign business practices that they tried to postpone indefinitely the opening of any other ports and even to nullify the existing treaties. As the Governor of Kanagawa province put it to Sir Rutherford (his tongue carefully loosened by frequent libations of best Chartreuse, which he considered a strange and marvellous potion): 'We have had nothing but expense, everything is getting dearer and if this be the result of foreign trade at its first beginning, what will it be in its development?'

But whatever fears the Japanese government and the foreign

diplomats might have had about the future of Yokohama, the port was bound to prosper. By the end of 1859 a makeshift jumble of shops, godowns and bungalows strung out for nearly half a mile from the jetties to the cliff on the other side of the southern creek – and this cliff, already and for ever afterwards called The Bluff, had recently been suggested as a desirable location for merchants' residences because of its naturally superior position overlooking the huddled port below. In spite of Yokohama's isolation at the end of the guarded causeway, Japanese shopkeepers from Yedo and Kanagawa had heard from afar the sound of coin jangling in the pockets of foreign sailors and had brought their goods for sale. They had already learned to say 'vely cheap'; they already understood that the foreigners, seeing the little lacquer boxes in which, for centuries, hair ornaments and letters had been carried, would buy them, call them luncheon or glove boxes or work-baskets and carry them away as 'souvenirs of Japan'.

For already, too, a few hardy and inquisitive tourists were beginning to arrive. There was the Right Reverend Bishop George Smith of Hong Kong, a man who liked little of what he saw anywhere. 'The population of Yokohama,' he announced after his visit, was made up of 'the disorderly elements of Californian adventurers, Portuguese desperadoes and the moral refuse of European nations'. The Bishop also made it his business to count the number of local grog-shops – which he found excessive – and to discover on the edge of the swamp the existence of an establishment euphemistically called 'The Gankiro Teahouse', in which 'at least two hundred females were dispersed over a spacious series of apartments'. The foreign merchants, he learned, were encouraged to negotiate a sort of 'woman price' through the local custom officials and, for a reasonable sum, could buy a mistress-housekeeper for an indefinite period if they so desired. The Bishop was scandalised; Yokohama was a snare and a trap for the innocent young Englishmen pure from home, it was a deplorable setting for 'demoralisation and profligate life' in which existed 'every facility for the perpetration of domestic vice and impurity'. It is fairly easy to estimate the Bishop's character from his writing and this impression is confirmed by an unexpected reference to him in the letters of Lieutenant George Preble – who was, of course, safely home again with his wife and family long before the Bishop reached Japan. Preble, apparently, had known Smith in his zealous and intolerant youth and was amazed to find, during the time that Perry's expedition was wintering in Hong Kong, that 'humble Mr Smith, Episcopalian Missionary, is now styled "Lord Bishop of Victoria" and receives a salary of 5,000 pounds'. Preble attended one of the Bishop's services, but was vexed by the formal theatricality of the responses and the irksome 'frequency of getting up and sitting down'. This newly-affluent, pompous and even more censorious ex-Mr Smith was not at all to Preble's simple Christian taste.

Another Englishman who visited Japan during 1860 was much more delighted with the country – perhaps because he was more interested in its plant and animal life than in its impurities and imperfections. Robert Fortune was a botanist who gathered a vast collection of Japanese plant specimens and shipped them home to his beloved Kew Gardens. The most exciting moment of Fortune's Japanese visit was when he discovered the male of the *Aucuba japonica* species. Europe, it seemed, was full of female *Aucuba japonica*, but their lack of male company meant that they had never produced any red berries in autumn as a truly fulfilled *japonica* should. And so Fortune sent some male Japanese *japonica* for all the deprived European female *japonica* and one assumes that they all berried happily ever after.

As Fortune's collection soon outgrew the bounds of his Yokohama hotel room, he rented a disused office-warehouse in Kanagawa. He pottered around there for months, his trays of butterflies, moths and beetles, his pots of cuttings, his boxes crammed with shells and seeds proliferating in ever-richer abundance over floors, balconies and shelves. He wandered extensively through the quiet, busy countryside noting how the rape-seed was harvested, how sweet potatoes were cuddled up in straw and how irises were grown on the flattened ridges of the thatched cottage roofs. The Japanese liked him, though they may have thought him a little mad. When there was trouble in Yokohama they sent men to reinforce his fences and gave him a couple of police-guards. But no one bothered such an unquestionably apolitical fellow and, the next year, when he left Japan, he was allowed to take all his beautiful and lively treasures with him.

However, to the occasional visitor such as Fortune, charmed by all he saw, a resident of Yokohama in 1859 would undoubtedly have pointed out a few of the port's deficiencies: there was no dairy and no beef, no bread and no library, no club and no town-hall, no park and no theatre and a lamentable insufficiency of respectable women. Moreover, and perhaps most galling of all, he was still strictly confined within the limits fixed by the treaties and so could travel only ten *ri* (about twenty-four miles) in any direction. So that, all in all, when there were few ships in port and mail-day was two weeks ahead and the latest batch of bills was neatly docketed in pigeon-holes waiting to be paid, there was little for a commercially-minded foreign gentleman to do but to take a stroll and look at the scenery and the people and meditate on the merits of the land he had come to exploit.

For as long as anyone could remember the Shogun had enforced a law which stated that no firearm of any kind could be used to kill bird or beast within a distance of fifty *ri* from his palace. And so, on the marshes behind Yokohama, just seventeen miles from Yedo, flocks of wild geese flew securely over the strolling merchant's head; storks moved with dignity after eels and worms; partridges and pheasants blinked amiably at him as he went by. And the merchant, who lived on a diet of rice, eggs, seaweed, fish and the occasional piece of tough chicken, rubbed his trigger-itchy fingers. As Alcock complained, a lack of beef and mutton was extremely undermining to the British constitution and to be denied even the consolation of munching the plump innocent breast of the nearby duck was hard indeed.

Given these circumstances, it was scarcely surprising that within about a year of the port's opening there was trouble. One Michael Moss, Esquire, Yokohama merchant, was tramping home through Kanagawa on a November evening with a gun over his shoulder and his servant behind carrying what was very obviously the gun's spoils – a large wild goose. As they neared the causeway, a body of Japanese policemen suddenly pounced on the servant, and Moss turned back to aid him.

There are two irreconcilable versions of what happened next. According to the Japanese, the policemen tried to arrest Moss who, with more malice than forethought, cocked his gun and fired – shattering the arm and chest of one of the officers. According to Moss himself, he was attacked from behind just as he cocked his gun, he fell forward, and as he did so the gun's trigger entangled in the ropes which the Japanese were trying to fasten round him and went off – the indisputable result of the shot being the same for the luckless policeman. Again according to the Japanese, Moss was then bound hand and foot and dragged off to a prison cell where he was left until the early hours of the following morning. But according to Moss's own more colourful account, he was not only trussed up and imprisoned but, in the middle of the night, carried out to the beach, dumped in the bottom of a boat and taken out to sea, transferred to another boat and brought back and dumped again on the floor of his frigid cell in a sort of nightmarish chaos during which he thought every moment was his last.

That Moss had been foolish was incontestable; he had violated the laws of the country, for which violation a Japanese could receive the death penalty. If, of course, he had also deliberately maimed a policeman who was doing no more than his duty, his crime was that much more serious. The next day the little settlement was a dark and fearful hive of rumour – the wounded policeman's brother had sworn to take revenge by killing at least one foreigner; Moss was to be secretly tortured and executed; a gang of outlaws was being organised in Yedo which would massacre every foreign male in the country within a week. The merchants oiled their guns, bolted their doors and kept close together for comfort.

There was a great deal of sympathy for Moss. Undoubtedly he was by no means the only foreigner who had been shooting the game, he was merely unlucky enough to have been caught. Moss stoutly averred, for example, that the British Consul in Kanagawa was the best shot in the settlement! Perhaps such an assertion partly explains why, when Moss was eventually tried in the British consular court, he was only fined one thousand dollars and sentenced to deportation.

But the matter did not end there. Sir Rutherford Alcock, who firmly believed the official Japanese version of the incident, was enraged at the leniency of the local Consul's sentence and ordered that a three-month stretch in a Japanese prison be added to it. Moss screamed in fury, the Yokohama merchants sent a protest deputation to Alcock and passed round the hat to help Moss pay his fine. By whose connivance it is, perhaps, wise not to inquire, but, in the event, Moss managed to take advantage of a series of blunders on the part of the local authorities and a legal oversight on Alcock's part and escape after he had spent but five days in prison. A month later he appeared unscathed in Hong Kong.

From that safe distance he instituted proceedings against Sir Rutherford for injury suffered during his short period of detention, won his case and was awarded damages of two thousand dollars. Even then Moss did not give up for, he argued, this sum by no means compensated him for the properties he had been forced to abandon in Yokohama. He continued to shout for justice and for Alcock's dismissal during the next two years – first in Hong Kong, where he besieged the courthouse and the home of the local judge, and later in London where he penned copious letters to Palmerston, the Law

Society, Earl Russell, the Duke of Edinburgh and anyone else whom he thought might listen. As a last salvo he wrote a pamphlet – an unsavoury mixture of self-pity, self-aggrandisement, cunning and hysteria – in which he described the affair from his personal viewpoint.

Eventually people got rather bored with Michael Moss and his wild-goose chase after an imaginary justice. Certainly, though Moss claimed he was the only loser, no one did well out of the business. The policeman lost his arm and his livelihood; Alcock lost his case, the respect of the local Japanese officials and any remnant of sympathy which had hitherto existed between him and the foreign merchants; the Consul of Kanagawa lost Alcock's trust; Moss lost his new warehouse and the hope, as he put it, 'of being on the high road to fortune'; and as for the wildfowl, they soon lost their faith in man. A merchant who secretly scoured the marshes with his gun a year later records that an early riser in the 'good old days' (that is, in Moss's time) could 'bag twelve birds before breakfast. Now he's lucky to get two'. A few years later still, there was seldom a goose or a duck or a stork or a pheasant to be seen anywhere. The western hunters' guns had done their work.

IV

The Moss affair, which occurred towards the end of 1860, was not the first incident to shatter the fragile peace of the Yokohama settlement that year. For, during the preceding months, the foreigners had already learned to recognise and dread the two chief hazards of pioneer life in Japan: fire and the sword.

From the first moment that three or four flimsy wood-and-paper dwellings are strung together to make a street on the precarious earthquake-ridden Japanese soil, fire lurks round the corner licking anticipatory jaws. Fire, say the Japanese, is the flower of Yedo which blooms throughout the year, and it is a plant which they seem more inclined to feed than to root out. A Japanese fireman of the nineteenth century armed with a hand-operated pump no more effective than a garden hose, from which emerged a trickle of water just sufficient for him to keep himself cool and soggy, and with a barbed pole for tearing down buildings and shooing away spectators, was a totally inadequate figure to fight the huge conflagrations which, at disturbingly frequent intervals, demolished whole areas of the towns. Nevertheless, perhaps because they never stopped trying, the firemen were – together with the *sumo* wrestlers – the popular heroes of Yedo. They wore quilted mantles, cotton quilted hats and wooden *geta* (pattens) – all good, fireproof material! At the sound of the alarm bell, they would form into procession and march towards the fire singing loudly. First went an officer bearing a paper ensign; then three or four juniors jerking along a thirty-foot bamboo ladder, then the other firemen, carrying firehooks and the pump. The fellow with the ensign would then clamber bravely on to the roof nearest the one in flames and stay there, trying to protect it from flying sparks, until he or his roof or his ensign caught fire also. Many a fireman perished in this fashion; but it was an honourable death and every New Year's Day the remaining firemen would celebrate their own survival and their comrades' heroism by marching to the public parks and performing acrobatics on their long ladders to the great admiration of all who saw them.

This situation had gone on for so long that the Japanese had learned to live with it. An efficient system of alarm bells usually gave sufficient warning of the approaching flames for a family to wrap its few possessions in a couple of *futon* (padded bed-rolls) and escape to safety. Next day, they would return to the heap of ashes which had been home and enjoy a picnic there-on, to which any neighbour with a roof still over his head was a particularly welcome guest. In return for hospitality offered under such depressing circumstances, the neighbours would lend a hand and, usually within a fortnight or so, a new one-storey dwelling of equal inflammability was erected to replace the old.

But for westerners things were not so simple. Not only were their houses more elaborately and expensively constructed and filled with heavy furniture which could not be carted away at ten minutes' notice, but the godowns near them might well contain goods which represented the total of a young merchant's capital – probably uninsured. And so, for some, the year 1860 began disastrously. The weather during the first week of January was sharp, bright and windy. In Yedo, Sir Rutherford Alcock had to break the ice before climbing into his morning bath; in Yokohama that same day the hot flowers of flame burst through the foreign settlement, climbing and twining over the houses of native and foreigner alike. Order was maintained during this first shared disaster, there was no pillaging and the firemen were briskly marshalled into their ensign-flying brigades. Nevertheless, damage was extensive, lives were lost and the high hopes of several young merchants were turned literally to ashes within an hour.

But in spite of the risk of financial ruin that fire threatened, the westerners, like the Japanese, learned, though with less resignation, to live with it. But the other threat, more deadly, more elusive and cruel even than fire, no foreigner could be expected to accept: the Japanese sword. This beautiful and terrible weapon, its edge as icily efficient as a diamond, its blade a slender arc of blue light, its guard tenderly wrought with designs of bird and blossom, was the embodiment of the silent, invisible, incalculable, unconquerable menace of bloody assassination which made the flesh creep on the skull of merchant, sailor and diplomat alike as he turned the dark corner in the passage-way or found himself in a quiet and watchful back street as evening fell.

Ever since the leading ship of Perry's squadron appeared over the horizon, the reactionary factions in Japan had fought obstinately to prevent western infiltration. Now that the battle seemed almost lost it was inevitable that they should turn to their traditionally violent ways of disposing of undesirables. The most actively hostile elements of the movement were, at first, concentrated in the powerful southern clans of Satsuma and Mito, and, as soon as it became clear that the westerners had come to stay, warriors from these clans banded into lawless, violent groups whose sole aim was to oust the intruders from the sacred soil of their land – by killing them, by firing their residences, even by murdering the progressives in their own government. These men, whose function in the old feudal order had been to support their lords and fight for them in time of war, understood that they could have no place in the new cosmopolitan society of a modern Japan. As special clan loyalties became meaningless, they had nothing left but the last desperate loyalty to the vanishing past and, with the fanatical, self-annihilating bravado of the *kamikaze* pilot, they intended to go down fighting. Such men were called *ronin* which literally means 'wavemen' – a descriptive term for those who, as the waves of the restless sea, tossed hither and thither from one disruptive venture to the next. And, for most of the 1860's, that word *ronin* conjured in the uneasy mind of every westerner and of every open-minded, liberal Japanese, the picture of a swaggering, reckless two-sworded monster who was lithe and swift as a panther and whose lovely weapon could pierce the heart, hack the entrails, slice the white neck before a man could close his own eyes for the last time.

The first four years of the decade were the *ronins'* heyday and one of their first victims was a man of their own race – Dankitchi. Dankitchi was Sir Rutherford's chief interpreter at the Yedo Legation who owed his exalted position to the fact that, years before, he had been shipwrecked in the Pacific and been picked up by a ship going to America. Dankitchi was, apparently, an overweening, intemperate man who wanted to display the new 'progressive' habits he had acquired to his 'backward' countrymen. Because he was invaluable at the time – one of a handful of living men who knew both Japanese and English – he had ample opportunity, says Alcock, 'to work out the errors of his mind and system' – in other words, to throw his weight about.

One quiet Sunday afternoon Dankitchi swaggered out of the Legation's front door, dressed, as usual, in dapper western-style suit, crisp white shirt, polished black shoes. He stopped at the gate and leaned against the entrance leading to a narrow lane which led to a few Japanese houses; above him the Union Jack flapped in the cold bright air. Perhaps he did not even hear the stones crunch under the feet of the man who buried a short sword in his back, the point of which protruded above his right breast; probably he did not see the man; certainly he did not live long enough to tell.

Sir Rutherford was convinced that there must, at such a time and place, have been some witnesses to the deed and even that the Japanese authorities themselves were fully aware of Dankitchi's danger. However, the murderers were never caught; there was too much fear and hatred abroad for that. Dankitchi's loss was mourned by the foreigners chiefly because he had been so useful; but it was also unpleasantly symptomatic that this, almost the first assassination, should have occurred under the very shadow of a foreign flag and that its victim was one who, despite his faults, had worked hard to establish contact between the westerners and the Japanese. In any event, though the murder of Dankitchi greatly disturbed and incommoded the foreign diplomats, its effects were soon forgotten in the uproar caused by the sensational assassination which was perpetrated two months later – the most audacious and ambitious of them all.

In accordance with a traditional oriental deviousness which invariably arranged for Japan to be ruled by some discreet authority whose power was sheltered behind a titular figure-head, the destinies of the country were, during this crucial period of her history, largely in the hands of the Gotairo – the Regent. The Gotairo was a far-sighted and resolute man who had negotiated and signed the first treaty with the Americans

and who had since advocated the gradual but continuous opening of his country to foreign influence of all kinds.

The Gotairo and his abundant, flamboyant retinue occupied
a stately residence flanked by courtyards and low, grey-tiled
outbuildings, from which a level line of road swept down to
one of three bridges graciously arched across a moat that
encircled the grounds of the Shogun's own castle. Every morning the Gotairo, escorted by his bodyguards and bearers,
climbed into his *norimon* and proceeded slowly down the road,
across a bridge and into the castle where he explained to the
Shogun what was going on in his country.

The morning of 24 March 1860 was, as far as the Gotairo
knew, an ordinary one, except that the weather was unusually
inclement for the time of year. Sleet and rain lashed the surface
of the moat; the ducks, their feathers disordered, crouched for
shelter along the wet banks and under the intermittent cover of
the willows and the crooked pines. It was in fact a day which
offered 'little inducement to mere idlers to be abroad', as Alcock
commented in his detailed account of the episode. The Gotairo,
being a man of such immense consequence, had attendants to
carry light wood screens on either side of his *norimon*, which
protected him both from the worst of the elements and the eyes
of the curious. The attendants, bowed against the wind, were
wrapped like parcels in rainproof cloaks of oiled paper with
wide lacquer hats tied on their heads and straw or cloth shoes
which squelched in the mud. But in spite of the relative infor-
mality and unseemly wetness of that morning's procession, it
was very clear, from the presence of the two standard-bearers
carrying spears tipped with ruffled black feathers, from the
quantity of liveried grooms, porters and umbrella-bearers and
from the occasional glimpse of a crest – an orange on a leafy
branch – that it was the Gotairo himself who swung beneath
the pole which supported the largest *norimon*. The straggling
body of men trailed along the road and the first bearers
stumbled towards the bridge, pushing aside a few muffled and
cloaked onlookers who were standing around. Just ahead of the

Gotairo's party, the last of the retinue of the Prince of Kyushu was leaving the same bridge and hurrying for the shelter of the castle enclosure.

On the instant that the Gotairo's *norimon* was swung down towards the bridge one of the seeming bystanders leaped forward across its path and, with equal celerity, the guards rushed forward to grab him. In less than an instant the idle watchers threw aside their cloaks and became armed warriors whose steel swords sang through the grey wind as they severed the wrists of the men carrying the *norimon*, slashed the bellies of the Regent's officers even as they reached for their weapons and hacked the sides of the *norimon* as it thudded to the ground in a welter of blood and mud. By the time the Gotairo's escort had mustered enough strength to reach the *norimon* it contained but a headless trunk slopped across the silk curtains, and two of the assailants, each carrying a severed head, were flying away into the rain. The officers, spotting one of them as he bore his gruesome trophy aloft, dashed in pursuit. But when, after a short desperate chase, he was overtaken and slain, the head he bore was found to be that of a bearer. A few of the attackers, who were all men of the reactionary southern Mito clan, got clean away and carried the Gotairo's head in gory state to their Prince. He, it is said, spat upon it in triumphant scorn and exposed it at the execution ground in the ancient city of Kyoto above a placard which read, 'This is the head of a traitor who had violated the most sacred laws of Japan — those which forbid the admission of foreigners into the country.'

This murder, which showed that even the Japanese themselves, even one of the most powerful Japanese in the land, were not safe from the assassin's sword, did nothing to allay the westerners' fears — especially when, wincing, they heard about the placard which had appeared below the frozen scream of the Gotairo's purple head. Yedo and Yokohama were in uproar; all barriers between the city quarters were guarded and locked; only policemen and soldiers, their padded jackets bulging with weapons, waddled importantly through the wet streets, and the Shogun's personal officers, mounted on horseback, jolted past on urgent missions, their faces half-concealed under folds of cloth and low, wide black hats, their fearful, suspicious eyes seeking the lurking, two-pronged shape of a lawless *ronin*. The foreign legations were stuffed with bodyguards and every westerner who ventured outside was accompanied by a small army of soldiers – who, snorted Alcock, 'would have proved but a useless and encumbering appendage in any emergency'.

Eventually, some of the assassins were caught and tortured, or managed to commit the comparatively attractive *hara-kiri*. But long before that the tension had subsided, particularly among the foreign merchants who were only remotely interested in the political affairs of the country. Much closer to their hearts was the fact that business was beginning to boom. In Yokohama a total of £1,000,000 trade was reported at the end of the second year; 3,000 bales of silk and 1,250,000 lbs. of tea were exported to Europe and America, and heavy nuggets of gold, beaten sheets of silver were already being shipped away to have their intrinsic values proved in the world's markets.

John Black, an Australian journalist who became editor of *The Japan Herald*, the first English-language newspaper in Yokohama, put it this way: 'The profitable results of almost every transaction that was entered into, kept all in good spirits, and as the society was very limited, everybody knew everybody, and kind feeling and good fellowship were the rule. The beauty of the surrounding country, the pleasantness of the climate and the vigour of the settlers, most of them in the heyday of early manhood, combined to make all look bright and pleasant. Hearty, robust and energetic, they could equally enjoy the climate and avail themselves of business opportunities; and it is not to be wondered at that any who heard of Japan either from the lips of those who had visited Yokohama, or the letters of residents, were charmed with the description, and pictured to themselves, if not a land of oil, olive and vine-yards and flowing with milk and honey, at least a terrestrial paradise where "all but the spirit of man was divine".'

V

Before John Black arrived in Yokohama he had already tried to start a newspaper in Nagasaki, the southern port which, compared to the rest of Japan, could claim a long, if distraught and fragmentary relationship with the rest of the world. It was here, on the tiny island of Decima which was connected by a narrow causeway to the mainland, that the Dutch, for two hundred years, kept open Japan's only outward-looking window. And a very odd and unhappy life it must have been. The spiked gates at either end of the causeway were guarded continually by sentries who had the right to search all comers; no Dutchman was allowed to pass through them except on very special occasions under heavy escort; only prostitutes, Japanese merchants, customs officials and, for some weird reason, 'mendicant priests from the mountains of Kofu' could go to the island – and all but the former had to leave at sunset when the gates were bolted. During most of their two-hundred-year stay the Dutch were not even permitted to converse freely with the Japanese; they were constantly watched by bevies of government spies and, if the whole situation so overcame them that they died, even a piece of the sacred soil was denied them and they had to be buried at sea. So, on this small, hot island – 'little more than a mudspeck' in one historian's view – with its rows of neat houses attached to huge barn-like warehouses, their windows framed by neat, green Dutch-style shutters, the Hollanders dozed their years' stint away, smoking their own cigars, drinking their own gin, begetting unwanted Eurasian children and waiting for the next ship to arrive from Europe.

Even when a ship did at last arrive things were not all plain-sailing. The vessel had to anchor outside the harbour where it was ransacked from stem to stern by the Japanese for forbidden cargo, and Bibles and firearms were confiscated. Oliphant tells the story of one old Dutch sea-captain whose breeches were so weighted down with contraband he was trying to smuggle through to his mates on Decima that he had to have two sailors supporting him as he walked. After this incident the Japanese were exceedingly suspicious and were even known to break open fresh eggs to make sure there was nothing inside other than yolk.

Copper and silver were exported on the Dutch ships and, surprisingly enough, silk was imported from China and Macao in those days. Apart from silk, cigars and Dutch gin, the arriving ships were laden with tribute – gifts from the remote West which, every year, the Dutch carried, as a kind of tax, to the Shogun's castle in Yedo. After being cooped up in Decima, the Dutch enjoyed the long overland journey, though they were still obliged to travel in closed *norimons* under constant surveillance and the landlords of the inns in which they stayed along the route were instructed to build high palisades round their premises so that the barbarians could not see even the streets outside. As a last indignity, when the Hollanders got to Yedo they were forced to crawl on hands and knees into the Shogun's mighty presence and, on occasions, perform western-style dances for his entertainment. It was, all in all, quite a price that the Dutch had to pay for their virtual monopoly of Japanese trade.

The restrictions of this situation chafed Japanese and foreigners alike. Naturally, a small number of Japanese had to be permitted to learn Dutch so that they could act as interpreters during trade negotiations, and, through these interpreters and a small band of scholars who gathered in Nagasaki and who were hungry for news of the West, some slight, out-of-date knowledge of western medicine, science and astronomy filtered from time to time into official government circles. Sometimes the reigning Shogun, if he was an inquisitive man, might set the Director of Decima the unenviable task of compiling Japanese-Dutch dictionaries or writing reports to explain what had been going on in Europe for the last hundred years or so.

By the beginning of the nineteenth century it had obviously occurred even to the Shoguns with their barely rudimentary understanding of the burgeoning world over the horizon that their exclusive idyll was doomed to invasion. Nevertheless, they managed to keep at bay a couple of French frigates which tried to land, some brave American missionaries and, in 1804, a full-blown Russian Ambassador named Rezanov who came as the personal envoy of Tsar Alexander I. Rezanov's ship anchored in Nagasaki Bay and, after weeks of wrangling, he was permitted ashore to meet an official who acted as 'a representative of the Emperor'. Part of the dispute had concerned the manner in which Rezanov should appear before this august personage. The Russian expected to walk up to him, bow and, perhaps, shake hands; the Japanese expected the barbarian to crawl towards him on hands and knees as the Dutch did. Finally, Rezanov compromised and agreed to sit on his heels for a few minutes. An American historian – after seeing a portrait of Rezanov – comments sympathetically that the Tsar's envoy 'must have been a superb figure in his full Ambassador's costume – red sash, cocked hat and orders blazing on his breast. He had a tall, straight, commanding figure; a long pale face, eyes humorous and brilliant under heavy lids and light hair which he wore short and unpowdered. At any other court but that of Japan he would have been the most imposing figure in the diplomatic corps, but what impression can a man make sitting on his heels?'

Clearly, a heel-sitting compromise was not the right approach; Rezanov was sent away empty-handed and it took the uncompromising, even menacing persistence of Commodore Perry to break down the Tokugawa shogunate's policy of isolationism. After the advent of Perry there was no more talk of westerners crawling into important presences; no more were westerners penned into enclaves quite so humiliatingly prison-like as that of Decima – though the diplomats had to negotiate for every extra mile of freedom for their countrymen. By the late 1850's when Lord Elgin and Laurence Oliphant and, a little later, Robert Fortune, all called in at Nagasaki, they could walk freely about the streets looking at everything – the fishmongers' stalls on the waterfront selling conger eels, mackerel, cray, star and cuttle fish; the dried-fruit stalls; the warehouses stuffed with barrels of soy and *saké*, bales of tea and rice; and, in the back alleys, the one-man businesses of herb-sellers, tobacco-leaf cutters, scissor-grinders, glass-blowers and makers of lanterns, shoes, incense-sticks, umbrellas, ink, idols and spectacles.

The worst restriction imposed upon these early foreign visitors to the port was that, in spite of all the tempting wares displayed, they could buy only from the Russian and Dutch bazaars recently established on the harbour front. The former of these, Oliphant comments, was 'like an Eastern caravan-serie', with a paved square and everyone drinking tea while they bartered and money-changers presiding vigilantly over boxes that contained the Mexican and Spanish dollars which had been exchanged by the foreigners for the local trading currency – which was, in 1858, in the form of paper notes and coins called by the Chinese names of *taels, mace, can* and *cash*.

At any rate, in spite of the restrictions which made it difficult for the westerners to buy what they wanted, they were all delighted with the beautiful Nagasaki. For one thing, it was such a clean, neat contrast to the Shanghai from which many of them had come: 'Along the entire length of the main street,' Oliphant enthused, 'no foul odours assailed our nostrils or hideous cutaneous object offended our eye-sight.' In fact, he continued, the port offered a superabundance of attractions, 'like being compelled to eat a whole pâté de foie gras at a sitting; the dish was too rich and highly charged with truffles for one's mental digestion'. The only slight flaw in the otherwise perfect picture was, to British eyes, the summer nudity of the natives. 'It does not seem', Elgin remarked, looking at the brown, lithe, near-naked bodies of his coolies, 'that there will be any great demand for Manchester cotton goods'; and added, with typically heavy-footed Victorian jocularity, after seeing the local inhabitants take their evening baths out of doors, 'I never saw a place where the cleanliness of the fair sex was established on such unimpeachable ocular evidence.'

Robert Fortune enjoyed the port too; particularly because he was able to visit the Dutchman Dr Von Siebold, a botanist and scientist who had spent many years in the country, first cooped up on Decima, then in a lovely, secluded Japanese country house surrounded by grounds in which he grew bamboos, podocarpus, mimosa, camellias, junipers, myrtle and a mighty profusion of azaleas. Von Siebold was friendly with everyone in the neighbouring village and spoke fluent Japanese – 'No revolver or guard was necessary for him', Fortune comments enviously – and indeed, as Fortune also proved during his stay at Yokohama, the totally vulnerable and guileless neutrality of men such as Von Siebold disarmed even the most vengeful *ronin*.

During the year 1859, which separated Lord Elgin's visit from Fortune's, the first British Consul for Nagasaki installed himself, his four-poster bed and his 'feminine appurtenances' as he called them, in a disused temple on a hill overlooking the harbour and, on 18 June, hoisted the first 'British Jack' to be flown over a consulate in Japan. Consul Charles P. Hodgson was a comfortable, affable man; his 'appurtenances' were his wife – a nervous, vain and undiscerning woman – his daughter, – a yellow-ringleted, blue-eyed little girl called Eva – and their stoical maid, Sarah. Poor Mamma Hodgson was terrified of leaving the 'good strong English ship' and going to live among the Japanese – demi-savages who thrust 'horrible sweetmeats' in Eva's hand and made quick sketches of everything she and the child were wearing. Perhaps, Mrs Hodgson thought, they did this because they coveted western clothes, for, just on the short journey from the ship to the consulate, she saw enough near-nudity 'to disgust any woman of delicacy'. As for the welcoming gifts from the Governor of Nagasaki— boxes of pickled radishes, four hundred eggs and a little pig— *they* did nothing to persuade her that she had actually arrived in a highly civilised society.

Once inside her new home Mamma Hodgson hardly ever bothered to go out again because 'everyone who has seen the town has pronounced it to be uninteresting'. So she reclined on a specially-imported sofa, read romantic novels, fanned the insects away and was 'refreshed by the pleasant idea that all my nice dresses from Paris and nearly all my linen, shoes and fineries are becoming mouldy and spoiled by the fearful damp and warm disagreeable steams which the earth is generous enough to emit to add to my agreeable situation'. Even this was not the extent of Mrs Hodgson's trials; indeed it was only the beginning. The frail, whining voice went on and on in endless letters to a sympathetic and anxious Mummy: mosquitoes bite her and even have the effrontery to nibble the chubby pink legs of poor little Eva; centipedes crawl over the floors; she could swear that it was a dead viper she saw hanging behind a picture; rats 'as big as cats' scuttle in the ancient thatch above; and then, oh, experience almost beyond endurance... 'the other night, whilst on my knees saying my prayers, I saw close to me another vile serpent of the same centipede family, but larger still. I was the only one awake and, not knowing what to do, determined not to sleep with such a neighbour in my chamber, I therefore seized a sword hanging close to my bed (a precaution which it is unfortunately necessary to adopt here) and after repeated blows which I gave, almost fainting with fear and horror at what I was doing, I managed to sacrifice it to my vengeance.'

Fortunately, no Consul's wife had to fight the animal and reptile kingdom of the country single-handed for long, nor stay indoors to keep away from the natives, because, soon after the Hodgsons' arrival, foreign community life began to perk up considerably. On the Bund the Commercial Hotel was opened by Mr William Warren, who begged 'to invite the attention of residents and visitors to his house and assure them that they will at all times find there supplies of liquors of every description and of the best quality'. Mr Warren also wished to mention that his establishment could boast a bowling alley 'for which he has recently received a new set of *ligumn vita* [sic] balls'. The Nagasaki Club, formed in 1860, held meetings at the hotel and its members and guests were a lively heterogeneous bunch of shippers, merchants, consuls, naval officers, travellers and various unexpected Russian women who wintered there while their husbands were whaling in the far north.

Announcements of club meetings, of items for sale such as Watchel & Company's 'Fine champaign Sparkling Sillery and La Tour de Bouzy' [sic] and of new business ventures – 'I have this day established a General Commission Agency at this Port under the style of Maltby & Co: John Maltby, 7th May, 1861' – appeared in *The Nagasaki Shipping List and Advertiser* which began as early as 1860 and persisted fitfully for years under different names and different editors. This was the paper which John Black edited for a time, but he soon realised that Yokohama was the real boom town and so he packed up his printing press and hurried north, after advertising just about his all for sale in his last issue: 'linen jackets, shoes, one escritoire, 1 milch cow, three sets tortoiseshell spoons and forks, 1 Shakespeare, a toddy kettle, an aquarium and 1 Dmub Waiter' [sic].

It was an indolent, haphazard, southern style of life that Black left behind. There was lots of time for billiards and bowling and single-stick competitions between the young bachelors; a letter sent early in August might, with luck, reach London by the middle of October; a gun boomed off every Tuesday and Friday noon so that one could – if so inclined – set one's watch or rate one's chronometer. There was lots of time for a fellow to rent a little wooden house on the hill and box a little butterfly-wife in it for a year or so until his company moved him elsewhere. There was lots of time to sit on the verandah and gaze at the lovely bay that enclosed the increasing number of vessels which, as the years drifted by, were listed time and again in *The Advertiser*: the *Whampoa* from Shanghai, with a cargo of black velvets, white Victorian lawns, turkey red chintzes, dark blue blankets, damasks and some good yellow peas; the *Flying Cloud* from Hakodate bringing whale oil and cuttlefish; the passenger ship *Anna Marie* whose captain once failed to wait for the mail at Shanghai and, in consequence, was verbally blasted out of port by the irate Nagasaki residents longing for letters from home; the grubby little *Dwarf* which had chugged in from Foochoo long ago and now just sat there month after month while her captain, apparently, tried to remember where he'd been going.

As well as the shipping lists, *The Advertiser* always carried a few news items tucked away in a corner for a chap to meditate upon. He would have learnt, if he had the energy: on 10 May 1861, that, in America, 'President Lincoln issued a proclamation calling for 75,000 troops'; on 17 July, that, in England, 'the Queen was suffering from an extreme nervous depression which, together with her time of life, a very critical period for ladies, and excitability inherent in the Royal Family, has given rise to great anxiety with respect to her future health'.

But the problems facing President Lincoln and Queen Victoria were thousands of miles away, on another planet, almost. Here it was drowsy and warm every afternoon and the only sounds were the rattle of the cicada in the near-by willow, the pad of white-socked feet on the *tatami*, the palpitation of a butterfly's wings against the rice-paper screens. So easy to live here, in a place where the natives had been used to the mysterious presence of foreigners for centuries and where the concept of 'east–west contact' had long since ceased to be a burning issue. The proximity of China, which was, of course, a principal reason for Nagasaki's comparatively broad-minded attitude, also meant that the foreigners felt less vulnerable and isolated than their compatriots in Yokohama and Yedo. After all, if life became too claustrophobic, one could simply embark on a 450-mile shopping spree to Shanghai – eat at the oyster bar of the Grand Hotel, spend a day at the races, buy a hat for the wife at Madame Wright's Millinery and Drapery Establishment opposite the Hanoverian Consulate. Naturally, as soon as Nagasaki opened, great numbers of Chinese, who always rush to fill any near-by vacuum, wanted to go and trade there, which they were not officially allowed to do because China had no treaty with Japan. This situation enabled less scrupulous westerners to build up a nice little racket: they brought the Chinese in (for a price) ostensibly as their personal servants and then let them trade in secret – often from their inviolate western homes. The Chinese, as Chinese will, smuggled in opium, tobacco and other illicit imports and ran several smoky gambling dens for sailors behind the Bund; they also did the cooking, which was a great relief to almost every westerner who found chow mein much more palatable than raw tuna on cold rice.

Another mixed blessing that resulted from Nagasaki's proximity to Shanghai was the frequent appearance of visiting western 'artistes', whose circuit stretched from Australia, through Colombo to Singapore and Canton and – now – as far as southern Japan. The members of the Nagasaki Club were enraptured in the summer of 1862 by the talents of Miss Bailey, soprano, Mr Marquise Chisholm, tenor, Mr Sipp (his accomplishment unspecified) and Signor Robbio, 'a violinist of exceeding merit'. Later there were other visits from, for instance, Baron von Hohenlohe and Signor Spectalini, who sang duets in costume from the opera *Stradella* and then, for light relief, took part in a comic drama by Chas. Matthews entitled *Little Toddlekins*. The men were pretty good apparently, but as for the ladies, oh, asks the reviewer in *The Advertiser*, 'What shall we say of Miss Belle Chimer as Mrs Whiffleton? Her dress was perfection; her deportment maternal; and from her knitting to her whist-table her acting was consistent and natural.' Indeed so great was the enthusiasm engendered by such impeccable professionals as Miss Chimer and Signor Spectalini, that an amateur theatrical group was soon formed among the members of the Nagasaki Club and *Mr Tweedleton's Tail Coat* was performed before an enthralled audience, with Mr Straw as Farmer Blackberry Thistletop 'rendering the dialect and boisterous guffaw of a country bumpkin most admirably' and Miss Toddles, who 'came forward with her usual elegance' to receive special praise from the reviewer for 'her exquisite toilette'.

How Mamma Hodgson, with her melodramatic bent and her nice Parisian dresses, would have loved to grace the front row, dazzling reviewer and audience with the exquisiteness of *her* toilette! But alas, long before the first curtain rose in the Club's lounge, the Hodgsons were, after only four months in Nagasaki, picked up by HMS *Highflyer* and carried tremendously far north to Hakodate. Mrs Hodgson, by the way, unwittingly left a memento to her hosts in southern Japan – her likeness, which some enterprising local manufacturer had drawn when she wasn't looking and which he used as a trademark on every bottle of his *saké*. However, according to the irritated, but ever-gallant Consul, it was not a good likeness, indeed it was 'as much like the original as a butterfly to a salamander'.

VI

One imagines that Consul Hodgson needed all his gallantry and tact to tide his wife over the first shock of Hakodate, which was so remote and spartan that Nagasaki seemed a bustling, comfortable metropolis in comparison, and where he found one British subject to put on the consular register and two American shipping agents, two French missionaries and a Russian Consul for company. Like Nagasaki, however, Hakodate was, after its fashion, a beautiful place in those days.

The quiet waters of the almost landlocked harbour reflected the lines of hills, the haphazard shapes of the wooden houses and shops which chequered the narrow strip between upland and sea. Icy wet winds straight from Vladivostock blasted down the wide main street for much of the year, and hares white as winter snow could be had for the catching. So strong and constant were these winds that each citizen had to take drastic measures to prevent his house from blowing away. Rain-grey pebbles, lemon-light shingle, creamy rocks and boulders were strewn over every roof to keep it in place, so that it looked, wrote an early visitor, 'as if a street had been unpaved and all the materials transported to the roof, ready for assault or defence'. To no one's surprise the method was not totally successful, and though most of the roofs kept on, many of the stones blew off. One of the duties of the local police, in addition to making sure that all snow was cleared away, that water tubs were kept full in case of fire, that no bad vegetables were sold on the market and that all lights were out by ten, was to check, once a week, that there were sufficient stones per roof to withstand the next inevitable gale. In the shops below the roofs the subtly-toned discreetly luxurious harvests of the north were for sale: skins and horns of the mountain deer, sleek otter fur and gruff bear hides, fifteen-pound salmon for a shilling each, gleaming piles of plaice, mullet and dab and great lacy skeins of green and golden seaweed ten feet long and two feet wide which the fishermen had cut away from submerged rocks with knives fixed on the end of bamboo poles. When it was fine the beaches were festooned with the stuff hanging out to dry; but when rain was imminent the weed grew dank and humid and was covered up, thus usefully providing its own barometrical warning.

After the first shock the Hodgsons enjoyed Hakodate surprisingly well. They were installed in the port's only remaining temple (the other three having been requisitioned by the Russian Consul, his staff and the American Commercial Agent respectively – where the people were then expected to worship is not recorded) and they hoisted a bright new British Jack and made another little outpost for Queen Victoria in a strange world. Hodgson was again content and busy; if his lively interest in the customs of the people and the flora of the countryside ever flagged, there was always his lovely suffering spouse to jolly along, his child to teach and the Russian Consul with whom to share a brandy.

In order to test the good intentions of the Japanese and satisfy his own insatiable curiosity, the Consul made several inland excursions when the weather grew warmer, and these were planned and conducted with the earnest determination of a pilgrimage. The First Major Excursion commenced on 14 June. From sun-up and even before the cicadas had wound themselves up for their daily clatter, Hodgson was bustling around the horses in the temple courtyard which were being loaded with bed-rolls, mosquito-nets, huge hampers filled with eggs, snipe, plum puddings and hams, parasols for the ladies and bottles of claret for the gentlemen. Hodgson had everything under control; he forgot nothing – not a corkscrew or a chopstick or an extra bonnet for Eva. 'Having been in Australia and Abyssinia,' he confesses, 'I am rather conceited as to my powers of making up a party.' And, under his supervision, the party was successfully made up – of himself, his wife and Eva, the maid Sarah, the French abbé, the wife of a newly-arrived Russian doctor and a small army of servants, both Chinese and Japanese. These functionaries all had to wear red belts with the arms of Her Majesty Queen Victoria embroidered thereon, a device which, Hodgson hoped, was sufficiently awesome to deter any attacker; though even he had a few secret qualms about having 'so many petticoats in train'.

He need not have worried, for, petticoats and all, the expedition was a huge success; in fact, as in Nagasaki, Eva's presence greatly increased the foreigners' popularity. The Japanese beamed in wonderment on her fair hair and blue eyes and the foreigners beamed back and, with intent presumably kindly, changed one of their silver dollars into 5,320 iron coins which they scattered among the watching natives 'who scrambled eagerly for them, much to our delight'. At night they slept in the uncharted interior under the shadow of a volcano and they kept fires going and guns firing at intervals to discourage any wandering bears. Early next morning, faithful to the Victorian spirit which could never leave a nearby mountain unscaled, they all — Eva in her frilly pink dress and Mamma in her feathered hat — clambered and stumbled up the crumbling ashy sides of the volcano and, sitting near its crater, drank several glasses of claret and water as a toast to absent friends.

Perhaps it was this grubby experience that made 'the petticoats' decide to stay at home when Hodgson embarked on his second excursion a month later. This time he went to have a look at the Ainu, the aboriginal inhabitants of the islands who had been pushed northward by the Japanese centuries before. They were a cowed, aimless, half-savage people, one of those pathetic remnants of humanity who get heedlessly trampled over in some great stampede by a more aggressive race. To reach their scattered villages Hodgson and his male companion rode through waywardly beautiful country. They passed ashes, pine and hazel, wild sloe, agrimony, rosemary and honeysuckle; ferns, orchids and weeping birch, rhododendrons, maple and vines hung with small black grapes; and, as for the unknown plants, they, says Hodgson, 'gave me their cards, the dear things, in the form of dried specimens, but referred me to their godfather, Sir William Hooker, for their names'.

The entrance to the Ainu village was guarded by bear-heads, for the bear was the Ainu's obsessional challenge — the test of his courage, the measure of his manhood, the thrilling focus of his glum and crude life. But when the foreigners, unarmed and unawed, rode confidently past these snarling tokens of the Ainu strength the villagers cowered before them, staring with their sad, doubtful doe-eyes into the big pink faces of the intruders. These people had made little impression on the lush land which lay beyond their village boundaries, unexplored interiors where, says Hodgson, 'bear and deer are landlords and tenants'. But who knew what mineral wealth might be stored there? Hodgson, as usual, was optimistic about the possibilities: 'Coal had made England what she is; may not coal, with the blessing of God, make Japan a mighty nation?'

The travellers stayed for a night in an Ainu hut, a smoky, smelly thatched dwelling with a fire in the centre and, swinging over the flames, a stew-pot from which was ladled the evening meal of shark-meat, pumpkin, beans and seaweed. The following morning Hodgson and his friend were encouraged to stroll around the village as they pleased. They saw everything – the stakes of whittled willow wood, their shavings left to curl like hair on the top, and the clusters of animal skulls which were placed as religious offerings at the east end of every hut; the spiritless, dirty women, their lips and foreheads tattooed bluish-black, who sat weaving or cutting up bears' fat in the open doorways; the chief himself, with wild hair, dangling earrings and melancholy eyes who pressed cups of *saké* on them as a gesture of friendship.

After his brief sojourn with the Ainu – who were, incidentally, destined before another decade had passed to become the target for the most indefatigable and remorseless zeal of the approaching invasion of missionaries, Lady Travellers and anthropologists – Hodgson was as grateful as ever to return to the security of his beloved wife and child. In fact, he never tired of proclaiming the therapeutic values of feminine society and of being astonished at the felicitous results which ensued from his wife's company. For one thing, the presence of the foreign ladies made it proper for the Japanese Governor of Hakodate to invite the Hodgsons to meet his own wife at home, and so Mrs Hodgson was undoubtedly one of the first western women to suffer the uncomfortable, exquisitely courteous rituals of being entertained *à la Japonaise*: the innumerable thimble-cups of insipid tea, the glutinous and garish sweetmeats, the numbing of the limbs after ten minutes squatting on floor cushions, the giggles over chopsticks or forks, even (at a later evening visit) the yellow soup in which floated the squelched bodies of indeterminate shell-fish, the slippery green trails of prehistoric seaweed. But the Governor's wife was beautiful in spite of the soup she served; Hodgson, ever a susceptible fellow, watched her in bemused wonderment. Her shining jet hair was coiled in swathes above her powdered-white face, her eyebrows were shaved off and, when she opened bright scarlet lips, her teeth were polished black as ebony. This exotic mask concealed, apparently, merely a rather commonplace inquisitive and acquisitive spirit. For, when Mamma Hodgson was conducted on a tour of the ladies' apartments, her hostess carried out 'a most indelicate inventory' of every article she and her daughter were wearing; and later when, in due season, the Governor's wife visited the British Consul's residence she was so utterly captivated by the material goods from the West that she coveted them all – up to and including a preserved prune and a pin, which items she popped surreptitiously into the sleeve of her lovely silk kimono.

The big event of the year in the Hodgson *ménage* was the early autumn visit to Yedo to see 'the Chief'. Mamma Hodgson was in her element at last. All the nice Parisian dresses could be worn for the benefit of the naval officers who happened to be staying at the Legation and for Sir Rutherford himself who insisted that the womenfolk take over his own suite of rooms overlooking the garden and lake. They all went to visit Townsend Harris and 'the amiable, intelligent and obliging Heusken'. Harris took great delight in showing Eva his favourite trick: he struck a couple of stones together under the surface of the water in his ornamental pond and hundreds of goldfish came rushing to the sound, their wet, pink mouths agape for food.

When the time came for the Hodgsons to return to Hakodate on HMS *Highflyer*, Sir Rutherford decided that he should accompany them to put, as it were, his official seal on the consular residence there. And, in order that the arrival at the remote port should be marked with due ceremony, the marine band was mustered to pipe Alcock, the Consul and Mrs Hodgson and Eva and Sarah ashore to the strains of *The British Grenadiers*. Never before had such stirring martial strains burst upon the ears of the Hakodatians. They left their seaweed-drying and their hide-cleaning, their fish-gutting and their pheasant-plucking, they hurried from tiny back rooms, from near-by paddy-fields and – greatly to the embarrassment of Mamma Hodgson and frilly-frocked little Eva – from their steaming bath-houses, all damp, innocent and quite naked and most heterogeneously mixed together, to see what had arrived.

While such an enthusiastic reception caused the foreigners some consternation, they, in turn, created consternation among the Japanese by the inclusion of twelve sheep among their party. These animals – whose melancholy function was to supplement the diet of the Consul and his family during the meatless months ahead – were almost unknown in the north, and Hodgson had great trouble in finding suitable quarters for them, as the consular residence, which had already been adapted from a temple to a house, could not further expand into a small farm. When the sheep were finally penned into a remote outbuilding the Japanese were constantly piercing the paper windows and removing the wooden slats so that they could get a closer look at the weird creatures inside; and when, in the winter, Hodgson ordered his Chinese servant to lead the first one to the slaughter, there was great horror among the townsfolk that such an absolutely woolly beast could be considered edible. By a later ship, incidentally, a pig arrived at Hakodate to perform the same function as the sheep. It too was a rarity there, though a priest of a nearby shrine had read in his scriptures what a loathsome and unclean animal it was, so he rushed to the quay as the pig was being unloaded and exhorted all true believers to help him throw the poor creature into the sea. However, the American Commercial Agent who happened to be on the scene took the pig under his special protection; and in due season all the barbarians shared their pork.

Sir Rutherford did not, of course, stay long enough to witness all these ramifications of the food question. Indeed, he inwardly agreed with the port's Governor who had told Commodore Perry years ago when the black ships first arrived there, that Hakodate was 'a pill of a place'. So, after seeing that the Union Jack was again hoisted from the consular roof and ordering the guns of HMS *Highflyer* to fire a salute, the Chief hastened back to the comparative comfort of Yedo. As *Highflyer* steamed away, leaving the little port and its inhabitants to the long bitter winter ahead, Alcock thought how desolate the bay looked and how much more desolate it would look when there was no western ship in its waters. And his sympathy went out to Hodgson as he adds that 'a functionary can hardly be much to be envied, though a fortune and honours were at the end of a short term. As neither of them usually fell to the lot of a British Consul, I could only hope that the Consul of Hakodate might carry within him and about him something to compensate such utter isolation and banishment in the prime of life.'

In fact, Charles Hodgson did have qualities within him and people about him to ameliorate his situation. In January the temperature dropped to twenty below zero; the local inhabitants were afflicted with 'colds, blindness, cutaneous eruptions, catarrhs, fever and other national maladies', he recorded; gales thrummed through the wall-cracks of their temple-home; snow-drifts grew as high as the fishmongers' slabs; in the slate-green boiling waters of the harbour ships buffeted on to the rocks. But cheerful, loving Hodgson and his 'appurtenances' survived intact and, in 1861, probably much to Mamma's relief, their tour of duty in Japan ended.

The following year the first Japanese representatives to Great Britain landed at Dover, and the first person to hurl himself forward with Japanese exclamations of greeting was Consul Hodgson. He wanted the Japanese to be as happy as he had been in their country, he explained; he wanted them to taste muffins and good beer as he had tasted seaweed soup and *saké*; he wanted to show them the Crystal Palace and Dover Castle as they had shown him Mount Fuji and the Imperial residence. Oh, said Consul Hodgson, it was grand fun being almost the only foreigners of one's kind in a country – if the country was as beautiful as Japan or England and its inhabitants as kind and hospitable as the Japanese or – he hoped – the English. It was a happy coda to the Hodgsons' stay in Japan, during which they had established such pleasant and trusting relationships with the Japanese. It was, perhaps, because the Hodgsons lived, completely isolated and unprotected, in places remote from the main European settlements that they encountered hardly any of the hostility which was soon to mar the beginning of so many western-Japanese encounters.

Part Three

Swords and Victims

'*From whencesoever these successive blows proceed,
there comes also, and always, a voice through the
organs of the Government (not ashamed to be the
medium of communication) which cries aloud: "So
are you all doomed; begone or perish."*'
– Sir Rutherford Alcock, *The Capital of the Tycoon.*

Sir Rutherford Alcock, his coat a little shabbier and his hair
more grizzled than when he first came to Japan, gazed into the
garden of his lovely and secluded residence in Yedo. It was
December; the rustic bridge which spanned the tiny lotus lake
was a treacherous arc of ice; a few wine-red maple leaves
scudded on the water's surface; only the pine trees which
soared nearly a hundred feet above the roof-tops thrived green
in the sombre air. December 1860 and his heart was heavy with
distrust. At this cold dead of the year Alcock felt most keenly
his melancholy sense of isolated alienation from all gay and
familiar things. He was, he wrote, in a 'wilderness of living
men' with whom he felt no touch of human sympathy and of
whom he was increasingly suspicious and afraid. The newspapers on his lap only served as a reminder that the very
bustling life they described was already past; it was, he
thought, like receiving 'a page torn out of the history of the
world ... a fragment telling of some distant period ... always
remote and which never can be linked to the present.' He felt
condemned to the past, to the irrelevant backwaters of the
world where he was an unprotected and unlamented exile.

At Christmas a British warship arrived bringing officers who
were exhilarated to be finished with a relatively successful
Chinese campaign. Cigars and port were distributed from

Alcock's precious store and, on Christmas Day, a sprinkling of officers and several members of the other western legations were invited to join the British diplomats round a board piled high with duck, venison and wild fowl. Yet, even as the glasses were raised to the Queen and the moustaches bristled proudly and the loud Christmas laughter guffawed out, Alcock was looking apprehensively over his shoulder, 'We sat down twenty-three,' he wrote with his usual quiet pessimism, 'and within that number of days one of the guests, perhaps the most light-hearted of the whole, lay wrapped in a bloody shroud.'

On the first day of the Japanese New Year, young girls in their best kimono, their high-coiled hair glittering with orna-ments, trotted pigeon-toed to visit relatives; children yelped for joy as they played battledore in their backyards and flew fledgling kites; in the homes, housewives crowded the low lacquer dining tables with bowls of vegetable broth, flat, dough-coloured *mochi* cakes made of rice-paste, crunchy lotus roots, fresh carp decorated with yellow chrysanthemum petals and bottles of the special New Year *saké* called *otoso*, thick, sugary and aromatic. Wide fringes of straw hung about with angular strips of white paper rustled above every house-entrance and everywhere, in windows, shops and shrines, were clustered the other traditional decorations – bunches of fern leaves surrounding an orange, to suggest the continuity of the generations, and a bent lobster to signify the peace of old age after a long and happy life.

That same day Henry Heusken arrived to see Sir Rutherford, looking tired and rather pale. The news from Townsend Harris was that several hundred *ronin* had joined forces with the intention of firing the Yokohama settlement and assassinating every member of the foreign legations in Yedo. This, as Alcock sadly remarked, 'was not an auspicious opening of the New Year'.

The Japanese government, remembering Dankitchi and the hapless Gotairo, begged that all the foreign representatives in Yedo would leave their separate residences and gather under one protected roof within the sacred precincts of Yedo castle itself, until the *ronin* could either be seized or their numbers dispersed. Alcock's first impulse was probably to flee for cover — as indeed would be that of any man with a head attached by mere flesh and bone to his shoulders. But he was extremely suspicious of the government itself and was firmly convinced that a large faction in it merely used such alarming rumours as excuses to further restrict the foreigners' movements and to so hedge them round with guards that they would finally leave the country altogether. And so neither Alcock nor the other western representatives sought the security of the castle grounds. They stayed put and waited. A *daimyo* was given charge of the British Legation and two hundred of his guards clanked and swaggered round the grounds all day and all night. The road from Yokohama clattered with patrols of government police spiked with ready swords and the remains of the New Year *saké*.

Night-time was, of course, the worst. A duck, disturbed, skittered ominously over the legation lake; every bush bristled bear-like; the flash of light from a sentry's lantern was sharp as steel. Henry Heusken, riding back late from the Prussian Legation where he had been visiting Count Eulenberg, saw, perhaps, the steel itself as it glinted under the globes of light which hung from the bamboo poles carried by his Japanese escort. There was a horrendous yell from the caverns of the dark street on either side of him; the lanterns swung and blew as men reached for their weapons. Heusken, his scalp prickling, spurred his horse and, armed only with a riding whip, tried to thrash a path through the terrible, vicious faces which suddenly surrounded him. In the jolting flood of movement, fear and anger he did not at first feel the warm channels of his blood on his shoulders and wrists and over the handle of his precious whip. He rode on for over a hundred yards alone, sinking in the saddle, calling from a slashed throat for his horse-boy, the lanterns all out, behind him and before. By the time Doctor Myburgh of the British Legation arrived to tend the mangled body that had been taken to Harris's residence there was nothing left to do but to hear from the dying man's hopeless lips that most of his escort had deserted him.

Every foreigner in the country was horrified. Heusken – surely not Heusken? The young Henry who had been there longer than anyone, except Harris himself, who was always so helpful, always ready for a ride, or a drink or a game of cards or just an amiable chat and who, above all, was one of the few who could ever make comprehensible that fiendish mad maze of a puzzle – the Japanese language. And if Heusken, who next?

Who next, wondered the group of foreign representatives who followed the funeral *cortège* from the American Legation to an orderly, shaded cemetery next to a Buddhist temple. It was 18 January 1861, a bright clear day, and the sun, Alcock said, flooded into the newly dug grave. Behind the foreigners a band of Prussian marines wailed a lament. Heusken's bier was covered with an American flag, for, though a Dutchman by birth, he had been murdered in the service of the United States. The ministers present each cast a handful of earth on to the coffin. By the side of the grave was a plain tablet – the only other one in the cemetery written in Roman characters – which announced the death of Dankitchi on almost the same day the previous year. Was this to be the pattern, mused Alcock, an annual victim to be furnished from one of the legations, 'a sacrifice apparently to the rage of unknown enemies'?

The melancholy, the mute indignation, the concealed fears felt by the black-suited westerners round Heusken's grave were strongly imprinted on Alcock's mind, and his dry, sombre, earnest temperament was roused to vehement, but helpless, protest: 'The beauty of the site and clearness of the sky only contrasted the more painfully with the moral features of the scene. A foreigner in his prime, the only son of a widowed mother – cut down in his strength and murdered by a band of political assassins in the streets of a great eastern capital, where all but the few members of the legations are still jealously excluded – lay in the grave – round which the representatives of the greatest Powers in the West stood, mourning a wrong they were indeed helpless to redress.'

As a gesture of strong revulsion against this outrageous murder, the representatives of Holland, Prussia, France and Britain struck their flags and moved out of the capital to Yokohama. Townsend Harris alone persisted in remaining at his legation in Yedo. This was not because the American Ambassador felt the tragedy any the less keenly, indeed, as he put it in an explanatory letter to the State Department, he considered that the relationship he and Heusken had enjoyed was 'rather that of father and son than of *chef* and *employé*'. But Harris liked and trusted the Japanese more than the other representatives of the time, he understood the nature of the anti-foreign fanaticism which the government, with the best will in the world, could not control, and he believed that to move away from the capital at this juncture was simply to play into the hands of the *ronin*. Moreover, while he mourned Heusken's death, he was the first to admit that the young man had been foolhardy. Many times, it seemed, he had warned Heusken about riding home late night after night from visits to his Prussian friends; but Henry had shrugged off the advice.

Townsend Harris's attitude roused the fury of the other foreign representatives who, from temporary, draughty bungalows on the Yokohama waterfront, demanded better protection from the Japanese for themselves and their compatriots before they would return to Yedo. After a month of diplomatic bickering, Sir Rutherford and the other western diplomats returned to the capital in what they considered to be a kind of triumph – at the Shogun's personal invitation, with the Japanese Governor of Foreign Affairs to meet them and with a battery salute of twenty-one guns when the foreign flags were again hoisted over the respective legations.

The crisis was over, ostensibly to the satisfaction of all parties: Harris congratulated himself for staying put; the other western representatives congratulated themselves for moving and for forcing the Japanese to pay marks of respect to their official positions; the government was relieved to escape without too much loss of face from a difficult situation; the assassins, perhaps, had the most legitimate grounds for self-satisfaction – they had killed their man and they were never caught.

II

Sir Rutherford judged, rightly, that a comparatively untroubled lull would follow the Heusken affair, so he took ship for Hong Kong in March, remained there until May and then returned to Nagasaki from where he proposed to travel overland to Yedo, a distance of some eight hundred miles. It turned out to be quite an elaborate exercise, as did most of the westerners' early invasions of the interior. On 1 June everyone assembled outside the Dutch Consul's house and a slow, wet start was made. There was Alcock himself with two new recruits for the British Legation staff, the Dutch Consul, Mr de Wit, the British Consul of Nagasaki, Morrison by name, who wanted a change of scene, and, surprisingly enough, one Charles Wirgman, an artist attached to *The Illustrated London News* who grabbed at this unique opportunity of sketching 'scenes of an unknown land'. And behind the Europeans came the inevitable entourage – guards by the score, with two large swords apiece poking evilly from under their loose jackets; *norimons* in whose stuffy insides curled quiet government spies; baggage-bearers and horse-grooms with their robes tucked up to their knobbly thighs and 'tea-whisk' brushes of hair bouncing on top of their scalps; low shaggy horses piled high with provisions, umbrellas and clothes; and a few odd men wearing black conical hats, whose function no one knew. Altogether, as Alcock says, 'the whole party, as we left the town, stretched in a line interminable'.

For the next eight days the interminable line drew itself slowly across the island of Kyushu to the southern shores of the Inland Sea. The decrepit horses kicked, bit, staggered and stumbled the whole way; the roads varied between sandy hill-tracks to quagmires of low-lying mud; the sun beat on the travellers' heads from ten in the morning until dusk, and the only respite from the glare came in occasional warm, heavy rains. And yet it was a splendid ride for the Europeans who, once away from the coastal settlements, found themselves in a Japan which, in 1861, was still a pristine, inviolate, unopened world.

Here, intact, was a feudal land, peopled solely with peasants, lords, ladies and their retainers, a medieval fairy-tale of thatch-cottage villages, wide open fields and withdrawn castles. All day the peasants bent their patient backs – to thrust the young rice-plants into the sloughs of the paddies, to roll spools of cotton for spinning, to flail the bearded wheat and to spread out on the straw mats the flowers of hollyhock and thistle which, when dried, could be used as crude dye. And in their castles the *daimyo* of the provinces, owners of almost nine-tenths of the lovely countryside, hunted and quarrelled among themselves, each one burdened with a load of idle, swash-buckling retainers before whom the peasants had to bend their backs even lower – in obeisance. It all looked so immutable that even the progressive-minded westerners could not imagine that it would take but ten years to destroy utterly that whole social pattern.

Perhaps because the *daimyo* half-consciously understood that these travelling westerners presaged destruction they tried to hide their world away from the prying eyes of the invaders. As the party rode through the main street of each village, Alcock was infuriated to discover that barriers of cloth bearing the crest of the local *daimyo* had been stretched high across every branching side road so that he was prevented from either making a detour or seeing the whole size of any one place. Everything of importance in the countryside – coal-mines, shrines and reservoirs for instance – were similarly guarded by flimsy barriers of bamboo, near which leaned insolent, armed retainers belonging to the particular province. Sometimes Alcock stubbornly asserted his diplomatic right – which stated that he was allowed 'to travel freely throughout the Empire' – by pushing aside one of the barriers and going to inspect what lay behind. But such action roused his own escort to a frenzy of horror, for they had never seen a man brush aside so lightly the crested screens of a *daimyo* and live to ride away.

But Sir Rutherford survived, and on the eighth day after leaving Nagasaki the party arrived at the little harbour of Kokura where they dispersed among the British ship, *Ringdove* and four accompanying junks for the voyage across the Inland Sea and then as far north as Hyogo (later known as Kobe). Mr de Wit was, apparently, an indefatigable tourist and, during the brief visit that they made to Shiminoseki on the north side of the Inland Sea – the harmless little port which was destined to have a very unpleasant encounter with the West two years later – he turned up a journal written about the place by the last Dutch commissioner, Donker Curtius, who had passed that way and, Alcock says wearily, 'with that sense of obligation known to all travellers by which they are driven to see everything written down for them, often in utter ignorance whether the objects will repay the trouble, we proceeded as a matter of duty to exhaust the catalogue and test out our sight-seeing capabilities'.

Shiminoseki's leading tourist attraction was an aged cartoon in an aged temple. The cartoon depicted an historically cele-brated sea-fight, of which, said Alcock, 'the most remarkable feature was the utter inadequacy of the vessels to carry a tithe of the warriors represented as most valiantly fighting on their decks'. But Shiminoseki's more sensational claim to fame was that Japan's 'social evil' flourished most blatantly there – encouraged in the past, it was said, by a wily general who wanted to keep his soldiers happy while they fought a long internecine war on his behalf. The prostitutes, who were also on Donker Curtius's list, were painted and powdered little creatures, their poor heads weighted with galaxies of glittering hair ornaments, silken tassels and jewelled combs, their limbs encased in robes of emerald, bronze or blue brocade. Brought up from infancy for their profession, their eyes were generally lustreless and vacant, their scarlet lips pinched – for they had no true childhood and their names, 'Silver Willow', 'Pearl Harp', 'Little Plum Tree', 'White Blossom', suggested an innocence they had not been permitted to know. The law, however, stipulated their release from servitude after a certain number of years and the ex-prostitute might then marry and have children; though Alcock thought that such an 'easy transition from the depth of pollution to the sanctity of married life and domesticity' was an amazingly unpleasant idea.

In the quiet seas between Shiminoseki and Hyogo the junks lumbered and lolloped enormously, their huge decks surmounted by thick trunks of wood which dipped and swayed towards the horizon as they ambled along like amiable old elephants. Because the waters were uncharted, the little fleet anchored each night, and then there was no sound but the tippling of the water against the prow, the slap of a loose rope and, below the steep main deck, the chatter of chopsticks and the tapping of pipes on tobacco boxes as the crews ate and smoked.

It was a pleasant interlude and its peace was quickly wrecked when the party reached Hyogo where they were met by the Governor of Foreign Affairs himself. This gentleman had been sent post-haste from Yedo to warn them that the *ronin* were abroad again in such numbers that the Government had fears for foreigners' safety and to beg them to return all the way by sea. This the party refused to do and there was another 'diplomatic joust', as Alcock termed it, which resulted in the foreigners continuing their land route, but agreeing to avoid Kyoto, the royal city which was the nucleus of anti-foreign sentiment in the country.

They did, at any rate, explore Osaka fairly thoroughly – a

medieval township peopled with craftsmen, merchants and hired hands and dominated by the grim grey castle of the Shogun. The whole population spilled out to see the hairy barbarians ride by and their escort had to clear a passage through the quiet, curious throng by banging citizens over the head with weighty fans. For part of one day the westerners were punted in small open boats along the city's bustling, fetid canals which were darkened by the shadows of overhanging balconies and edged by the granite outer walls of merchants' residences and warehouses. The canals were spanned by wooden bridges which vibrated under the constant pad of coolies' feet and whose rails, that day, were knobbed with rows of watchful heads as the foreigners passed beneath. Osaka, decided Alcock – who was adept at coining the cliché which bevies of subsequent globe-trotters would find useful for their journals – Osaka, said Sir Rutherford, 'is the Venice of Japan'.

The party also visited Kabuki and saw the theatre in its original, pre-westernised form in which the whole of the auditorium was divided into separate wooden compartments. A family would hire one of these for the day and, squatting comfortably on the *tatami*, father, mother, children of all ages and grandparents would alternately watch the action, smoke, sleep through the dull bits and chat among themselves. During the leisurely intervals, lacquer lunch-boxes were opened, servants arrived bearing more food and the floor of the little compartments became a glorious messy heap of fish-bones, chopsticks, thimble-sized *saké* cups, beans, bowls and teapots as the family feasted – feasts which often continued long after the actors had returned to rant up and down and kill each other all over the stage. Sir Rutherford enjoyed the audience immensely, but found the drama so indelicate that, after making all possible allowances for different cultural tastes, he still could not 'conceive how anything of purity or sanctity could enter into the lives of the young girls and respectable matrons who find their recreation in witnessing such plays'.

When Alcock wrote about his visit to Kabuki several months later, he found that one particular scene was fixed indelibly in his mind, more because of what had ensued in the intervening period than because of its intrinsic merit. The scene showed a large dark house surrounded by a wall. Over the wall silently appeared several muffled figures who crept menacingly towards the house, swords glinting in their hands. The house and its occupants were asleep, cradled in the light of a full moon. Cat-like the men leap on to a low balcony, slide slim shutters, raise their bright weapons. There is a scream, noise of a scuffle. . . It was an unpleasant thought.

The next day the party left Osaka for Yedo and were, at first, annoyed by groups of peasant boys who popped from around corners and behind trees bawling something that sounded like '*Tojin Baba*' at them from a wary distance. It was not, apparently, a compliment, as '*Tojin*' meant Chinese and '*Baba*' meant an old woman or a wily merchant – or both. After a time, however, they outpaced their detractors and fell into an easy loiter through a sweet countryside which dozed and buzzed in the summer sun. Occasionally they passed primitive refreshment stalls and on the counters of these, displayed among the sticky yellow buns and the pink beancurd pastries, were light wooden frameworks from which hung rows of tiny tortoises, suspended by their hapless middles in the air. These desperate little creatures turned their scaly heads and constantly pawed at space in a vain endeavour to make some progress towards the earth below them. The plight of these tortoises worried Alcock considerably, not only because of its essential discomfort, but because it aroused in him a strong sense of fellow-feeling, for, he writes, 'I was struck with the analogy to my own position as Diplomatic Agent in Japan. Doomed, like them, to unceasing effort, without any very sensible progress.' Poor Alcock, he could rarely escape from the impression that he was being put upon and that the world, on both its oriental and occidental sphere, was against him.

But the journey, at least, progressed smoothly enough.

Alcock and de Wit usually rode ahead, discussing the way that the corn was flailed and the rice was ground and the fields were tilled. Behind came Morrison and Wirgman – the latter making furiously rapid sketches at every halt – of a wandering minstrel with a hugely over-size cloche straw hat pulled down over his nose, of a post-runner dressed like an ancient Greek in loin-cloth and sandals and carrying over his shoulder a parcel of letters slung from a bamboo pole, and of a peasant woman moving patiently across a backyard full of children, cooking pots and bath-tubs. Behind them came the two wide-eyed young men of the British Legation and the motley collection of bearers and servants and cooks cumbered with the whole *batterie de cuisine* and everyone rather more sunburned, irritable and dirtier than when they had left Nagasaki three weeks before.

It was a long journey. It was, after a time, a monotonous journey. Alcock marked off in red letters the slow stages of their progress and yearned for even the comparative tranquillity of his Yedo temple. Indistinguishable and numberless thatched villages jogged into view, each with its quota of walnut-faced old men, shy women with staring babies on their backs and batches of hens, dogs and little boys who all scurried away at their approach. Occasionally they saw the castle of a local *daimyo* in the distance encircled by a moat, its outer mud wall surmounted by roughly hewn parapets behind which rose a few sturdy towers, grey tiles pulled down in gracious curves over their square heads. And they came to wide, pebbly rivers with sudden chasms in their centres across which they had to swing in *norimons* held aloft by bearers up to their shoulders in the swift bubbling water. A nerve-racking procedure, for, as Alcock remarked, if a bearer were to lose his balance and let his burden fall, the closed *norimon* would be an effective watery grave.

But at long last, when they were all so tired and blistered and insect-chewed and saddle-sore that there was no sweeter thought than that of cool rain on a cloudy Yorkshire moor, they saw Mount Fuji rising out of the plain ahead, and behind Fuji was home. Thirty-two days after their departure from the south Sir Rutherford and his companions rode in quiet triumph through the gates of the British Consulate at Kanagawa – the first Englishmen for many a century to have travelled the whole way from Nagasaki to Yedo by land.

III

The next day, when Alcock crossed the river between Kanagawa and Yedo, he was delighted to see some familiar English faces waiting to greet him – among them the smiling, open-air countenance of Laurence Oliphant. Ever since his first brief, fascinated visit to Japan three years previously Oliphant had been hoping to return for a longer stay, and so, when he was offered the chance of being *Chargé d'affaires* for a year while Alcock went on home leave, he grabbed at it. As Oliphant's arrival promised Sir Rutherford's own release from duty (a false promise, as things turned out) the weary and frustrated diplomat was particularly pleased to see him and the two men rode to the Legation together, Alcock discoursing in his sober, rather pedantic way about his journey, Oliphant explaining that he had used his first week in Yedo to start an entomological collection for the British Museum. He had already found a couple of rare beetles, he continued, which were neatly speared on trays in the Legation dining-room – oh, and he had also collected a dog, a poor cur that had wolfed his lunch-scraps one day and was back at the Legation too – guarding the beetles. Alcock listened and nodded and thought of his approaching vacation and did not envy his companion in the least.

Lulled into security by the unusual number of familiar faces around him and, if he needed additional reassurance, by the numerous Legation guards whose strength had been increased to a hundred and fifty, Sir Rutherford spent all the next day reading dispatches and writing reports. At seven in the evening he joined his less industrious companions for dinner. They had spent a pleasant time – Wirgman had been making sketches of the local shops, Oliphant and Morrison had been insect and curio hunting, Gower, one of the young secretaries, had been trying to develop some of the photos he had taken during the journey. It was a clear luminous evening and, said Oliphant, a comet was predicted to flash through the sky around midnight, surely the Chief would join them in waiting up for such a spectacle? But Alcock's eyes ached and his body felt sapped from the day's heat; before eleven he left the chatting group and retired to his room. So warm and gentle was the night that the whole of the front of the low wooden house was left open, with only wire sliding-screens between rooms and garden. Clad in his night-shirt, Alcock paused to look out at the stars; no comet had yet appeared; the purple slumbering shadows of oak, pine and maple swayed mildly. So tired was he, so soft the night, that he did not even bother to take out his revolver from its case on the dressing-table and put it under the pillow as was his custom. He slept almost as soon as he lay down and dreamed, perhaps, of home.

But the younger men sat in easy basket chairs, sipping brandy, watching the blue cigar smoke curve away and idly strolling across the lawn now and then to see if they could spot the comet's tail. One of the Legation staff had a fine tenor voice and he sang a few old songs to which they all hummed the chorus. After midnight the comet came; a rent in the dark so swift that they hardly saw it. They drained their glasses to it; there was no further excuse for staying up. And so, bidding each other a sweet sleep, they padded off to their respective rooms which were dispersed among the low passages of the sprawling building.

On reaching his room, Oliphant later recorded in his memoirs, he was greeted by his dog who had already decided that it was his duty to guard the door for his new master. Dozily, Oliphant looked at the revolver-case on his dressing-table. Where the hell was the key? Oh well, it didn't matter. As he climbed into bed he heard the approach of the watchman whose job it was to patrol the grounds all night and wind a wooden rattle at intervals to scare away ghosts, rats, *ronin* and other undesirables. The irritable, sputtering sound, which was presumably intended to reassure the sleeper, aggravated Oliphant, creaked through his head like an aged and boring omen of disaster. He tried covering his ears with the sheet, but it was so hot that he felt smothered. Suddenly the dog began to bark outside his door and he heard a distant scuffle. He jumped out of bed and felt again for the key to his revolver-case, but the damn thing had vanished. Going to the door he nearly stumbled over a box which he had not yet unpacked and which contained a suit of armour – visor and all, he had been told – which a friend had given him as a farewell joke when leaving home, to protect him from those bloodthirsty *samurai*. He grinned, imagining himself striding out of the room with a breastplate over his night-shirt. The dog was yowling desperately and he thought he heard the thud of a quick, surreptitious footstep. From a corner he grabbed his heavy-handled hunting whip which, he imagined, would be enough to quell whatever little domestic strife it was that had caused the dog's distress.

Oliphant slid back his bedroom door, stepped over the trembling dog and tiptoed barefoot along the narrow, low passage which led past Consul Morrison's room, past the young interpreter's room and on to the main front section of the house. The passage was lit only by a flickering oil lamp at the far end and, as he padded along, breathing rather quickly, the lamp began to swing and he heard noises of some distant commotion. He gripped his whip more tightly and, on the instant, from nowhere, out of a nightmare, an armoured figure with sword raised and arms uplifted came hurtling down the corridor towards him. Oliphant stopped and raised the whip which entangled in the folds of his night-shirt and, as he ducked

135

instinctively back, the figure was upon him, its sword slashing down towards his skull. In the first breath of terror Oliphant hardly realised that he was still alive, that his scalp was merely tingling from the expected death-blow. Again and again the figure slashed at him and yet, for some reason that neither he nor his assailant could see in the desperate darkness, the blows did not seem to reach him. Frantically aware that he was fighting now for his life, Oliphant lunged out with his whip, cursing and moaning for the revolver which lay securely in its case back in his bedroom.

Just as the nightmare seemed to be reaching its grotesque climax, Oliphant saw, felt, touched a blinding flash before his face and, at the same second, his left arm seared with half-numb agony and dropped useless to his side. Certain that he had been shot, Oliphant recoiled into the steadying arms of Consul Morrison who, rushing up from behind, had placed his revolver on Oliphant's shoulder and fired point-blank. Even as Morrison pressed the trigger, the swordsman had inflicted a fierce wound into Oliphant's arm which cut to the bone. Oliphant had not time to blink the flash out of his eyes before another Japanese was upon them both and sprang at Morrison with a driving thrust which left a deep gash across his fore-head. Morrison, half-supporting Oliphant, emptied the second barrel of his gun into the new assailant. After a grunt and a slump, there was a sudden odd silence, during which both men realised the significance of the dark, warm fluid which was flowing down and away from their bodies. Nauseated and dizzy, they stumbled towards the only light they could see. Thus it was that Sir Rutherford, who had been awakened by a junior interpreter and had just grabbed his revolver from its case, had gone but five quick steps from his bedroom when he was confronted by the staggering figure of Oliphant covered with blood, followed by the almost equally gory shape of Morrison, his weapon still smoking.

Aghast, Alcock pushed the two wounded men behind a large screen which separated his bedroom from part of the dining-room and prepared to meet their assailants, who, he assumed, must be in hot pursuit. But, for the moment, there was nothing other than the fearsome noise of distant fighting – and no visible evidence of any one of the hundred and fifty Legation guards. Hurrying behind the screen, Alcock saw Oliphant stretched out on the floor livid pale and semi-conscious, bleeding profusely from neck and arm; one of the interpreters, armed, was defending the entrance, the other was helping a Chinese servant load a double-barrelled rifle; Morrison, crouched on a stool, was desperately staunching his head-wound and trying to see out of eyes filled with blood. Realising the severity of Oliphant's plight, Alcock dropped his weapon and, tearing his handkerchief into bandages, began to improvise a tourniquet. Even as his trembling fingers tried to secure the knot, he heard a grinding crash in the room he had just left, the sound of wood and glass splintering under heavy blows. Two assassins had jumped through the dining-room window and landed barefoot upon the trays of pin-impaled insect-specimens which were spread out on the table. At such painful contact, they had fallen sprawling on the floor, one of them careening full-tilt into the sideboard as he tried to regain his balance. It was apparent from the confusion that the assailants were being attacked in their turn and also that they had lost their bearings in the dark and could not, for the moment, find the Europeans whose lives they sought. Nevertheless, it was very much a matter of touch and go. There were seven men behind the screen – including two badly wounded and a ser-vant – with three revolvers and a rifle between them. And, by the sound of it, there might have been fifty attackers approach-ing from different quarters. Furthermore, though the fracas was constant and ever nearer, they could not ascertain whether the Legation guards or the attackers were in control without exposing their vulnerable hiding-place. They held fire and waited; sweaty fingers coiled aching round the triggers of the precious guns.

Oliphant, lolled back on the floor, could see the quiet night sky through the window behind him. The others could perhaps escape to the cover of the garden? He raised his head to suggest it in a weak low voice; but was hushed by the servant bringing water. 'Do you think they'll torture us before they kill us?' murmured the servant in his ear. Torture. Oliphant shut his eyes again, weak with pain and fear, and closed his throat on a scream. Throughout the house the uproar suddenly increased into a passion of violence; the wooden floors trembled; windows shattered and fell; bodies thudded and there was the sickening screech of steel on steel and the crack of distant shots. They waited; again the noises surged away. By now Alcock, who was desperately anxious both about the wounded and about the three Europeans who were missing – Gower, who lived in a building slightly apart from the main house, Macdonald, one of his assistants, and Wirgman, the artist – decided to reconnoitre.

One of the young interpreters was posted at an angle of the corridor, his weapon ready to cover the advance of Alcock and his companions and to guard the other approach. Alcock had scarcely progressed ten quiet, sliding steps when the interpreter, who had seen a group of armed men appearing from the other direction, fired at them. As Alcock and his companions fled back to the comparative safety of the dining-room, there was a rush of feet behind them and there – at last – were the house-guards, harassed and distraught and very relieved to find most of their charges unharmed. While the guards were shaking hands with the beleaguered British and congratulating them on their narrow escape, Macdonald, swathed incongruously in a flowing kimono, broke through them in search of Alcock. He, apparently, had escaped through a side-gate and made his way unobserved to the front of the Legation where he had come upon a wild scene of tumult and blood. Groups of men were fighting for their lives in the courtyard, thrusting into unguarded flesh with sword and dirk or coming to grunting, clumsy hand-grips as they rolled over each other in the dark bushes. Servants and grooms scurried in all directions, globes of lantern-light bobbing in their hands. One of them recognised Macdonald – a feverish and conspicuous figure in his flapping white night-shirt – and offered him a Japanese robe for conceal-ment. Macdonald threw it over his shoulders and hurriedly ordered some of the guards to break from the mêlée outside and get inside the Legation to protect the foreigners there. Morrison had scarcely told his breathless tale when another odd figure pushed through the gathering crowd – Wirgman, his chest and stomach covered with a breastplate of thick gar-den mud and his hair festooned with ancient leaves and cob-webs. He, hearing the approaching onslaught and having nothing more defensive to hand than paintbrush and palette, had decided early in the game to take no part in it. Leaping from his bedroom window, he flattened himself on the ground and crawled into the eighteen inches of space between the raised foundations of the Legation and the solid earth. And there he had stayed, while the violent footsteps thudded over his head and the shock of bullet and steel shuddered through his ears.

At about this time, Oliphant, lying swathed in bandages in an armchair behind the screen, roused from his semi-coma sufficiently to watch, with the detached interest of the weakly bloodless, as more and more guards filed past him through the house, their armour clanging and their headpieces and swords glinting blue in the moonlight, like, he wrote later, 'a scene from *The Huguenots*' – a dream of medieval horror in which he had no more part. When Oliphant became conscious enough to move, his servant and the interpreters helped him to his feet and supported him as he tottered round the screen and through the dining-room. The scene there was fearful. Windows and furniture were shattered; from under the broken sideboard a man's severed head lay like a huge, bloated, mangled ball and, in the middle of the room, the headless body slumped, foul with its own blood. Under his bare feet Oliphant felt some-thing slippery, cool wet like an oyster. He shook his foot and looked down – into the remains of a human eye. A wave of nausea broke over him, he clutched the shoulders of his companions and was half-carried away, to face what was to be, for him, the anguished ordeal of the next two weeks.

During the rest of that shattered night and the next day, Alcock pieced together the tragic story. The assailants were a band of about fifteen *ronin* who had signed a declaration – a copy of which was found on one of their bodies – that they 'had not the patience to stand by and see the Sacred Empire defiled by the foreigners'. Each of them had further declared that 'though being altogether humble myself, I cannot make the light of the country to shine in foreign nations, yet with a little faith and a little warrior's power, I hope within my heart separately, though I am a person of low degree, to bestow upon my country one out of a great many benefits – that is, to cause the foreigner to retire'. They had gathered at an inn in Shinagawa that evening and, about midnight, marched in force on the front gate of the Legation. Finding it closed, they scaled the high fence at the side and crept towards the house – exactly, in fact, the same strategy as that employed by the attackers whom the foreigners had watched on the Kabuki stage three weeks before. The gatekeeper, who first heard a noise, was instantly cut down, as were a hapless groom, a cook and a dog – the latter, says Alcock bitterly, being 'the only sentinel awake' out of the hundred and fifty Legation guards!

Sir Rutherford, who had never held the Japanese guards in much esteem, had some very bitter things to say about them now. The guard-houses throughout the capital were, he wrote, 'generally occupied by boys or superannuated old men, who spend their whole time squatted on their knees and heels and either dozing at their posts or smoking the pipe of apathetic idleness'. And, he adds, as the Gotairo of Japan himself was slain in the middle of an escort before the Shogun's very palace, it was hardly surprising that he himself was nearly slain just at the time that he was in the midst of the Shogun's own body-guard with the armed contingents of two *daimyo* ranged round for his protection and the whole Legation building surrounded by specially-constructed barricades.

At any rate, Alcock wrote, after making a dawn survey of the situation, it was clear that all these men and materials had been no proof against the reckless violence of the *ronin* swords. In every room wooden panels had been crushed and broken, sheets, mosquito-nets and even bed-posts slashed by the searching steel, fragments of furniture and glass strewn across blood-spattered floors and screening partitions hurled down and trampled over. In the corridor where Oliphant had faced his assailant a low central beam was brutally gashed with sword-cuts. Apparently Oliphant had been standing beneath and just slightly behind this beam so that, in the darkness, none of the powerful thrusts intended for his skull had quite found their mark.

Miserably, the Japanese Minister of Foreign Affairs sent his personal doctor to attend the wounded Englishmen and a basket of ducks and a jar of sugar as a 'gesture of amity' to Sir Rutherford. The gifts were returned with a note which stated that the British Minister wanted justice and redress instead of ducks and sugar. The government then tried to persuade the Legation staff to retire temporarily to Yokohama for safety; but Alcock determined to reduce their numbers to a minimum and stick it out. Even higher stockades were constructed round the grounds – each separate bamboo pole of which, Alcock commented, could easily be slid upwards to allow a man to creep underneath; contingents of armed marines from one British and one French corvette at Yokohama landed and established twenty-four-hour watches; a couple of warships were summoned from Nagasaki. The Legation, during that hot month, resembled a besieged castle, with bells ringing alert signals each night, desultory shots being fired as tense guards aimed at shadows and every foreigner going to bed with a loaded pistol beneath his pillow and an armed man posted outside his door.

In such circumstances rumours circulated and accumulated

in shuddering whispers and the nastiest of these was that the Legation attack had been a revenge for some outrageous insult which the westerners may have unwittingly paid to the pride of a *daimyo* during their overland journey from Nagasaki. Therefore, it was suggested, Mr de Wit's Dutch Consulate came next on the assassins' list. A week or so after the attack on the Legation two armed Japanese warriors broke into the foreigners' hotel at Yokohama, but, on seeing the alarmed face of some innocent merchant, they silently withdrew. It was Wirgman they had been seeking, the merchant declared the next day – for Wirgman was staying at the same hotel and he had been on the journey from Nagasaki.

Laurence Oliphant meanwhile, though removed from the constant fear of further attack, was, nevertheless, suffering his own private purgatory. As soon as an escort could be arranged, he had been taken from the Legation to HMS *Ringdove* which was lying off Yedo harbour and there he was given a bunk in the captain's own cabin. Both his left arm and his right shoulder were severely slashed and so, with arms bound to his sides, he was fed and cared for by his harassed Chinese servant. He had lost so much blood that he broke out in boils all over and the next day he caught the eye-infection ophthalmia which was raging among the ship's crew. The doctor bandaged his eyes and poured in doses of nitrate of silver which stung like sword-points; the thermometer stood at ninety-five degrees and the stifling cabin swarmed with mosquitoes and flies; his face and arms were scarlet with prickly heat. Oliphant lay in the humid darkness, itching and sweating and hurting and swelling, cramped like a paralytic, helpless as a huge dying baby. But the man had the tenacity of the tough adventurer. 'It is', he wrote in a descriptive letter home afterwards, 'for such emergencies that a beneficent Providence has especially provided tobacco.' After about a week the boils subsided, soon he was allowed to move his right arm and then, at the end of about the worst fortnight he had ever experienced in his eventful life, he was able to stagger up into the cool evening breeze on deck and to receive his new orders from Sir Rutherford.

The orders were that he was to return to England. Alcock had decided this mainly because he correctly judged that Oliphant still needed prolonged and expert medical attention and also because he wanted the Foreign Office to receive a full account of the Legation attack – an account which Oliphant could verify only too well from painful, personal experience. In addition, Oliphant was to bear to Queen Victoria the Shogun's own letter pleading for a delay in the opening of more ports (Hyogo and Yedo in particular) on the grounds – so recently confirmed again – that the Japanese were not yet prepared for further drastic change. So, in the middle of August, after but two harrowing and turbulent months in the country, Oliphant left for home, and Japan did not, after all, profit from the sympathetic scrutiny of the most talented British writer to land on her shores up to that time and for several years to come. The experience, incidentally, had a very long-lasting and profound effect on poor Oliphant. His wounds took a year or so to heal properly and, partly as a result of them, he resigned from the Foreign Service and devoted himself to a private life which became increasingly entangled and melancholy.

As for Sir Rutherford, who longed desperately for his overdue leave, he felt it his duty to remain at his post and await further instructions from Her Majesty's government. Carpenters came to repair the shattered Legation building; guards relaxed into their habitual sleepy postures; Alcock wrote numerous dispatches, more detailed accounts of everyday Japanese life, many wistful letters home. And again, when he looked from his study window, the Legation grounds seemed secure and beautiful, as the first red maple leaf of autumn scudded over the water of the garden lake.

IV

During this latter part of his stay in Japan, Sir Rutherford Alcock became increasingly concerned, not only about the security of foreigners in general, but about the behaviour of certain foreigners towards the Japanese and towards each other. For, by the early 1860's, Yokohama had become rather like a boom town of the Wild West – flimsy, raffish, jaunty and harsh, and populated largely by Jacks-of-all-trades, rootless, incurably optimistic men who liked to make up laws to fit their own particular needs as they bowled along from one adventure to the next.

The port itself was an ever more sprawling collection of clap-board lodging houses and bungalows (in which lived about one hundred and forty permanent foreign residents), of tattered commercial offices, black-roofed godowns, insecure banks, a few shops and, from 23 December 1861 onwards, the ramshackle shed which housed the printing presses of John Black's *Japan Herald*. When a merchant disembarked from some slow, smutty little cargo boat, he had only to rent a piece of swampy land, stake a fence round it, build a shack on it and he was equipped for trade. His address would be conveniently fixed for him according to the time of his arrival and his nationality – thus the third American to start a business lived at 'American No. 3', the second Dutchman at 'Hollande Niban No. 2' and so on. A pictorial map of Yokohama produced in 1862 shows about fifty-five foreigners' houses all told, not including, says the cartographer, 'a Dutch carpenter's house, an American woman's house and a Seamen's Hall'.

From the *Herald*'s advertisements it would appear that the Selfridges of the settlement was Baker & Company, whose address is given as 'First store left above Yokohama Hotel,

American No. 14'. Baker & Co. was a glorious emporium which sold – 'with attention, civility and punctuality' – such heterogeneous items as oil, flour, hats, pickles, solidified milk, stationery, merino-wool underpants, cordage, champagne, tarpaulins and 'good fresh water' to ships.

Baker & Co. was expansive; it allowed Bill Baillie, former master of a cargo vessel, to open a butcher's shop in the rear of the premises and Bill sold venison, ducks and pork most of the time and beef when he could lay his hands on it; but he shuddered, as most foreigners did, at the skinned monkeys which hung whole over the counters of his Japanese competitors and which looked so terrifyingly human that it was not even funny. Baker & Co. was solid and reasonably honest, and would not, perhaps, give shelf-room to the spurious imitations of Lea & Perrin's Worcester Sauce which, that indignant company informed its customers, were being sold locally. 'Make sure', Messrs Lea & Perrin command, 'that our name appears on the wrapper and on the label and on the stopper and on the bottle itself' – for only by making such a quadruple check could a fellow be sure that he was not pouring over his precious fillet an evil Japanese brew of soy sauce, vinegar and water. Baker & Co. was a chaotic and colourful establishment to which came ships' *compradores* who bargained for hours over the price of lard and biscuits, Chinese servants who, while buying tinned hams for their foreign masters' dinners, also offered cut-price rates on Mexican dollars, and the foreign merchants themselves, who tramped through the mud in thigh-boots to see if a new consignment of cigars or whisky had recently arrived from the civilised world over the horizon.

For commodities of most kinds were still scarce (though Freeman & Co., a rival of Baker's, *did* have a special supply of French capers and mustard for Christmas) and a man with an eye for a quick deal might go far, as Raphael Schoyer, the town's first auctioneer, realised. Schoyer was always eager to put up for sale in his shed on the Bund such items as 'two pianofortes, a dozen sperm candles, three well-known and excellent ponies, four Crimean shirts, a picnic junk or sampan, pilot bread, a barrel of best Bass and a supply of Dr Miller's bitters' – and any other goods and chattels that a newly-ruined merchant might wish to dispose of in a hurry.

Such an unfortunate young man had probably signed a few too many chits a few too many times. The chit system, which came from the Chinese ports along with many of the merchants themselves, was a great success in Yokohama where the local currency was cumbersome to carry about and where most of the new arrivals were living more on hopes of their ships coming in than on a quantity of ready cash. And so any foreigner who looked sufficiently like a resident could sign a chit for practically anything – a brandy, a meal, a woman, a haircut or a game of billiards – and, if he was lucky, it might be months before his creditors caught up with him. When they did, the gay signatory might be able to pay them thrice over without batting an eyelid, or he might already be ripe for the auctioneer's gavel. For small fortunes were made or lost in the space of a few months, according to the luck of the draw. Mr Bush, a young hopeful from Shanghai, was in Yokohama just long enough to invest all his capital in tea, store it in a godown and begin preparations for exporting it at a sizeable profit, when fire swept like a blight down his street and devoured all he owned in under ten minutes. On the other hand, another merchant, by name Mr Hunter, arranged for a shipment of 8,000 *picals* of sapan-wood to be brought up from Malaya, where it had been unsaleable at a dollar and a quarter a *pical*, which was what he paid for it. In Yokohama, the Japanese grabbed it up at thirty-five dollars a *pical* and Mr Hunter was well on the road to living happily ever after.

Prices plunged up and down with less predictability than a yo-yo in the hands of a baby and, as no one could have foreseen, the imports which realised the greatest single profits in 1861 were two tigers brought up from the Malay Straits by a Dutchman. When the Japanese customs first saw the tigers they refused to allow them to land, because they were not an item on the agreed trade tariff. At this the Dutch Consul was called in to help decide what should be done with the animals – whose owner could not afford to take them back, refused to kill them and was not permitted to keep them ashore. 'In that case,' said the Consul sadly, 'the only thing to do is to let them free to fend for themselves.' 'Let them free,' gasped the customs men, 'why, they will eat us all up.' The two Dutchmen sighed in acquiescence. And so the interdict on the tigers was hastily waived and their owner made a very large profit by arranging for them to be exhibited in towns and villages throughout the land.

This readily-acquired money went as easily as it came. There was an ever-increasing number of grog-shops and of livery stables which hired out nags for shore-visiting sailors to ride; the foreigners' hotel on the Bund was equipped with two bars, a bowling alley and a gambling saloon; and, in the swampy area behind the town, a whole local 'Yoshiwara' – entertainment quarter – had grown up around the expanding and expensive Gankiro Teahouse. From Gankiro's balconies hung two or three pennants of cloth proclaiming in Japanese that 'this place is designed for the amusement of foreigners'. Between the Yoshiwara and the harbour a space had already been filled in for a quarter-mile racecourse which was opened in 1862. Every resident owned a pony or two for racing and for riding excursions within the treaty limits, and merry, prolonged champagne-picnics were quite the order of the summer days. Alcohol, fortunately, was cheap, owing to the convenient ability of the Japanese customs to overlook the full import duty and allow in huge quantities of bottles 'for personal use only'.

In such a precarious and shifting society no one really trusted anyone else. Not only were the native customs officers eminently bribable, but the local tea-packers were accused of substituting poor quality tea for good when the foreigners' backs were turned, silk-growers were said to adulterate the raw silk with sand and all the Japanese merchants were notorious for breaking contracts as often as they kept them.

The western businessmen labelled the Japanese as a thoroughly corrupt lot and grumbled at their own diplomats for negotiating with them in what one foreign resident termed 'a soft and too-reasonable way'. The diplomats, in their turn, considered the foreign inhabitants of Yokohama to be uncouth, un-principled and greedy and Sir Rutherford once went so far as to call them 'the scum of Europe'. The foreign merchants, for their part, furthered this reputation by cheating the Japanese over currency transactions and swindling each other over land prices and godown rents.

A kind of bastard language had been invented by this time in which Malay, Dutch, French, Chinese, Japanese and Eng-lish words were garbled together into a horrid, totally un-grammatical jargon which foreigners and Japanese shouted at each other. The easiest way to communicate without actually having to learn anything was for the westerners to impose upon the Japanese a few compendium words which could be adapted almost infinitely according to circumstance. Thus the word *piggy* (from the Malay *pekke* – to go) had a large number of generally negative meanings, such as 'to remove', 'to take away', 'to clear the table', 'to get out of the way'. In some cases English words with an added vowel were used – boat became *boto*; sometimes French half-triumphed – a stove-pipe hat was *nang eye chapeau*; then there were Japanese words as foreigners misheard them – the pronoun 'I' was *waterkoosh*. One young linguist tried to produce a phrase-book for this mongrel dialect, in which he informed newcomers to Japan that, in order to tell a native to 'make less disturbance driving nails in the wall, or I shall be obliged to punish you', they should shout '*O my pompon bobbery waterkshee pumgutz*'.

Most of the shouting, apart from such peremptory com-mands, was about tea (*o cha*) and silk, for these were the principal exports, apart from a few 'ventures into Rags' which were, Black wrote, extremely unsuccessful. Compared to these the imports were diverse and exotic in the extreme, and a list of them which includes such items as lucraban seeds, rhubarb, gypsum, cloves and putchuck sounds more appropriate for a sixteenth-century apothecary than for a nineteenth-century Japanese stall-holder.

Animals were popular exports as well as imports, for the Japanese soon realised that a sailor who churns for months over the monotonous waters likes to have a bit of land-life around – some perky, bright creature to remind him of hill and grass and tree. And so one of Yokohama's streets was called Poultry Row and the shops there were backed by small court-yards filled with cages and pens. A wandering seaman with more money than sense could buy a baby bear, with springy black fur and vicious eye, caught in the mountains of Yezo; pheasants with gold, silver or copper plumage; dogs with eyes like saucers and no noses to speak of; long-bearded lanky goats; red-faced apoplectic monkeys; motley mandarin ducks and, if he was lucky, a Japanese *ugisu* (nightingale), a solitary plain-tive bird who was so accustomed to the dark recesses of the woods that he was kept in a closed box with only a small paper window through which dim, leaf-shadow-like light filtered.

Yokohama's first bookshop was established near Poultry Row where, in addition to some tattered dictionaries and works of history and travel, there were for sale scrolls on which native artists had drawn their impressions of the 'hairy barbarians'. The impressions were not, on the whole, flattering. Hugely bearded and moustachioed white faces glower under chimney-black hats, often with glasses raised to wide lips; pudding-cheeked, beady-eyed women stand square and solid in a weight of patterned skirts, fussy trailing bonnets and shawls; stiff children in sailor suits or puffy frocks loiter joylessly at Mamma's side. Grim, heavy, large and stuffy people were the westerners apparently, in the eyes of the local artists.

While many foreigners bought these scrolls 'just for a joke', the item they most wanted from the bookseller – a map of Japan – was not usually available. The Shogun's government was still obstinately convinced that it would be dangerous for the barbarians to learn the contours of the land, the position of its cities or even the depths of its surrounding waters; so, for as long as possible, the publication of any kind of map was suppressed and arriving ships were prevented from making accurate surveys of the coastline. Robert Fortune, for instance, explained how, in 1860, he visited the Yokohama bookshop and, after various preliminary introductions, was taken into a back room and shown a map of Yedo which he was allowed to buy as a special favour and for a very high price. The bookseller, however, justified its price as a kind of danger money by drawing his finger across his own throat to give a graphic indication of what would be his fate if the authorities found out about the transaction.

A second useful piece of equipment which the stranger might seek in vain at the bookshop was an English-Japanese dictionary. Ernest Satow, who arrived in Japan as a student-interpreter to the British Legation two years after Fortune's visit, enumerates the following pitifully small number of linguistic aids available at the time: a thin pamphlet of phrases in the Nagasaki dialect by the Reverend J. Liggins, a vocabulary published by a certain Mr Medway in Batavia, a Dutch-Japanese grammar translated into French, Hoffman's Japanese-English dialogues and Alcock's grammar.

To begin a serious study of Japanese with such inadequate tools was a discouraging grind, but nevertheless, Satow, after only five years in the country, was one of the leading Japanese linguists. Satow was a serious, shy-looking young man, with flat dark hair parted straight down the middle and a droopy moustache. The course of his future life was fixed on the day that he picked up a newly-published copy of Lord Elgin's account of his mission to China and Japan which Ernest's elder brother had happened to bring home from the lending library. The book, Satow wrote, 'inflamed my imagination with pictures verbal and coloured of a country where the sky was always blue, where the sun shone perpetually, and where the whole duty of man seemed to consist in lying on a matted floor with the windows open to the ground towards a miniature rockwork garden, in the company of rosy-lipped, black-eyed and attentive damsels'. Well, as he was to discover, Japan was not quite like that; but Satow was never totally disenchanted. On the brilliant day in September 1862 when, from the deck of the steamer *Lancefield*, he first saw the gracious cone of Mount Fuji and the billowing junks blowing over the waters of Yedo Bay, he confirmed a love affair with Japan which was to be his passion for the next twenty years.

V

When Ernest Satow landed he did not, as he had anticipated, have to go to Yedo to join the Legation, but had simply to turn left along the Bund and there was the British flag—flying from the second storey of an undistinguished wooden building facing the sea. In March of that same year Sir Rutherford Alcock, strained and careworn after his nerve-racking three-year sojourn in the country, had at last gone on his overdue home leave. Though his staff may have missed his authoritative support, many foreigners were frankly glad to see the back of him.

Alcock had infuriated the Yokohama residents by adopting what they termed a policy of appeasement towards the Japanese government. He had, for one thing, agreed with the Shogun that a Japanese delegation be sent to Europe in order to negotiate a postponement of the opening of Yedo and Osaka to foreign ships, on the grounds that Japan was ill-prepared for such a step. This delegation arrived in London early in 1862 and spent six hectic weeks there. The Japanese ministers, resplendent and exotic in their stiff silk robes and gauze hats, went everywhere—from the Zoo to Woolwich Arsenal, from a Midland coalmine to the Crystal Palace. The interpreter attached to the party was one Fukuzawa Yukichi, who later gained a considerable reputation for his philosophical analyses

151

of western thought. At this time Fukuzawa was a handsome and indefatigable young man who scribbled copious notes about everything he saw abroad – schools and street-lamps, newspapers and nannies, lavatories and law-courts. Practically everything surprised Fukuzawa and the ministers, and nothing more so than the Duchess of Northumberland's ball where they watched in bemused wonderment the odd spectacle of ladies and gentlemen actually grasping each other's waists and jogging and hopping and prancing around together under the elegant chandeliers. On his return home Fukuzawa published his extensive and accurate observations in a book which became a best-seller overnight because it contained just the sort of information that the Japanese longed to know about the strange western world.

The delegation succeeded in its mission and the opening of more ports was postponed; but whatever advantages accrued to the Japanese from such postponement, the foreign merchants saw it only as a criminal waste of trading potential. As 'Mr Opening Wedge' wrote irritably to the *Herald*'s editor: 'In Yedo you would be enabled to purchase any amount of silk and a thousand tubs of oil in a single transaction', whereas in Yokohama, the writer continued, there was but a paltry supply of goods available for export and few of these were at competitive prices. But Alcock, who knew much more about the unstable political situation in the country than Mr Opening Wedge and his fellows, understood that, if foreign merchants had been given a completely free hand at this time, the internal economy of Japan might have collapsed entirely.

But Sir Rutherford did not think it necessary to explain such matters to his compatriots; and then he made himself even less popular by publishing in the *Herald* a restrictive ordinance which stated how British subjects should behave themselves. This notice, expressed in the admonitory and severe tones of a headmaster addressing a wayward class, declared that a Briton was not allowed to fire a gun without the Consul's written permission, nor ride at speed through a busy street, nor enter a

Japanese house without formal invitation, nor sleep away from the settlement area, for, he wrote, 'those who come to Japan as residents have other and more serious objects in view than to wander about the country in pleasure excursions'. Alcock also promulgated a rule of the road which, though it sounded extremely fussy and circumlocutory at the time, was to prove very relevant in the light of later events. If a foreigner happened to meet a procession or *cortège* of any kind, Alcock suggested that he 'take and keep to the left hand side of the road, and on overtaking and wishing to pass before any such person, *cortège* or procession ... shall leave the left hand side and if practical without collision but not otherwise ... pass on the right side of the road'. 'Well, now,' one can almost hear a carefree young merchant snort, 'what a brilliant and unusual idea!' – and later raise his glass to Sir Rutherford's departing ship.

In the period between the Legation attack and Alcock's departure the British diplomats had been in a pretty jittery state. In February the new British Legation, which was being built in a beautiful Yedo park, was burned to the ground. 'They have cut down our beloved cherry trees to make a place for the houses of the foreigners,' growled the anti-barbarian men as they watched the construction going on. 'But it will be a very red blossom before it is full grown.' So the Legation staff, who had removed themselves and their archives from Yedo to Yokohama and back to Yedo, now again returned to Yokohama, where Ernest Satow joined them.

In fact, all the foreign legations were at Yokohama during most of 1862, with the exception of the Americans who stuck tenaciously to Kanagawa where, they affirmed, the first treaty stated they should reside. Townsend Harris remained so anti-Yokohama that he vowed he would never set foot in the place and, when he finally left Japan – at about the same time as Alcock went on leave – he had kept that vow as doggedly as he kept all his other unalterable and uncompromising promises.

But, in effect, the Yokohama-Kanagawa controversy was

already out of date and the newly-arrived diplomats accepted the former town as readily as the merchants had done three years previously. Of the legations there at the time, the British definitely had the most influence, if only because about two-thirds of the foreign residents were British. However, according to Satow, the efficiency of the Legation staff was hardly commensurate with its importance. There was a Secretary who neither had nor intended to gain any knowledge of Japanese and who was 'kicked up the ladder' at the earliest opportunity. 'All the domestic virtues were his,' Satow comments, 'and of actively bad qualities he had no trace.' Next in line was a First Assistant who, as many a man, loved music and painting more than administration. In his insouciant hands the accounts fell eighteen months in arrears and the registers of Legation correspondence were two years out of date. There were a couple of doctors, one of whom soon resigned to begin an extremely lucrative private practice; the other, Dr Willis, was a good-natured giant of a fellow about whom a friend wrote that 'how he got into his little Japanese house and how, once in, he ever got out again, remained as big a mystery as that of the apple in the dumpling'. And there was a cavalry escort which went by the honorary title of 'Pig-Drivers' and which was commanded by a lieutenant who adored glittering gold-festooned uniforms to wear and tasselled horses to ride above all things under the sun. Chief of this assembly was Colonel Neale, a last-minute replacement for Laurence Oliphant as *Chargé d'affaires*. Neale was a short wispy-haired man whose temper, said Satow, was 'sour and suspicious' and who 'did not understand the circumstances amongst which he was thrown'. A man of military background, Neale had at least the military virtue of keeping his head when all around were losing theirs, as he demonstrated very shortly after Satow's arrival. But, for the most part, Neale greatly aggravated Satow by making him copy out dispatches every morning instead of giving him a free hand to get on with his real job – which was to learn Japanese.

In spite of such minor annoyances Satow was happy. He shared rooms with the other student-interpreter at the rambling end of the Legation building and there spent what time he could grappling with that fearsomely unpredictable labyrinth of swirl and line within which the Japanese have constructed their unique calligraphy. During the warm evenings he often rode over the marshes to visit a friend in Kanagawa, or he would go bowling in the hotel's alley with Wirgman or, when in conscientious mood, he might make a further sortie to the bookshop and dig around its higgledy-piggledy stock in the vain hope of finding some new linguistic clue to his studies.

Along the same street as the bookshop, most of Yokohama's first curio shops were, by now, firmly established. There was a brisk turnover in skinny wooden dolls, *netsuké*, porcelain, cheap lacquerware and all the quaint, garish Japaneserie which was to proliferate so indiscriminately in years to come. The foreigners' insatiable appetite for lacquerware had, incidentally, already begun to undermine the traditional structure of the lacquer trade. In the secluded 'pre-barbarian days', a skilled gold lacquerer would be invited by a *daimyo* to go and stay in his residence for as long as it would take him to decorate some exquisite box or tray. After a month or two of unstinted free living, the lacquerer would present his finished work to the *daimyo* and would be entitled to charge whatever extortionate price he thought fit. But now things were different. A foreigner could not wait several weeks for a match-box-size lid to be perfected – and he was not willing to give the lacquerer board and lodging while he did the work. A foreigner wanted a reasonable facsimile of good lacquer for a reasonable, specified price which he could purchase while his ship was in port. Lacquerers – the younger ones at any rate – adapted themselves to the new demands; and the aging *daimyo* looked wistfully at his few beautiful pieces, wrapped them in soft blue silk to store away and mourned that such patient craftsmanship would never again be at his disposal.

But the old *daimyo* were walking against the tide; their

sacred land was becoming ever more defiled by ever more barbarians. In that same busy street where the new pseudo-lacquer was for sale, Russian whaling men, Chinese tailors, French missionaries, English merchants and American doctors jostled along together exclaiming at the natives exclaiming at them, and every ship brought its small contingent of globe-trotters who wanted to add experiences in exotic Japan to their lists of travellers' tales. Japan's tourist attractions were, how-ever, still few: a ride down the Tokkaido highway as far as the treaty limits would permit; a meal of seaweed and raw fish; a close examination of what was called by the westerners 'indis-criminate tubbing', that is, the traditional native habit of taking an open bath in a wooden tub outside one's own front door. These delights exhausted, the average traveller would, fairly rapidly, seek the sturdier pleasures of San Francisco or Hong Kong, according to which way his ship was point-ing.

In the hope of making Yokohama a more attractive place to live in and visit, a few responsible citizens formed the first Municipal Council in 1862. The council planned to deal with such thorny subjects as 'streets, lighting, bund and jetties, police, nuisances and cargo boats'. And certainly there were many matters needing constructive attention. Trade, for in-stance, was increasing; but amenities for trade were not. There were not enough warehouses to hold supplies, not enough small boats to carry them and not enough coolies to load them – at least, there was potential labour in plenty, but the coolie-masters of the Custom House had quickly learned the trade union principle, so that only those labourers within their groups were allowed to work and then for double the hire-fee of a year previously.

Another problem was that the port had already begun to haphazardly separate itself into a native and a foreign quarter, and the former of these was intersected by narrow, stagnant canals which ran directly below the back entrances of the poorer houses. Not surprisingly, the canals were soon rank and fetid; garbage was thrown into them together with the offal from pigs and fowl which were slaughtered by Bill Baillie and his fellow butchers in a makeshift abattoir just off the main street. It was not in jest that visitors to Yokohama were advised to carry 'large handkerchiefs plentifully sprinkled with aromatic spirits of vinegar'. Quite often, a late home-goer took an unsavoury tumble into one of these canals, for there were but a few unreliable paper lanterns to light the way and the undrained roads were permanently slippery with mud.

In addition to these deficiencies, the Municipal Council was promptly informed by other irate citizens that the town had no fire brigade, no public transport and no sewage system and what was going to be done about it? As is frequently the case with well-intentioned committees, there were, at this time, more problems than members with ideas or money to solve them; and the only tangible results of several stormy meetings were that more pony races were arranged for the new season and that plans were suggested for the founding of a Protestant church. Even this latter proposal ran into trouble because, although the foreign consuls agreed to jointly finance a church with the money they had gained from renting land to arriving merchants, each consul wanted one of a slightly different Christian hue to be built first. And while Episcopalians and Anglicans and Baptists and Methodists were politely quarrelling among themselves, the Roman Catholics had been quietly getting on with the job and dedicated a chapel, The Sacred Heart of Jesus, on 12 January 1862 – the first officially-sanctioned place of Christian worship in the land for nearly three hundred years.

Anyway, apart from the pony races and the ecclesiastical disputes, matters tended to slide rather – as matters often did in a long hot summer when only a few ships rode listlessly at anchor in the bay and foreigners, tilted in basket chairs on their balconies, sipped languidly at whisky-sodas and the Japanese idly flipped their fans at flies as they lay sprawled in siesta on their soft *tatami* – until the day of 14 September 1862, when

everyone in Yokohama was suddenly shaken out of his summer
torpor by a tragic event which was to have far-reaching consequences for foreigner and native alike.

VI

The two principal actors in this drama of consequence were
one Shimazu Saburo, prince of the southern clan of Satsuma,
and a certain Charles L. Richardson, Esq., English merchant
from Shanghai. The two men never actually saw each other
face to face; but as a result of their close proximity on that
particular day at one certain time, Yedo and Yokohama were
to be in uproar, Britain was to gain the dubious distinction of
being the first western power to bombard Japanese territory
and the Shogun himself was forced to acknowledge the limits
of his power.

Even at the time it was difficult to assess how greatly events
were influenced by the characters of the two men themselves;
by now any such assessment would be mere guesswork. The
Satsuma clan had, from the days of Commodore Perry, been
associated with the 'barbarian-expelling party', fanatical members of which murdered the Gotairo, attacked the Legation
and, probably, killed Henry Heusken. Shimazu Saburo, however, was a more moderate man who wanted to reconcile
Shogun and Mikado and who had wit enough to see that many
of the products of western technology had too much potential
to be summarily rejected. Nevertheless, the prince was undoubtedly a proud man, a man of authority and courage who
was accustomed to the unquestioning obedience and homage
of his own people.

And Charles Lennox Richardson? He was just an ordinary
merchant who, on his way home to England, was visiting business friends who had come up from China a year or so pre-

viously and settled in Yokohama. 'A fine manly specimen of young Englishman, mild and conciliatory,' Robert Fortune wrote of him. 'A choleric man,' wrote Edward House, an American diplomat, fifteen years later, who 'already had a reputation for violent and high-handed treatment of the "natives"'. Richardson was about thirty-five; his friends probably called him Charlie; and he rode out on a bright clear morning from Yokohama with two of them – William Marshall and Woodthorpe Clarke – to see the sights along the Tokkaido highway.

It was such a lovely day, the first hint of cool autumn in the air, that Marshall decided to take his sister-in-law Mrs Borrodaile with them, for she was on a visit from Hong Kong and was also interested in the local tourist attractions. They clopped at a leisurely pace over the causeway, through the guard-gate and on down the main street of Kanagawa. They talked about Japan and the problems of living there – both Marshall and Clarke were on the Municipal Council and were apt to get hot under the collar about the inertia of the British diplomats on the one hand and the Japanese authorities on the other. Mrs Borrodaile contributed the latest Hong Kong gossip and Richardson was anxious to make comparisons between the trading prospects in Shanghai and in this new country. After lunch they continued along the Tokkaido towards the small village of Namamugi, a one-street, one-horse little place with a few shops open to the road and a row of shabby, jumbled one-storey houses.

As they neared the village they passed an increasing number of two-sworded men on horseback and bustling grooms on foot. On the back of the men's jackets, on their sleeves and scabbards was the emblazoned crest of a cross within a circle, which denoted, though the foreigners probably did not know it, that they were all retainers of the Shimazu family from Satsuma. Though some of the servants gesticulated at them and the men on horseback scowled, the English party continued to ride forward, chatting casually among themselves and only half-aware of their surroundings. In the centre of the village the road narrowed and the foreigners formed into pairs – Richardson and Mrs Borrodaile ahead, Marshall and Clarke behind.

Abruptly, the two front riders were confronted by a solid phalanx of mounted *samurai* whose broad silk sleeves gleamed in the sun as they waved their arms angrily at the barbarians. Prudently, Mrs Borrodaile dropped behind Richardson and the two of them reined in, edged on to the left side of the road and paused – but still craned forward to get a good look at the elaborate gold-hinged *norimon* which swung regally in the midst of its guard. There was a second's harsh, tense pause and a low growl, a deep impassioned protest of hostility and outrage fumed through the ranks of the Japanese as they saw the barbarians approaching so closely and casually towards their lord.

Only then did the two strangers fully understand their danger. Richardson began wheeling his horse round, signalling that Mrs Borrodaile should do the same. Even as he raised his left arm, a *samurai* burst through the crowd of attendants surrounding the *norimon* and with one powerful upward thrust of his sword slashed across Richardson's side. Another warrior made a high sword-sweep at Mrs Borrodaile which severed hair and hat from her ducked head. The street was in tumult, red-faced, yelling soldiers, their weapons raised, surrounded all the foreigners in a ghastly scuffle of blood, dust and noise. Marshall was wounded in the side, Clarke's shoulder was slashed, Richardson, deeply cut, slumped across his horse's head. 'Ride on,' cried Marshall in agony to Mrs Borrodaile, 'we can do nothing for you.' She spurred her horse fiercely against the threatening crowd and, miraculously uninjured, galloped back towards Yokohama, sobbing hysterically, her hair lopped and bedraggled, her skirts spattered with her friends' blood, her body rigid in a blind panic of flight. In this state she reached the settlement and gasped out a few horrifying details of what had happened.

Sir Ernest Satow

Laurence Oliphant

The Gankiro tea-house in Yokohama was from the first a popular resort for westerners. Here a sailor demonstrates a hornpipe to an amazed audience

Westerners seen through Japanese eyes: a couple, probably Americans . . .

. . . an Englishman and a Russian woman

横濱休日
亜墨利加人遊行

Pleasure riding in Yokohama on a Sunday

'The firemen were, with the sumo wrestlers, the popular heroes of Yedo. At the sound of the alarm bell they would form into procession and march towards the fire, singing loudly.' An engraving based on a Japanese print

'Outrage on the British legation at Yedo. Attack on Messrs. Oliphant and Morrison', as recorded in The Illustrated London News

Western houses at Yokohama

The murder of Richardson — '*Even as he raised his arm, a Samurai burst through the crowd . . . and with one powerful thrust of his sword slashed across Richardson's side*'

*On 24th June, the Prince of Satsuma paid over £125,000 in Mexican dollars
as reparation for the murder of Charles Richardson*

Charles Wirgman sketched the scene. The pig-tailed figures in the foreground are
Chinese *shroffs*—experts in the detection of base coin.

Now it was the foreigners' turn to be in uproar. Revolvers were loaded, horses hastily saddled and practically every able-bodied western male in the town thundered over the causeway towards the scene of slaughter. There was Lieutenant-Colonel Vyse, the British Consul of Kanagawa with the Legation mounted escort, there was the volatile Monsieur Bellecourt of France with half a dozen French troopers, there were merchants from America, Prussia and Holland, two doctors, a few visiting marines and an assortment of hangers-on – all of them spoiling for a fight. They surged through Kanagawa, past some of the Satsuma retainers and into Namamugi, where, at first, there was no sign of any English, only flies and dogs buzzing and snuffling round the trodden blood in the road. No one, it seemed, knew how the blood had got there.

But the principal victim was not hard to find. Richardson's corpse lay near a tree under a couple of mats, hacked in pieces, his bowels spilling on the grass, his right hand severed as he had raised it to protect his throat from being cut.

With trembling hands, some of the men raised the mangled body and carried it back to the American consulate at Kanagawa – which Marshall and Clarke, though both wounded, had been able to reach alive. When the whole sorry story was pieced together it seemed that, immediately after Mrs Borrodaile's flight, Richardson, while galloping after her, had fallen from his horse and was left for dead. Not dead but dying, he had crawled to a tea-shop on the outskirts of the village and begged for water. At that very moment a Satsuma noble's *norimon* drew level with the shop, a warrior jumped out and inflicted the final savage wounds on the helpless man. As soon as the Satsuma men had departed, the corpse was removed to a near-by field by the terrified, innocent villagers.

This murder inflamed the foreign community as no previous – and, indeed, no subsequent – assassination did. It was the first time that a completely harmless non-combatant civilian had been so brutally attacked. Soldiers, sailors, even diplomats and their assistants might find themselves in the line of fire while performing their official duties, but that a merchant should be murdered, and this merchant but a young, quite disinterested visitor to the country, and that two respectable businessmen should be wounded – and perhaps most abominable of all – that an English lady should have barely escaped with her life; this was quite unforgivable.

A tempestuous meeting was held in Yokohama that evening at which all the westerners clamoured to set off at once for Hodogaya, where the Satsuma contingent were thought to be staying for the night, to exact immediate and total vengeance. And, indeed, if all the men from all available foreign ships in the harbour had been mustered, reinforced – as they would have been – by the enraged residents, it is quite possible that such a force could have captured Shimazu and his men. The murder of Richardson teetered on the brink of becoming another Jenkins's ear, for who knew, or at that point cared, what would have been the ultimate consequences of such an attack?

In the long run, it was fortunate that the cooler, more far-sighted command given by the British *Chargé d'affaires* was obeyed. The foreign settlers, complaining bitterly at what they considered to be a gesture of appeasement on Neale's part, were told to return home, put away their revolvers and let reparation for the crime be exacted by more civilised, if less quixotic, diplomatic methods. Naval guards patrolled the settlement at night during the next few weeks to give extra protection for foreigners; a Volunteer Corps was formed among the merchants themselves, who kept their rifles at the ready for any fresh emergency; for a while every foreigner held his breath as he passed a two-sworded *samurai* on the highway, and in the quiet loneliness of the warm nights, his flesh quailed at the memory of Richardson's fate.

Meanwhile the cumbersome machinery of British diplomacy creaked into action on the dead man's behalf. When Lord John Russell at the Foreign Office heard the news of the affair a few months later, he demanded heavy and stringent reparations from the Japanese: the payment of £100,000 as the

Shogun's penalty for allowing a civilian Englishman to be murdered and for failing to arrest his assassins; coercive measures to be taken after twenty days if the penalty was not paid in full; a revenge attack on the Satsuma clan, who were ordered to execute the assassins in the presence of English military officers; a payment of £25,000 by the Prince of Satsuma which would be distributed to Richardson's relatives and other injured parties.

Considering the strength of the British naval force which, during April 1863, steamed up the Japanese coast towards Yedo Bay in readiness for the 'coercive measures' which were to be taken if the Shogun did not pay, it looked as if Shimazu Saburo had run up quite a bill for his country on that September afternoon six months previously. Inevitably, the Shogun pleaded for a delay and, when the twenty days expired (from the time that the Japanese government had received the British ultimatum) and the money had not been handed over, the natives were convinced that the British ships were about to bombard Yokohama and Yedo harbour. Japanese servants and shopkeepers bundled their belongings together and fled towards the safety of the inland towns – Satow recalls that his cook and boy disappeared during the night of 5 May, taking with them a little cutlery and 'the remains of last night's dinner wrapped in a tablecloth'.

It was another uneasy period for the foreign residents. Throughout the next month rumours abounded that the Mikado had ordered the closure of all the ports and that the Yedo government was not strong enough to prevent this; it was suggested that all western women and children should leave Yokohama at once and that their menfolk should keep a twenty-four-hour watch, in case of a surprise attack by royalist forces from the south. However, after much bluffing and blustering on both sides, the Shogun, who feared schism within his own country as much as the threatened foreign reprisals, paid the indemnity.

At dawn on 24 June, sleepy Yokohama was roused by the

guttural '*Hai, huida, ho, ho, hai*' shouts of the coolies as they dragged heavy boxes crammed with Mexican dollars from the treasury to the British Legation. Canny Chinese *shroffs* (experts in the detection of base coins, and money changers) were hired to check that the coins were genuine and then the money was crated and put aboard the squadron waiting in the harbour. A month or so later Charles Wirgman published a drawing of the extraordinary scene in *The Illustrated London News*. In the foreground the pigtailed *shroffs* are bending over piles of coins which they are testing and scrutinising as ardently as any Silas Marner. Behind them sit three Japanese dignitaries in stiff robes who, understandably, look rather peeved. On either side stands a group of British Victorian gentlemen in attitudes of casual power, hands in pockets, faces righteously grim, covertly watching the bright metal which shiningly proliferates at their feet. It is not, a hundred years later, a very pretty picture.

But though the Shogun himself had been brought to heel by the British squadron, he was powerless to influence the behaviour of Shimazu Saburo, who obstinately refused to pay any part of the indemnity or execute Richardson's assassins. At length and with some reluctance, Lieutenant-Colonel Neale determined to go down with the British force to Satsuma in order to present officially Her Majesty's ultimatum and to take 'coercive measures' if its demands were not met. Ernest Satow accompanied his chief on this mission and, in his unquestioning, cool way, seems to have enjoyed it more than most of his companions did.

The little squadron looked very portentous and business-like as it steamed southwards for five fiery August days. There was HMS *Euryalus* – the flagship of Admiral Kuyper, the squadron's commander; a couple of corvettes, whose names, *Perseus* and *Pearl*, made them sound as if they would, at any moment, burst into a song-and-dance routine; a paddle sloop, *Argus*, with Satow and his friend Doctor Willis aboard; a dispatch vessel and two sleek, efficient gunboats, the *Racehorse* and, ominously, the *Havoc*. On 11 August, they anchored in the bay facing the provincial capital of Kagoshima and a letter which stated the British demands was sent ashore. An unsatisfactory reply to this was received from the Satsuma clan on the following day, and without more ado, the squadron went into action.

Three Japanese steamers were seized and plundered; 'I secured a Japanese matchlock and a conical war-hat,' Satow tells us, and adds that the worthy British tars grabbed anything they could lay hands on – glasses, benches, decanters and even old pieces of matting. The steamers were then fired and scuttled and a line of battle was drawn. At about noon several shore batteries opened fire on the squadron which was rolling sickeningly in an almost typhoon-force gale. The *Euryalus* did not return the fire for an hour or two because, says Satow, its crew was engaged in moving the huge boxes of the indemnity coins which, when put aboard at Yokohama two months before, had been piled against the door of the ammunition magazine. It was a nicely ironic touch but, if correct, did not say much for the foresight of the ship's officers.

When the battle did begin in earnest it was hotter and fiercer than anyone had imagined. The aim of the Japanese gunners soon became alarmingly accurate and a single shot killed both Captain Josling and Commander Wilmot as they stood together on the bridge of the *Euryalus*. A ten-inch shell exploded on the flagship's main deck, another on its upper deck; the *Racehorse* had grounded in the gale and had to be towed off; the *Pearl* was considerably damaged. In return, British rockets had fired the town and the proud factories, where the famous Satsuma porcelain was made, burned to the ground. 'I shall never forget the interest and excitement of the whole affair,' Satow exclaims, 'from the bursting of the shells high in the air against the grey sky all round the flagship as she lay at anchor before we weighed, till we came into action ourselves and could see first the belching forth of flame from the middle of a puff of smoke.'

A further perfunctory shelling of the town and the batteries was carried out the next day and then the Admiral decided that the Satsuma clan had been taught their lesson. The squadron sailed back to Yokohama to report what was, at best, an indecisive victory. There were sixty-three British killed and wounded, no landing had even been attempted and no one really had any idea of how extensively Kagoshima had been damaged – though the official dispatch states, with satisfaction, that £100,000-worth of Satsuma property had been destroyed.

A few certainties emerged from the affair: a number of people who were totally innocent – even ignorant – of Richardson's murder had been vengefully killed; a classic piece of gunboat diplomacy in the time-honoured western style had been perpetrated; the British government was richer by several thousand Mexican dollars; Richardson's torn remains were buried in Kanagawa cemetery; and his assassin, later known to be one Narabara Kizaemon, a fanatical swordsman, lived to a ripe old age. Back in Yokohama the merchants had put away their guns, their nervous wives had returned and, wrote Satow, 'we settled down quietly again and trade went on pretty much as usual'.

VII

By the time that Sir Rutherford Alcock returned from his home leave early in the following spring, it seemed that the Satsuma clan had been bombarded into complete silence – though its members were profiting from their experience by busily learning how to manufacture armaments in the effective western manner. Sir Rutherford brought back to Japan with him a K.C.B., a wife to lighten his solitude – the widow of a Hong Kong clergyman – and authority from the Foreign Office to take further drastic measures against any continuing hostility from the southern clans.

When, therefore, soon after his arrival, the British Minister heard that another clan of the region, the Choshiu, were in the habit of firing on any foreign ship that ventured through the Straits of Shiminoseki on the voyage from Nagasaki to Yokohama, he felt empowered to follow his usual tactics when confronted with Japanese resistance. These tactics were, simply, to gang all the foreign powers together, present a united front to the Yedo government and then threaten combined military action which, in this instance, would follow unless the straits were made safe for foreign ships. The Prince of Choshiu refused to be intimidated either by the westerners' threats or the pleas of the Shogun, and so Alcock (who felt he had to act quickly to circumvent an impending new Franco-Japanese alliance) ordered immediate combat. It was, as Ernest Satow wrote, 'an immense responsibility that he had assumed. There was no telegraph in those days to any point nearer than Ceylon, but a dispatch dated July the 26th was already on its way to him positively prohibiting the adoption of military measures in the interior of Japan and limiting naval operations.' Blissfully unaware of the new Foreign Office decision, eight British ships supported by French and Dutch corvettes and an American steamer chugged southwards down the blue sunny coast to see peace restored and to teach the upstart Prince a lesson.

The operation was carried out in a fairly leisurely and haphazard manner. The western ships fanned in stately array across the Inland Sea to the mouth of the Shiminoseki Strait; the next day they began to fire at the Japanese onshore batteries and the Japanese fired back; the day after that they all fired again and then some of the foreign marines landed, climbed up the steep grassy hills under fire, upset a few of the Choshiu gun emplacements, broke up the carriages, threw the shot and shell into the sea and burned the powder; late the same afternoon more 'blue-jackets' landed, scrambled around the paddy-fields taking pot-shots at mostly imaginary foes and bore off as many trophies of war – armour, bows and arrows, spears – as they could find; the eastern end of the little port of Shiminoseki was set ablaze and its inhabitants fled; the following morning 'working parties' of sailors landed on the deserted shore and either carried away or destroyed the rest of the Japanese bronze guns; in the afternoon the westerners counted their casualties (eight killed, thirty wounded) and buried their dead on the bright hillside.

After that there was nothing to do but negotiate a peace. The Prince of Choshiu agreed to cease firing at foreign ships – indeed he had no guns left with which to fire – to refrain from building any forts overlooking the straits and to pay an indemnity to the westerners which would help finance their expedition against him – a cruel twist of the knife. While this settlement was being negotiated the local Japanese and the foreigners from the ships fraternised happily, and Satow, who was interpreter to the expedition, long remembered the welcome meals of stewed terrapin, melon and tough boiled rockfish which he shared with the villagers.

By the time the foreign ships returned in triumph to Yokohama, Lord Russell's dispatch to the effect that it was not British policy to adopt military tactics had been received; this was followed by an 'invitation' to Sir Rutherford to return to England and explain matters. Eventually, Alcock was able to explain matters to everyone's satisfaction and – in the way that long-distance dispatches had of missing the people for whom they were intended – another one reached Yokohama after Alcock had left again for England which stated that the writer, Lord Russell, now understood the full background to the Choshiu incident and was convinced that the British Minister had acted correctly after all! When the Foreign Office finally sorted out all their dispatches, it seemed that Sir Rutherford was not only totally exonerated, but that he deserved some reward for his endeavours. And so Alcock was given the post of Her Majesty's Minister in Peking – a sweet plum compared to the rather bitter aloes of Japan – and henceforth was able to confine himself to his true *métier*: Chinese affairs.

While Lord Russell was being thus reminded of Japan's

existence, he also decided that, because of the frequency of the alarums and excursions in the new settlements, a contingent of British troops should be permanently stationed in the country. Consequently, during that same summer, men of Her Majesty's XXth, the 'red regiment' as the Japanese called them, arrived and were quartered in a hastily erected barracks on the Bluff, overlooking the harbour.

The soldiers were not, apparently, very pleased to be there. Ralph Jephson, guardsman, horseman and huntsman, remembered his army hut as 'a spacious apartment of ten feet square, bounded by walls, whose weather-beaten and mouldy sides, the temporary owner had fondly attempted, on more than one occasion, to conceal with Japanese screen-paper'. Wind, raking the exposed cliff-top, howled through 'various well-designed chinks', rats chewed large holes through the floorboards. In the centre of the hut a low stove, 'most conveniently placed for tumbling over', emitted suffocating fumes which refused to go out of the appropriate pipe but hung heavy in air already turbid with cigar smoke.

'Home' being such a cheerless place and the demands on their martial skills being few, the men of the XXth devoted most of their energy to wasting time in the pleasantest possible manner. They drank large quantities of 'b & s', ran billiard competitions, strolled down to meet the sailors at the United Services Club on the Bund and listened to the regimental band on Sunday afternoons. But above all the soldiers practised what Jephson calls 'that exercise in the field which gives a clear healthy tone to body and mind, and preserves the keen sense of enjoyment that English blood and breeding teaches us to find in the exciting pastime of the chase', in other words – fox-hunting.

Before the barbarians came the fox had been an animal of considerable standing in Japan. Foxes were messengers and guardians of the local Inari shrines and the fox-images that guarded the shrine-gates held keys in their mouths to symbolise their right of protection over the rice stores. Fox masks were popular at festivals and many were the legends of the fox who assumed the shape of a beautiful woman and married the man who had saved it from death while it was in its animal shape. Usually the marriage was a happy one, for the fox had a dignified and devoted spirit.

The men of the XXth bought up all the tough local ponies, which were known as 'griffins', imported a seedy pack of hounds from Shanghai (kept alive by frequent doses of sulphur and castor oil) and took to the paddy-fields. Foxes were the main quarry, though, in the earlier days before the huntsman's horn became such a familiar sound, foreigners also slaughtered deer and wild boar. There were dawn hunts, with the riders coming to an early breakfast, 'all breeched and booted with revolvers in our belts', Jephson notes, and calling for a stiff whisky with the gammon and eggs; there were afternoon hunts which often finished at a country tea-house so that the hunters, tired of their four-legged prey, could chase the pretty waitresses round the *shoji* (screens); there were 'drag-hunts by moonlight' – jovial, rollicking expeditions when the 'lads', already roaring with wine and brandy, leaped from the mess-table into the saddle and went galloping and hallooing into the night, breaking down the irrigation ditches and trampling over the rice.

Inevitably, the arrival of such a vociferous horse-loving fraternity increased the activity on the settlement's racecourse, and such sterling military characters as 'Mister Pop', 'Aaron' and 'Captain Puffles', riding such shaggy nags as Black Bob, Smiley and Batavier, careened round in the hot dust of the summer afternoons, the cries of their mess-mates goading them to the post. The 'Equine Deity', as Jephson fondly called it, was in ascendant, and the next best status-symbol to a race-winner was to harness one's pony to a brisk bright little trap and go clipping along the new road which ran round part of Mississippi Bay.

In November of 1864 the insouciant mood of the Yokohama regiment was temporarily disrupted. When the officers were not hunting or racing it was their custom to pursue their equestrian-worship by making bridle-path excursions to Kamakura, a small town farther down the coast. On the twenty-first of the month two officers, Major Baldwin and Lieutenant Bird, buckled on their revolver belts, saddled their griffins, filled their bags with claret and sandwiches and went to look at the famous 'sight' of Kamakura – the giant bronze statue of Buddha, the *Daibutsu* (called, invariably, 'daiboots' by visiting westerners). After a cursory look at the brooding, vast and somnolent mass of metal, the two men continued their ride towards the sea-shore. As they were about to turn a corner, a couple of *ronin* leaped from the bushes and inflicted fatal wounds on the soldiers before they had time to grab their revolvers. Baldwin died at once; Bird lingered for a few hours only.

Naturally the excitement in the settlement was again intense and naturally the men of the XXth brandished their fists and their weapons and wanted nothing more than to be ordered to march down to Kamakura and fire the whole village in reprisal. Luckily no such foolish measure was permitted. The victims were, after all, armed soldiers in uniform and the correct response to their murder was to capture their assassins and dispose of them in a military manner. It was a sign of the new times that, on this occasion, the Japanese government exerted every possible effort to trace the murderers and, before the month was out, one of them, Shimadzu Seiji, was a marked man and two of his associates were imprisoned and sentenced to death.

In order, presumably, to purge the British of their lust for revenge, the sentence was carried out with medieval thoroughness and the maximum publicity. Ernest Satow was one of the many foreigners who, on a drear December afternoon, gathered in an enclosure outside the local gaol to watch the spectacle. 'A little after three o'clock a whisper ran round that the condemned were being brought out,' Satow wrote. 'A door opened and a man blindfolded and bound with cords was led through the crowd. He was made to kneel down on a rough mat placed in front of a hole dug in the ground to receive his blood. The attendants drew his clothes downwards so as to lay the neck bare, and with the hand brushed his hair upwards so as to give full play to the sword. After this last, ghastly caress, the executioner secured a piece of cotton cloth round the handle of his weapon, and having carefully whetted the blade, took up a position to the left of his victim, then raising the sword high above his head with both hands, let fall with a swoop that severed the neck completely. The head was held up for inspection of the chief officer present, who simply remarked, "I have seen it", and it was thrown into the hole.'

A couple of weeks later the chief assassin, Seiji, was captured, bound tightly on a packhorse and led through the grey Yokohama streets. Before him, officials carried a placard on which his sentence of death was announced in huge bleeding red characters. On the last day of 1864, Seiji jumped jauntily out of his guarded litter, walked across the execution ground and bowed his head over the last hole. As his executioner approached, he threw himself back on his haunches and spat at the watching British soldiers, 'I do not regret being taken and put to death, for to kill the barbarians is the true spirit of a Japanese.'

As his head fell a single gun discharged. Later, the head was impaled on an iron spike and displayed at the sea end of the main Yokohama bridge, the story of its crime and punishment duly inscribed beneath.

Part Four

Feuds and Peacemakers

'Knowledge shall be sought for throughout the world, so that the foundations of the Empire may be strengthened.' – Article 5 of the Imperial Oath of Five Articles sworn by the Emperor Meiji in Kyoto Palace, April 1868.

The brutal assassination of Major Baldwin and Lieutenant Bird and the subsequent, hardly less bloody execution of their murderers did not bode well for the New Year of 1865; but, in the event, the worst savagery was over. The crucial issue for the Japanese during the next few years was not so much about who was to come into their country from the outside as who was to rule it from the inside. The two matters were, of course, intimately linked and, at this time, it still seemed as if the Shogun's councillors favoured increasing communication with westerners, the Mikado's party wanted their expulsion. But alignments were not as clean-cut as that. There were fanatics on each side whose sword-hands still itched at the very sight of a hairy barbarian and there were enlightened men in both Yedo and Kyoto who understood that growing contact with the West was desirable and inevitable. There were further deeds of violence against foreigners to be perpetrated by the 'barbarian-expellers' (as they called themselves), but they were the isolated desperate acts of men who lacked organisation and a clan-leader's support. All in all, the New Year brought for the majority of ordinary, well-disposed Japanese and for most reasonable, moderate foreigners the beginning of that happy state of affairs which is now called 'peaceful co-existence'.

The Municipal Council of Yokohama bestirred itself again with the spring and on 6 March a public meeting of all foreign land-renters was held. It was agreed that the Council should consist of eleven British members, five Americans, four French, two Dutch, two Prussians, one Portuguese, one Swiss – the numbers being proportionate to the amount of land rented by each nationality. Raphael Schoyer, the American auctioneer, was elected chairman. The Council, in the habitual fashion of councils, at once began to proliferate into committees: a road committee, a sanitary committee, a police committee – and a finance committee which obviously had the toughest job of getting enough money from taxes on grog-shops, rents and fines to pay for the measures recommended by the other committees. The Council dutifully began to meet at regular intervals and to pronounce ordinances. Its first ordinance was about the number of rabid dogs that prowled the settlement and had already caused two or three deaths; its second was to forbid the slaughtering of animals intended for food within the settlement boundaries – the same suggestion which a similar council had made a couple of years previously, obviously to little effect; its third was that all Explosive Substances should be stored on a hulk in the harbour out of fire's way.

From its inception the Council wrangled with the foreign Consuls who had granted its 'charter'. Rather tactlessly, the Consuls used their right of veto over the Council's affairs to stop the very first 'dog ordinance', which thus became an inflated and inflammatory issue – example to the Council members of the obstructiveness of the Consuls and example to sceptical non-members of the Council's impotence. Once again as summer swamped the land enthusiasm dwindled. It was, after all, a great deal more pleasant to gather together a few friends, some cases of claret and champagne and all ride off for tiffin among the hills than to sit in a hot room near the harbour trying to decide how to eliminate the stench that drifted in the windows.

Towards the end of August, however, a few of the more energetic Council members tried yet again. A well-attended meeting was held in the court-room of the British Consulate and Mr Schoyer made a passionately incoherent speech denouncing Consuls and Japanese alike. According to John Black, who was present, it sounded, in part, like this: 'If we have no power to conduct the affairs of the settlement, what is our position? We have full power over every indecent act although no power to punish... If Japanese are found obscene or endangering the lives of others, the Municipal Police shall arrest them... Ladies within the last ten days have been insulted and their lives endangered by *bettos* (grooms) furiously riding; and I say it shall be put down. Obscenity to be tolerated? And in places too where ladies are promenading with their children? The very notion is absurd, and for any Consul to say that we cannot prevent it, is a gross insult to our common sense.' Poor Mr Schoyer! It was his last tirade – and he had, apparently, been celebrated for them. As he resumed his seat, flushed and breathless, he suffered a heart attack and, in spite of the efforts of a doctor present, died without regaining consciousness. At the same meeting, Mr Black coolly notes, 'Mr J. Allmand was elected member of the Council, in place of Mr Schoyer.'

Plainly, local fame was still an ephemeral and casual attribute, but clearly too, as the continuing existence of the Municipal Council shows, the Yokohama community was becoming ever more aware of itself as an entity. By the middle of the 1860's, in fact, it was sufficiently defined and self-conscious to support its own satirical magazine – *The Japan Punch*. This was a haphazard, rice-paper-and-Indian-ink publication which appeared at irregular intervals for several years and contained some very vigorous caricature-drawings of local personalities by the omnipresent Charles Wirgman. The British and American diplomats in particular are pretty savagely depicted as a bunch of vacillating, short-sighted fellows who were invariably willing to sacrifice the interests of their compatriots in order to appease the Japanese. Compared to the art-work, the text is feeble and heavy-footed and is burdened with the ponderous facetiousness of not-very-bright young shipping clerks. There are several mock-advertisements: 'Timely warning – Quintius Curtius begs to notify that he has commenced slaughtering this day.' (That Yokohama stench again.) 'For Sale – A soda-water machine. The buyer will have to buy the Chinaman belonging to the machine.' There are the inevitable puns – hats for sale are not purchasable at the *hatoba* – and a variety of jokes about the writers' debts, occasional orgies and allied activities which young men like to tell the world they are indulging in.

The magazine, for all its laboured humour, certainly suggests that, by this time, the businessman of Yokohama looked upon himself as a real resident, that he took a certain pride in the oddities, 'quaintnesses' and minor deprivations of settlement life and that he felt secure enough to express his views about the diplomatic establishment in no uncertain way.

The new sense of cohesion and local pride was undoubtedly necessary to a community which was still, on its peripheries, fluid and precarious – the rich and the ruined constantly leaving and the sanguine, the industrious, the feckless and the simply colourful constantly arriving. Flamboyant even among the colourful arrivals at this time was one Professor Risley, 'a man', wrote Black, 'who never did himself justice'. Risley had made his name – though not, presumably, his title – as an acrobat during the 1840's, and he once appeared at the Strand Theatre in London where he amazed his audience by his ability to toss his young sons in the air from the soles of his feet; later he joined the Australian Gold Rush, but 'never saw the colour'.

Risley had first arrived in Yokohama during 1864 with a travelling circus. In the heat of the summer many of his performing animals died and Risley quickly decided that, rather than a circus, the citizens of the new settlement needed an ice-house. He built one near the harbour, imported hundreds of tons of ice from Tientsin on the Chinese mainland and soon accumulated a cool pile of Mexican dollars. After spending most of these on his favourite pursuits of rifle-shooting, whisky-drinking and billiards, Risley decided that the next thing

Yokohama needed was a dairy. So, late in 1865, he went off to California, bought half a dozen cows and their calves and proceeded to ship them across the Pacific on the trading schooner *Ida D. Rogers.* This trim, spritely, lucky little vessel, which had been plying regularly between San Francisco and Japan since 1860, was renowned for the celerity of its passages; but this particular voyage lasted seventy days and the cattle nearly died of thirst. Risley, loquacious and relieved to be ashore again, went to tell Black about it as soon as he landed: 'We were close to Yokohama a month ago – and blown right off to the north, and had to beat up against a dead head wind and thought we should never get here. Waal! One day I was wretched seeing the poor beasts licking the sides of their boxes and the deck, and lapping everything they could – b'lieve me, I could hardly stand it – I can't bear to see a poor dumb animal suffering – but – if you'd only seen the poor creatures. At last I'd made up my mind that they must all die, and I was only thinking whether I should throw them overboard or shoot them, and not yet able to make up my mind – when God was merciful and sent a night's rain. I worked like a horse; and all that night I was employed in catching water and I saved six thousand gallons – I did – all with my own hands! Waal! You may smile, but I did you know, and the cows were saved. I never was so relieved in all my life. When the rain came the ship was rolling terribly – and the Cap'n said, "Professor, don't you go forward – it's like tempting Providence – you'll be sure to go." Waal, said I, I'm not very comfortable here, so if I must go I must – but the poor cows shall have some water first. And so they did.'

The dairy, like the ice-house, flourished. But Risley was not a man to sit around and watch something grow; he always believed in ever-greener pastures. So, pretty soon, he gathered together a troupe of Japanese acrobats and rushed off to exhibit their extraordinary talents throughout the United States – 'the biggest show on earth', it would be, Risley said.

Another 'character' arrived in that year, a man who, in his

very different sphere, was no less colourful and enterprising than Professor Risley: Sir Harry Smythe Parkes, K.C.B. Sir Harry, who landed at Yokohama in July to take over as the new British Minister at the Legation, was a compactly-built man with vigilant blue eyes and a steady, kind expression, 'the last man in the world', wrote his biographer, Frederick Dickins, 'to let the grass grow under his feet'.

Because he was orphaned at thirteen and sent out to join his elder sister in the new colony of Hong Kong in 1841, Parkes completely by-passed the typical establishment education of the British diplomat; instead he acquired fluent Chinese and an intimate knowledge of how a colony really worked during his years as interpreter to various trading companies and consulate offices in Shanghai, Hong Kong and Canton. While on home leave in 1856, Parkes met, proposed to and married within six weeks one Fanny Plomer, a brown-eyed, intelligent young woman who enjoyed following her husband to the ends of the earth. By 1865 Parkes had already gained a considerable reputation; a man who, according to Ernest Satow, 'in the eyes of all European residents in the Far East held a higher position than any officer of the crown in those countries'.

After living in Japan for only a few months, Sir Harry satisfied himself of one fundamental truth, at which his diplomatic predecessors had only surmised: the real power in the country was shifting from the Shogun in Yedo to the Mikado in Kyoto. This transference was, of course, gradual and disorderly at first and had its early roots in the discontent and frustration of those Japanese clans which, for years before the arrival of the West, chafed under the restrictive bridle of Tokugawa supremacy. The violent murder of the Gotairo in 1860 (which had been perpetrated by the anti-foreign Mito clan) had deprived the Tokugawa house of an effective leader just when one was most needed. From then on the Shogun's government had been constantly challenged – on the one hand by the traditionalists who saw they would be dispossessed when

Japan was fully open to world trade, on the other by the westerners themselves and their progressive Japanese friends who felt that the Shogun's policy towards them was dilatory and dishonest.

In fact, by the time Sir Harry arrived in the country, many intelligent men of both factions were realising that it was impractical and irrational to try to expel all the new foreign influence; nevertheless, both sides exploited the barbarian invasion for their own ends – the Shogun by playing his domestic enemies off against the foreigners, the Mikado by channelling the reserve of anti-western sentiment into the struggle against the Yedo government. To Parkes it seemed clear that, once the powerful clans around Kyoto had sorted out their own differences – which they did by making a formal alliance in 1866 – the Imperialist forces were in an extremely strong position and were likely to gain control of the whole torn, dissident country. Parkes built his policy on that fact and, by so doing, cemented the British position and stole a march on many of the other foreign representatives. In retrospect, such a truth is less than startling; but all the western powers had to deal, usually through interpreters, with a succession of bland, courteous, traditionally secretive and unashamedly equivocal Japanese princes and ministers. In these circumstances and hampered by the continual surveillance of the native authorities, it was by no means easy for foreigners to assess what was happening in the country – especially now that it was approaching a period of internal flux and, soon, revolution. Monsieur Roches, the 'swashbuckling' French Minister, for example, put his money squarely on the Shogun and lived to rue the day.

By that autumn Sir Harry had reached the conclusion that the Shogun's ratification of the treaties with the foreign powers was not sufficient; the Mikado must ratify them also. There followed consultations with all the foreign diplomats and the upshot was that, on 1 November, a squadron of British, French, Dutch and American ships, all supplied, wrote Satow, with 'a sufficient quantity of foolscap paper, silk tape, quill pens and bottles of ink', sailed to Osaka to negotiate with the Mikado's advisers. The squadron anchored in Osaka Bay and there was, inevitably, a great deal of coming and going and message-conveying and *yaku-bio* (known to the Japanese as 'official sickness') and *daimyo* threatening to sever western heads from western bodies and westerners making bellicose preparations aboard ship; but finally, on the twenty-fourth of the month, the first officer of the Mikado was ordered to bring forth the *Book of the Irrevocable Wills* – and the sanction to ratify the treaties was given. It was Sir Harry's first triumph.

I I

Sir Harry followed his triumph by quietly fostering alliances with the royalist factions in the country. The next summer – July 1866 – he paid a visit to the Prince of Satsuma, the very man whose retainers had viciously cut down the unfortunate Richardson four years earlier and who had been notorious for his hatred of the barbarians. Now, however, all was sweet amity between the British and the Satsuma; Parkes and his wife were entertained with rare oriental lavishness. Their arrival was heralded with flags, gun-salutes and champagne; there was a five-hour feast of forty courses laid on for them; a royal hunt in a forest bristling with deer, monkeys and wild boar; and stately tours of the palace grounds, in which, according to one of the escorting naval officers, 'were miles of shady walks, with fine umbrageous trees, paths covered with a carpet of moss and fringed with ferns and the perpetual music of a clear brook which gushes and bubbles along at one's side until, in the garden beneath, it forms a charming cascade, supplies the artificial streams and fish-ponds and, finally, adds utility to beauty, by turning a rice mill just outside the garden boundary'.

Back in Yokohama the summer, as usual, was easy and genial. Yachting regattas were the newest craze; a party of Europeans made the ascent of Mount Fuji – the first to do so since Sir Rutherford Alcock made his primarily political pilgrimage six years earlier; Ernest Satow, after threatening Parkes with his resignation, got a rise of £100 a year – from £400 to £500; an Italian and a Belgian delegation arrived and both successfully negotiated trading treaties with the Japanese.

But the scandal of the season came from Hakodate. Hakodate had always been the real 'hardship post' – the Siberia of chilly, isolated, uncomfortable reputation to which no one wanted to be sent. British Consuls who followed the indefatigably amiable Hodgson there complained that it was impossible for them to work efficiently when communication between themselves and their 'chiefs' in Yedo was almost non-existent. At one stage, the few foreign residents – British and American shipping agents, a couple of French priests, a Russian consul and a Russian doctor, a coterie of disconsolate wives – organised a four-hundred-and-fifty-mile 'overland courier service' which, it was hoped, would get letters from Hakodate to the capital in twelve days during the summer, fifteen during the winter. But the scheme fell through because, apparently, hardly anyone in Yedo could bother to send letters back to Hakodate and, in any case, the Japanese postmaster started charging double rate every time it snowed.

So bad were the communications that, one year, the all-important Consular Returns, showing shipping movements and commercial activities in the area, which every Consul 'had the honour to forward' to Sir Harry at the end of each year, did not reach Yedo until April. It was not, the harassed Consul explained in an accompanying note, *his* fault: the Custom House records were hopelessly behindhand and had to be returned and then there were the New Year holidays (when nothing happened except *saké*-drinking) and then the records were still inaccurate and each firm's had to be checked individually and then there was no boat leaving for Yedo until

20 March and, anyway, it was just as well the Returns hadn't been sent earlier by junk as half the junks were shipwrecked that winter and never seen again. And when Sir Harry finally did receive the Returns they brought him little satisfaction – the saw-mill near Hakodate was 'at a dead stand-still'; coal-mining was proving 'insuperably difficult'; the only exports were sharks' fins, 'long and cut comboo', the horns and feet of deer and fish manure.

It was, perhaps, with the idea of infusing some spirit into the torpid export market (and paying for some of the more exotic imports which were needed to support existence there, such as four hundred baskets of Chinese wine, beef, brandy and baked beans) that a few of Hakodate's foreign residents had, since 1864, been operating a lucrative little side-line in Ainu skeletons. Several famous anthropologists had become interested in this primitive people and had begun to wonder if their remains might provide a clue to the elusive 'missing link'. In order to satisfy the learned curiosity of the West (it was rumoured that one anthropological society had offered two thousand dollars for a perfect female Ainu skeleton) certain settlers had made marauding expeditions to Ainu villages, opened graves and removed what bones they could find.

The poor Ainu, very upset and bewildered by this, reported the matter to the Japanese governor of the province who complained in turn to the British Consul in Hakodate. The Consul, however, who did not happen to be an unbiased arbiter, dismissed the case against the accused foreigners, obviously hoping that news of these nefarious activities would spread no farther. But it did. That summer Parkes heard the full story and sent for the Consul and his grave-robbing companions. He also dispatched a new Consul, Mr Gower, to the two villages whose cemeteries had been plundered. Gower called a meeting outside the local inn and then, standing on the verandah overlooking the wondering villagers, he explained that the grave-robbers would be punished and that he had come to apologise for their crime. He then distributed to every relation of those

184

whose graves had been desecrated a small sum of money done up in a packet, with an inscription inside indicating that it was a present from Her Majesty's Government. Sulks turned to smiles, the Ainu, still perplexed, cheered softly and then rushed to the other side of the inn to spend this amazing and unlooked-for bounty on a *saké* binge. The marauders, who were shunned even by the broad-minded settlers for this odious deed, were tried in Yokohama by Parkes and sentenced to a stretch of hard labour in a Hong Kong gaol.

And after the summer, the autumn, also as usual, brought disaster. The day of 26 November was cold and clear, a strong wind blew in from the north, raising and scattering the sea-spray in bright curtains over Kanagawa Bay. Most of the foreign residents of Yokohama were still at breakfast when the harsh sound of the fire-bells clanked through the early-morning streets. Ernest Satow and Dr Willis were two of many who hastily swallowed the last drop of tea and climbed on to their roof to see what was happening. The conflagration was quite a way off, Satow thought, but he pulled on his boots and an old hat and hurried towards the flames which 'were mounting to the sky exactly to windward of us'.

As Satow drew near the quivering waves of heat he found himself suddenly embroiled in a scene of panic and disorder. All along the narrow street people were trying to get their goods and chattels out of the little timber houses and away to safety. Here a family was piling upon father's back a load of bedding and mats; there a distraught mother, a baby in her arms, was trying to herd two sons, some hens and a dog away from the danger zone; near by, an aged couple struggled with a handcart on which were stacked a few pieces of plate, a cracked stove and a cricket in a cage. Soon, hordes of the already homeless were fleeing with their baggage, loaded pack-horses and carts towards the higher ground of the new settlement area and the little alleys were becoming hopelessly jammed. As the flames clacked nearer, people were forced to abandon even their remaining possessions and scramble for safety over roofs, through windows and down the fetid back passageways leading to the river.

This river, bordered by a muddy swamp, separated the part of the native town where the fire was fiercest from the rest of Yokohama, and the one ramshackle bridge over it was bulging and sagging with the weight of the fugitives. 'There were', Satow explained, 'one or two boats available, but they were already overcrowded, and their occupants were so paralysed by fear that they never thought of landing and sending back the boats to take off others. I saw a few poor wretches plunge into the water in order to escape, but they failed to reach the nearer bank. It was a fearful sight to see flames darting among the roofs of the houses on the causeway and sending forth jets here and there where the fire had not yet attained full mastery, when suddenly one half of the street nearest blazed up with a tremendous flash and a volume of black smoke arose which obscured the sky. This was an oil merchant's shop that had caught fire. . .'

The blare of this explosion reminded Satow of the vulnerability of his own house, which was situated near the edge of the native quarter. Flying back, he and Willis were just able to rescue some of their clothes, books and an immense harmonium; but when they returned from storing these in the nearest fireproof godown, their little home was a heap of ashes. Still the wind continued to provoke the flames and, wrote a spectator, streets and buildings melted 'like gun cotton passing through a burning candle'. The main street of the native town went up in a cascade of sparks which were whirled by the wind straight at the solid residences of the foreign quarter and some of the oldest-established merchant-houses – Jardine Matheson, Walsh, Hall & Co – and the whole row of consular buildings – French, Prussian, Portuguese, American and British – were levelled to the ground within the space of a searing half-hour. Next to disintegrate were the so-called 'fire-proof' godowns, whose copper-coated shutters and sturdy stone pillars were no match for the ravenous monster that the fire had become.

By this time, obviously, every available fire-engine was on the spot, but, as John Black sadly noted, some of them were so rusty from disuse that they would not function at all, there was no water-supply for those that did function – and no attempt at organisation left among the distracted members of the Volunteer Fire Brigade, who were watching their years' savings go up in smoke. By this time too the men of the recently-arrived IXth Regiment were on the scene, together with every able-bodied sapper and rating from the ships in harbour; but no one seemed capable of disciplining the chaos. Men ran about handing buckets, rescuing odd bits of furniture, getting water from the sea, douching flames in a dozen different places, blowing up buildings which stood directly in the fire's path – the debris from which subsequently ignited and merely spread the conflagration farther. By midday, the toll of destruction included, in addition to the native quarter near the swamp, the Japanese Custom House, two rows of bungalows and godowns, the Netherlands Trading Company, the fire-station itself and 'Bonded Warehouse A'. It was, perhaps, from the latter building that the military, in their zeal, rescued crate upon crate of hard liquor. They certainly got it from somewhere. For, about this time, Black wrote, many of the soldiers became 'almost uncontrollable' and rolled around the burning streets searching for plunder and women or stood tippling bottles and jeering while the civilians battled frantically against the flames.

For a time it seemed as if the whole of Yokohama would be a cinder by nightfall; but the wind abated during the late afternoon and, Black noted, at last the fire seemed 'to content itself with the victims it already had, without seeking for more'. As the embers sullenly burnt themselves out during the next couple of days, the citizens took stock of their losses. Satow had nothing except the clothes he was wearing, the manuscript of an English-Japanese dictionary and Alcock's *Colloquial Japanese*. But he was not a materialist and was able to find a certain exhilaration in the very purity of his bereft state.

Few, at first, shared Satow's monastic enthusiasm. One or two merchants whose goods were not fully insured (and insurance was still hard to obtain) went bankrupt overnight; house-rents doubled as a hundred and seven homeless foreigners searched for new roofs to keep over their troubled heads; the price of western clothes rocketed and Chinese tailors did a roaring trade among gentlemen whose four-year supply of suits and shirts from Swan & Edgar had been destroyed; food too was scarce, and the day after the fire the Governor of Kanagawa sent Sir Harry and his wife a couple of roosters 'to assuage their hunger'. The Governor's accompanying note was sympathetic but resigned: 'The Calamity of the Dancing Horse' had struck Yokohama and against such an enemy mere man was powerless. The expression, Satow discovered, was borrowed from a Chinese classical story in which a famous tower known as the 'Tower of the Dancing Horse' had been gutted by flame. The descriptive title became attached to the ravening element itself and happily stayed there.

For a few days the foreign merchants, unused to coping with such uncompromising disasters, were stunned into inactivity and several thought of leaving on the next steamer. When they pulled themselves together, they saw that the Japanese were already clearing their quarter, and that shanties, just as flimsy and combustible as their former homes, were mushrooming among the smouldering rubble. Was the calamity such a calamity after all? So much that had been shoddy, dirty and makeshift had been swept away; it was, in one sense, a challenge – as Satow wrote, it had given the enterprising among them a new idea, the idea of 'beginning the world afresh'.

'I think', wrote Sir Harry Parkes in a letter to a friend, 'that I shall get some good out of the Yokohama fire... My idea is to have a good broad boulevard of sixty yards or even two hundred feet in the centre of the settlement, to have it planted with trees and to allow of no wooden buildings being constructed upon it.' Well, the port did not turn out to be quite such a western idyll as that, but improvements were made.

The rest of the swamp behind the settlement was filled in, removing a major source of infection and noisome smells. The part of the pleasure quarter which had long teetered on the swamp's boundaries became less a collection of grog-shops, brothels and grubby tea-houses, more a lively district of cook-houses, curio stalls, public baths and rows of trim one-storey houses in which lived carpenters and dyers, umbrella-makers and wharf-porters, junior *banto* (shipping clerks) and *saké* brewers, tea-packers, Chinese tailors and boat-repairers. Another part of the old swamp was enclosed and levelled and became a Recreation Ground for foreigners where members of the new Cricket Club could bat, members of the new Pony Corps could trot and members of the new Rifle Club could take pot-shots.

Other western institutions which had functioned sporadically in the past regularised their existence around this time: Brother William Monk became the Worshipful Master of Masonic Yokohama Lodge No. 1092 E.C. which met, says Black, 'in an excellent Hall designed expressly for them'; a Chamber of Commerce was formed to protect the merchants' interests and present a united front – usually of opposition – to the Consuls; and the 'officers of the Diplomatic Service, the Army and Navy of all nations and members of the Yokohama, Yokohama United and German Clubs' all banded together in a wondrously rare display of unity to finance the permanent opening of the Race Club, whose meetings on their new site soon became the liveliest landmarks in the local calendar.

There were several other schemes afloat which would eventually enhance the settlement's respectability. One Mr Pease from San Francisco was trying to get the town lit by gas-lamps; a hospital was built to deal with the numerous cholera and fever cases; a Mr Smith and a Mr Lindau paced out the boundaries of a Public Gardens with flowery paths for promenading ladies on the eastern end of the Bluff overlooking the sea – for ladies, noted Black, 'were increasing in numbers and imparting a charm that had been wanting in the locality'; Mr Charles Rickerby started the daily *Japan Gazette* as a deadly rival to the *Herald* which had maintained an intermittent appearance for nearly five years; and machinery for a dock and an arsenal were ordered from France.

French businessmen at this time were exceedingly active and landed a number of fat contracts with the Japanese government through, it was rumoured, the influence of the French Minister. The imputation was stoutly denied; but it was certain that the Consuls of one or two less powerful countries who were also merchants mingled their diplomatic and commercial activities rather indiscriminately – a practice which was called 'official trading' by other western businessmen who were not lucky enough to enjoy diplomatic privileges.

According to Black, by far the most important innovation of 1867 was the building of 'the noble road which divides the foreign and native settlements, and which is lined on the one side with Japanese official buildings – the Custom House, the Post Office, the central Police Office – on the other by the British and American consulates and other buildings, with a pretty shrubbery bounding the road in front of the edifices throughout its entire length'. And so, at last, Yokohama had acquired edifices. It could boast of two respectable banks and a row of straight-walled houses with balconies and entrances flanked by stone pillars and windows flanked by heavy shutters and rooms which became increasingly filled with high polished tables and chairs and beds and sideboards and carpets and all the other impedimenta of affluence which the Japanese had lacked for centuries without even noticing the deficiency.

But now they did notice it. By the middle of the 1860's, it became quite customary for a Japanese gentleman to call at a western residence on some pretext and then ask to see all the rooms. After examining everything carefully – the framed windows, the quantity of china and mirrors, the comfort of armchair and sofa – he would hurry home and proceed to set up a 'western room' of his own. He would buy a patterned carpet to throw over his pristine *tatami*, stick in the room's centre a table covered with a tasselled tablecloth, hang a mirror or two on the walls and put glass panes in a section of his paper sliding screens. Then he would invite a few friends in and they would all sit very solemnly on wooden chairs and eat meat with a knife and fork and drink champagne and be generally very sophisticated. Up to this time, though the trappings were foreign, the natives retained the essential naturalness of their kimono; but this too would change and within a few years every Japanese businessman was to have his western suit in which he could be as uncomfortable as he was in his western room.

An air of general sobriety and respectability was further imparted to the local scene by the increasing numbers of foreign missionaries and teachers who were arriving to 'convert the heathen' and instruct them in western tongues. Pioneers in the field had been two Americans – Doctor Hepburn and the Reverend Brown – who, with their families, had started missions in Kanagawa at the time when Yokohama was still little more than a fishing hamlet in the middle of a marsh. Hepburn had already been a founder-member of at least three municipal councils, helped to bind the wounds of Marshall and Clarke inflicted by the assassins of poor Richardson and was to crown his missionary endeavours six years hence with a presentation of a Bible to the Mikado himself; Brown had guided Ernest

Satow in his early struggles with the Japanese language and had been among the first to open a school of English for the sons of rich *samurai*. Now the two were reaping the beginnings of their resolutely-sown harvest, and several other little schools, run by missionaries and their wives, were springing up in Yokohama, where English and the Christian virtues were taught together. It was, probably, the growing missionary influence which convinced the Governor of Kanagawa in 1867 that the state of being clad was a virtue and the state of nakedness an offence to public dignity. So the Governor issued a 'notification' to all the 'porters, carters, labourers and coolies and boatmen', who had for centuries been 'in the habit of plying their calling in a state bordering on nudity', which decreed that, henceforth, 'no one who does not wear a shirt or tunic, properly closed by a girdle, will be allowed to remain in Yokohama'.

It was a significant notification. The girdle of western respectability was closing round the port which had been such a lackadaisical, brusque and rollicking place only a few years before. As Doctor William Griffis, the American scholar and a later arrival in the land, remarked with satisfaction, 'the Great Fire seemed to purify the place municipally, commercially and morally': 'houses became homes', 'night-lodgings became hotels', 'ladies and children came in scores', and 'the solitary were set in families'.

This wave of moral respectability and refinement was exceedingly overdue – at least in the opinion of one Margaretha Weppner, who visited Japan for a few months at about this time. Miss Weppner, a German woman writing in English, soon came to the sorrowful conclusion that, in Yokohama, it was her misfortune 'to see Man in the lowest state of depravity and degradation'. The foreign men, idling over their drinks and cigars, eyed her lewdly from head to foot whenever she ventured into the shabby dining-room; as for the natives, they 'never wear clothes and live very much like the beasts of the field'. Poor Miss Weppner cowered for several miserable weeks in the Yokohama International Hotel and the Yedo 'Hotel for

Foreigners', nightly barricading her door against the alarming sounds of the settlers' evening festivities which, in her opinion at least, consisted entirely of whisky-drinking, followed by bottle-and-glass-smashing, gambling and vociferous, even violent, liaisons with the local prostitutes. So wholeheartedly and continually had the western males of Yokohama indulged these pastimes that, almost to a man, their eyes had taken on 'a kind of idiotic stare' and they saw and heard 'only what directly attracts the stomach and senses'.

Miss Weppner was, undoubtedly, a little unbalanced, for she was convinced that every foreign man in the place (with the exception of a few 'upright and honest' English and American gentlemen) were plotting to rape her; nevertheless she gives a credible enough picture of one of Yokohama's second-class hotels, with its tatty, stained furnishings, creaking, ill-fitting doors and windows, primitive bathrooms, noisy billiard-room and, over all, a prevailing odour of liquor, fish, stale smoke and ancient soy sauce. Most of the guests were men waiting for something – a ship to arrive or leave, a friend or wife to meet, a miracle to happen – and the Japanese staff, always so scrupulous about their own utensils and clothes, had not yet learned to cope with western things. To Miss Weppner's horror, her maid unthinkingly piled ashes from the fire on a spare dinner-plate, used her towels as dusters, borrowed her walking shoes and took a quick nap in her bed. Towards the end of her unhappy stay in Japan, one of the 'upright English gentlemen' took Miss Weppner to see some of the 'native sights'. The odd charms and lively beauties of the streets, the shops and the people eluded her, but she remembers two things with her usual gruesome prurience: the practice of mixed bathing in the bath-houses – which, apparently, foreign merchants attended with great regularity – and the sight of monkeys for sale in the butchers – 'If Mr Darwin is to be credited', she remarks primly, 'there is something very wrong in feeding on such near relatives'.

In spite of Miss Weppner's jaundiced views, Yokohama was,

by now, the most comfortable town in Japan for westerners to live in. Sir Harry Parkes had, however, been trying for many months to re-locate the main Legation in Yedo, for he considered it an undignified anomaly for the British Representative to be kept so safely far away from the seat of the country's rulers. Before the end of the year, Parkes succeeded in making his point with the Japanese and he and some members of his staff moved back to the capital. Among those to go was a newcomer who arrived a month before the fire and who had, like Satow, lost everything he owned except 'a pea-jacket, singlet, trousers, shoes and socks'. The name of the bereft newcomer was Algernon Bertram Mitford.

Mitford, later Lord Redesdale, was another of those wealthy young men of the period who, like Oliphant, had already been practically everywhere and done practically everything before he was thirty. He had spent part of his childhood in Paris and had watched old Louis Philippe, in a grey greatcoat and a steeple hat, pacing the terrace of the Palace gardens; he had been a member of Pop at Eton and had learned his maths from Charles Lutwidge Dodgson; he had spent a year in the Embassy at St Petersburg, where he attended the most brilliant salons, met Tolstoy and celebrated the 'mad week' before Lent with balls, picnics and skating parties; he had wandered through the palace of the Governor of Nif (Nymphi) near Smyrna and coaxed the pet goats under the oleanders; he had been to Ephesus and Constantinople and Samothrace; and then, one foggy day in February 1865, a Mr Hammond walked into Mitford's room at the Foreign Office complaining that he could not find a man to go to Pekin. Mitford leapt at the chance. He ran out and bought sun-helmets and insect-repellents and tropical trousers and, a month later, was drifting across the Indian Ocean on board the sailing ship *Simla* – a lovely vessel, Mitford thought, 'with beautiful, free, white decks and a view of the sea all round!' So much more delightful than 'the modern floating castles, with all their extravagances and luxurious discomforts'.

Mitford had enjoyed Pekin immensely. Quartered in a secluded monastery called 'The Temple of the Azure Clouds' he had spent the time learning Chinese, writing dispatches and strolling through the lovely grounds of the ruined Summer Palace. In the autumn, Sir Rutherford Alcock arrived there as the new British Minister, a man, Mitford says, 'of great ability and high courage', who had, nevertheless, been sadly miscast in his role of 'Envoy Extraordinary' to Japan – an appointment, Mitford adds, resulting from the British government's delusion that 'China and Japan were one and the same thing, and that experience in the one country must of necessity specially fit a man to take up work in the other'.

About a year after Alcock's arrival in Pekin from Japan, Mitford, making the next move in the endless inter-Embassy game of musical chairs, was sent from Pekin to Japan. His landing at Yokohama was drab: 'The sky was grey, sad and unfriendly; gusts of wind turned umbrellas inside out and defied waterproofs... The low eaves of what seemed to be a Custom House were mere runlets of water. Drip, drip, drip! In front of the building a number of *yakunin*, small government employees, bristling with sword and dirk, clad in sad-coloured robes with quaint lacquer hats, a mob of coolies with raincoats made of straw, looking like animated haycocks sodden in an unpropitious season; a woman or two clattering and splashing in high wooden pattens, carrying babies sorely afflicted with skin diseases slung behind their backs – a melancholy arrival in all truth and sufficiently depressing'.

IV

Algernon Mitford did not forget his first unfavourable impression of Yokohama and, in common with most of the diplomatic contingent, never liked the place. They felt that the port, even at this relatively early stage in its development, was an enclave, a little bit of the West defiantly self-sufficient and starchy, a town that looked away from Japan for its life and its increasing prosperity. In Yedo, on the other hand, one was completely in and at the mercy of the country itself, as the Legation staff soon found.

The new Legation, situated near the ancient temple where the Forty-Seven *ronin* of Japanese legend were buried, consisted of two draughty ramshackle bungalows which were guarded by men of the IXth Regiment, and both diplomats and soldiers were guarded in their turn by hordes of *ometsuke*, whose 'eyes in attendance' watched their every move. Oppressed by this unremitting vigilance, Satow and Mitford persuaded Parkes to let them hire their own temple a few hundred yards from the Legation grounds, and here they set up a private retreat which was more like home. Meals were supplied from a near-by Japanese cookshop (dishes of duck and chicken on good days, strands of dank seaweed buried in cold rice on bad); a few officers could be entertained with *saké* and song; and, from their verandah, they could see all Yedo Bay sweeping away into the blue distance.

Probably they watched a most momentous arrival to that Bay early in 1867: the 3,750-ton passenger ship *Colorado* which provided 'hotel-like' accommodation for three hundred first class, two hundred second class and 'an almost unlimited number' of third class passengers. The *Colorado*, which was chartered by the Pacific Mail Steamship Company, consumed 950 tons of coal and twenty-two and a half days to come from San Francisco and was the first of the Company's ships in regular service between Japan and America. These steamers carried hundreds of Chinese homewards (smaller steamers connected to Shanghai), hundreds of other Chinese to California and, of course, an ever-increasing number of globe-trotters for whom, in the next decade, Yokohama became 'a positive must'.

For Satow and Mitford, however, whose principal concerns were diplomatic, the beginning of 1867 was memorable chiefly because it then became apparent that events in the country were moving towards an inevitably belligerent climax. In autumn of the previous year the reigning Shogun had died; during the Japanese New Year celebrations held in February the death of the Mikado was announced. This announcement was a signal for fifty days of national mourning, and John Black remembers seeing men 'going about the Japanese town pulling down in all haste the emblems and decorations placed over the doors and in front of the houses at this season: holiday costumes were set aside and visiting and pleasure-seeking of every kind were decorously brought to a close'. For, however little political power this Mikado had wielded, he was a moral force in the land and had inspired great reverence, and his distrust of 'the barbarians' had been a hindrance to all the western diplomats. Superficially, after the mourning period was over and an unknown sixteen-year-old prince had come to the throne, the silken round of court life spun slowly on as before. But new men were in the ascendant and there was a great deal of intrigue going on behind the *shoji* (screens). The factions were forming; the leaders, many of them as yet unknown, were consolidating their supporters; both the Shogun's government and the Mikado's court were riddled with conflicting clan loyalties; the two basic issues of who was to really rule the land and what was to be the future policy towards the West were still unresolved.

The position of the Foreign Representatives remained crucial and hazardous. For a western country to align itself with the losing side at this juncture might seriously jeopardise its future standing after the conflict. Now that Townsend Harris had gone and the Americans were, in any event, still recovering from the aftermath of their own savage Civil War, Sir Harry and M. Roches were the acknowledged doyens of the foreign diplomatic circle; but they, like everyone else, could do little but bluff and spy and wait. And so when, in April, the new Shogun invited them, together with two other western representatives, to see him in Osaka and discuss the opening of the new port of Kobe (formerly called Hyogo), they accepted with alacrity, in the hope that they might learn more about the state of the government and that the invitation boded an increasingly liberal policy towards the West in general.

Both Satow and Mitford accompanied Sir Harry and his wife on this occasion, and it was, as Mitford wrote, 'an absolutely unique experience'. They were received in Osaka castle, 'that stupendous monument to feudalism' built of 'great blocks of granite piled irregularly one above the other without mortar in cyclopean pattern, or rather no pattern, massive, wonder-raising'. Inside the castle, walls glowed in gold leaf and their upper panels were decorated with subtly-toned paintings of peacocks, storks and cranes, azaleas and bamboo groves and clusters of twisted pine; above, the ornate tracery of the ceilings was slashed by beams of rich black and gold lacquer.

After the ritual tea-drinking in the ante-room, the Englishmen were ushered into a hall of state, sliding screens parted noiselessly and the Shogun appeared before his barbarian guests. 'He was', decided Mitford, 'the handsomest man that I saw during all the years that I was in Japan. His features were regular, his eye brilliantly lighted and keen, his complexion a clear healthy olive colour. He was a great noble if ever there was one. The pity of it was that he was an anachronism.' This was indeed the case, for the young Shogun had never been encouraged to develop any modern talents he may have possessed. A poorly-translated description of the young Shogun's formative years written by one of his pages is given by John Black in *The Japan Herald* about this time. The Shogun, apparently, rose late and first of all his hair was elaborately dressed. 'The strings with which his hair was bound were, of course, new every morning and he never wore anything twice. I distinctly wish it to be understood', the careful page adds anxiously, 'that I do not mean that underclothing only was new, but every portion of his dress, which was principally of the richest silk.' Stiffly garbed thus, the young ruler nibbled at a breakfast of delicacies brought to him 'from all parts of the Empire', then he would give audience to one or two of his advisers. After lunch he would usually 'follow his fancy' – a fancy which led to an hour of pistol-practice perhaps, a game of horse-polo, duck-netting on the still lake or an archery competition with his admiring courtiers. He would end the day with a long, leisurely dinner in the 'palace of ladies' and they would entertain him with drink, food, the playing of the *koto* and high, soft, sad Japanese love-songs. It was hardly surprising that such a life had bred an anachronism in the new world of the eighteen-sixties.

The foreigners stayed for dinner with the Shogun, who drank the Queen's health and presented them with silken tobacco pouches and slender pipes. Following the private audiences came a round of receptions for all the Foreign Representatives, during which forty men of the IXth Regiment were put through a bayonet exercise, the French marines staged a drill display, Mr Sutton of Her Majesty's Survey Ship *Serpent* had the honour of a sitting from the Shogun and 'took a capital photographic likeness of him' and everyone ate lots of huge breakfasts and dinners all courtesy of the castle and prepared under the superintendence of a specially-appointed French chef. In short, the whole visit went off remarkably well and everyone hoped that the opening of the ports of Osaka and Kobe to foreign trade the following year would be accomplished as smoothly.

While Sir Harry and Algernon Mitford returned north by the conventional sea-route, Ernest Satow and the artist Charles Wirgman (who must, by now, have seen as much of the development of Japanese–western relations as any living foreigner) decided to make the classical journey from Osaka to Yedo. They resolved not to burden themselves with the usual travel-impedimenta of knives and forks, napkins, tins of beans and claret but to rely completely on the country's resources. They bought a couple of *higido-kago* which were primitive palanquins slightly less cramped than the ordinary *kago* but more spartan than the padded *norimon*, they arranged for a mere ten-men strong Japanese escort to accompany them and set off in high spirits on 10 May.

Inside the *higido-kago*, Satow wrote, 'one cushion of silk damask thickly stuffed with raw cotton was spread on the bottom, and there was then just room enough to sit in it cross-legged without discomfort. In front was a small shelf above the window, and underneath a small flap which served as a table. The sliding doors also had windows, furnished with a paper slide to exclude cold and another covered with gauze to keep out the dust while letting in the air. If it rained, blinds made of slender strips of bamboo were let down over the windows. The body of the vehicle could also be enveloped in a covering of black oiled paper, in which a small aperture was left for the occupant to peep out.' In addition, each of the travellers 'had a pair of oblong wicker-work baskets to hold our clothing which were slung at opposite ends of a black pole and carried by one man over his shoulder'. Their bedding, bed-gowns and pillows were also carried in wicker boxes and on each box 'was fastened a small deal board on which my name and titles were inscribed with Indian ink in large Chinese characters'.

In this fashion they journeyed north. They soon joined the Tokkaido highway which was jammed with lumbering broad-wheeled bullock carts laden with bales of rice for the use of the Shogun's garrison at Osaka. At the lovely lake of Biwa they stopped to inspect a tea-firing establishment where neat young women were dampening the fresh fragrant leaves, spreading them on a flat table that was heated beneath and then twisting them by hand. At the broad river near Seta they watched fishermen spinning for carp and, in the shallows, fish jostling, with unconscious bravado, near the reed traps that had been set in the mud to catch them. Each evening they stayed at the best inn in town where they dined on fish, *saké* and any particular local delicacy – pheasant meat preserved in rice paste perhaps, chestnut-meal cakes topped with pickled radish, buckwheat vermicelli or 'a horribly tenacious kind of gruel, resembling bird-lime in appearance and made from the powdered root of the *Dioscorea Japonica*, a species of wild potato'. After dinner they flirted with the demure waiting-maids, who invariably offered to scrub their backs in the bath and who looked in some puzzlement at Wirgman's costume of wide blue cotton trousers, a loose yellow pongee jacket and a conical felt grey hat; and then they slept on soft eiderdowns and hard pillows, with a fire-box and a pot of tea ready at their elbows in case they should feel like a drink or a smoke at three in the morning. Naturally the travellers collected souvenirs as they went along: two of the famous, unglazed hand-moulded *banko*-ware vases; some fans made in Nagoya, delicate and light as lace; agates, ink-stones and green-streaked crystals; rolls of fine grey and blue crêpe from Kuwana and the jetty lacquer cabinets of Shidzuoka. Unfortunately, as Satow remarked, the prices of all these articles 'were such as befitted the supposed exalted rank of the travellers. In those days in Japan it was a well-observed doctrine that "noblesse oblige" in the matter of payments.'

On 27 May, after a glorious zigzag ride down hills covered with rain-washed pine and bamboo and past fields of young rice and golden barley, the two men stopped for the night at Kakegawa. Here they were attacked while sleeping by a group of *rei-sei-shi*, hired junior retainers of the Mikado's court who were journeying back to Kyoto and whose sense of increasing power had got rather out of hand. The assailants broke through the inn windows and rushed upon the Japanese guard, demanding to be shown the barbarians; but they soon took fright and fled, slashing a few mosquito-nets over the beds and ripping a couple of screens as they went. As in the much more serious attack on the Legation five years before, the assailants lost their way in the dark and, also as in that earlier attack, Wirgman took to his agile heels and was found an hour later crouching in an alleyway behind the inn.

After extracting promises from the local officials that the attackers would be caught and punished – as indeed they eventually were – Satow and his companion continued north and before very long saw the classic shape of 'The Peerless One' springing from the plain ahead. Happily they dawdled nearer, Wirgman sketching the famous mountain from every aspect – at dawn stark against a backdrop of eggshell blue; at noon with a hot belt of cloud encircling its firm centre; a purple cone perched above pine-clad hills; finally 'a mere molehill' in the distance, seeming to rise from the sea itself. The mountain, incidentally, was to have its sanctity more seriously violated later that year when Sir Harry Parkes made the ascent with his wife. It was October and the summit was already draped in snow, the wind so abrasive that it chapped and cut the faces of the climbers. Nevertheless they all got to the top, 'even Lady Parkes', Black wrote, 'persevering to the end, until she stood on the highest ground in Japan. The first foreign lady and – as Japanese females were forbidden to ascend the mountain – probably one of the first of her sex who had ever reached that proud and sacred eminence.'

Satow's overland journey and the Parkes' climb were the last respites of the year for the diplomats, who were soon busily engaged in preparations for the opening of Kobe and Osaka. 'Rules' were proclaimed for the guidance of future foreign residents of Kobe who were to pay an annual rent to the Japanese government, which then accepted responsibility for the upkeep, cleansing and lighting of roads, the control of small boats and so on. Merchants who had already consolidated lucrative firms in Yokohama endlessly debated over the after-dinner port the pros and cons of branching out again in the new settlements. Many, recalling the early precarious days, chose to stay put; but there was also a dash of adventurers around who, weeks before the appointed opening, gathered their piles of Mexican dollars together, bought one-way tickets south and waited impatiently for, as Black expressed it, 'the coming event which, they fondly hoped, was to place them in the groove that should direct them to fortune'.

A month before the opening, Satow and Algernon Mitford, in their habitual roles as general factotums to the Legation, again went to the ports to see how things were progressing. On the site of the future settlement in Osaka, warehouses, bungalows, barracks and custom-sheds were burgeoning daily – all constructed of bamboo, rope and paper and all looking flimsy, spindly and as temporary as a stage-set. In addition, the settlement area was already completely encircled by high, spiked palisades which, Mitford dryly commented, 'were not a very encouraging indication of the intentions of the Government to promote intercourse between East and West'. In Kobe, the diplomats found the populace to be in particularly jubilant mood about the whole scheme. Seven days of feast and merry-making had given a riotous send-off to the settlement building and the streets were still thronged with people dressed in festive red crêpe swinging red lanterns and wheeling carts full of earth to dump on the foundations, in an attractive little bay some distance from the native town.

But though the local citizens were delighted at the prospect of foreign trade and the developments it would bring, they, like the rest of Japan's people, feared that the new year of 1868 would bring trouble as well as wealth. At the end of the old year, in Kyoto, the Shogun submitted his resignation to the Mikado's councillors; around the capital the royalist clans, led by the Princes of Satsuma and Choshiu, gathered in quiet, determined hordes. The winter air throbbed with feverish rumour: that the office of the Shogunate had been abolished, that, if the Shogun did not retire utterly, the opposing clans would massacre all foreigners in order to provoke intervention from abroad; that the Togukawa generals would fight to the last bamboo-grove and then commit *hara-kiri*; that the Shogun's resignation was a feint and that he was massing troops to march on the royal capital. Grimly the foreigners prepared to lay low and avoid involvement; some sent their womenfolk off to Shanghai, many put extra locks on their flimsy doors and again got out their revolvers. All had to face the inevitable and unpalatable fact – as Mitford expressed it, 'the dogs of war were loose in the land'.

V

In spite of the fragile state of the country – it was, a Japanese friend wrote to Satow, 'like an eggshell held in the hand' – the actual opening of both Kobe and Osaka on 1 January 1868 went off quietly, almost casually. In Kobe, Mr Myburgh and, in Osaka, Mr Lowder – both appointed vice-consuls for the respective settlements – hoisted the British flag over their low wooden bungalows, and the ships in the harbours, which had brought Sir Harry and other foreign representatives down for the occasion, fired appreciative salutes. Hopeful merchants landed and began to haggle over land-prices with the Japanese; gay foreign sailors bartered biscuits and trinkets for tobacco and women; local boatmen and wharf porters cheerfully trebled their charges; the various settlers had fierce disputes among themselves over who had first staked a claim to what; and there was the general sense of bustle and zest and boundless opportunity which attended the openings of all the ports.

But while the foreigners were making firm their precarious new footholds in the land, the land's rulers were manoeuvring towards a confrontation. By the third of January the royalist clans were in total control of Kyoto and the following day all the Tokugawa titles and distinctions were abolished and new royal ones announced to supersede them; on the seventh, the Shogun withdrew to the fortified castle at Osaka in which Sir Harry had visited him the previous year. Early that same day, Satow and Mitford, who were staying at the newly-established Osaka Legation, which was situated behind the castle itself, strolled through the restless city to watch history being made.

It was a drear, bitter day. The streets were spiked with soldiers whose cold heads were swathed in grey mufflers and whose red fingers were never far from the icy steel of their weapons. Horses, breath steaming, clanked stolidly to and fro; at the corners of narrow alleyways field-pieces were being hauled into strategic positions. Presently, the Englishmen heard the wail of distant bugles and stood aside to watch the Shogun and his men approach the grim castle. It would have been hard, wrote Mitford, to imagine a more extravagantly weird picture. 'There were some infantry armed with European rifles, but there were also warriors clad in the old armour of the country, carrying spears, bows and arrows, falchions curiously shaped, with sword and dirk, who looked as if they had stepped out of some old pictures of the Gempei wars in the Middle Ages. Their *jimbaori*, not unlike heralds' tabards, were as many-coloured as Joseph's coat. Hideous masks of lacquer and iron, fringed with portentous whiskers and moustachios, crested helmets with wigs from which long streamers of horsehair floated to their waists, might strike terror into any enemy. They looked like the hobgoblins of a nightmare.'

In the midst of a troop of horsemen rode the fallen Shogun, his head covered with black cloth, his young face old. At the castle gate the whole army dismounted excepting only the Shogun himself who rode through the grey archway alone. It was the last entry of a Tokugawa Shogun into that magnificent building which had, for over two hundred years, withstood so much, indomitably contained so many rulers. 'A wild and wonderful sight,' Mitford concluded, 'and one of the saddest I have ever seen.'

Precarious and tense though the situation was, the British and French diplomats determined to remain at their Osaka Legations a few miles from the foreign settlements on the harbour-fronts. While Sir Harry had one or two inconclusive conferences with the depressed and harassed ex-Shogun in his castle, Satow and Mitford pursued the clandestine British alliance with the imperialists. The ex-Shogun's guard still kept all foreigners under close surveillance, but the two junior diplomats had become adept at climbing over the Legation wall about midnight and making their devious ways to the

Satsuma *yashiki* (nobleman's residence). There, over hot *saké* and sweetmeats, surrounded by vigilant swordsmen, they tried to persuade the Satsuma leaders that the Mikado's wisest course was to invite the foreign representatives to Kyoto and to negotiate with them openly.

As the first month of that stormy year drew to a close, waves of violence crashed nearer to the waiting city. On the night of the twenty-seventh the sky towards Kyoto was lurid with the flames of camp-fires lit in the streets by clansmen gathered there; on the twenty-eighth, the elegant, secret Satsuma *yashiki* was burnt to the ground by Tokugawa men who, perhaps, knew of the meetings between its residents and the foreigners so recently held in the building; on the twenty-ninth came news that the Tokugawa forces had been defeated in the decisive battle of Fushimi, twenty-five miles from Osaka; the next day a message from the ex-Shogun, who had departed by ship to Yedo, was handed to the British Legation – it stated that he, the erstwhile ruler of the land, could no longer guarantee the safety of the westerners within the city boundaries.

It was no time to effect a very dignified or orderly retreat. Boats, horses, carts and porters were at a premium, but, after much bickering, the diplomats left Osaka for Kobe in a commandeered houseboat, Satow in the prow hugging a huge pot of mincemeat, giant Doctor Willis squatting gingerly on the boxes containing the Legation archives. All the foreign diplomats arrived at Kobe about the same time and junior men such as Satow and Mitford found themselves quartered in draughty outbuildings or, as the latter wrote, 'a Japanese version of a fifth-rate Margate lodging-house'. However, the jolly Prussian Consul, with appropriate care for the body's needs, had unearthed a bottle or two from under his archives and acquired a pig, so that, in spite of the cold and discomfort, everyone became quite festive on pork and curaçao and congratulated themselves on their successful retreat from Osaka.

As it turned out their narrowest escape awaited them in Kobe. On the afternoon of 4 February, most of the foreign representatives, their staffs and a few merchants rode to the new settlement to see how things were progressing. They had all dismounted and were scattered in haphazard groups over the open, sandy building area, discussing, presumably, who should live where and which sites were of greatest value, when a troop of men from the pro-Mikado, anti-barbarian Bizen clan came out of the town gate, halted and, with no more warning than a shout from their commanding officer, opened murderous fire on every foreigner in view. Luckily for the westerners, who were so many sitting ducks, the Bizen men did not understand how to use the sights of their rifles which had but recently arrived from America. The volleys were high and wide and whined over the heads of the astounded and outraged settlers. Signals were immediately flashed to the western ships riding at anchor in the harbour; a contingent of British and American marines lunged off in pursuit of the assailants; the mounted escort of the British Legation, Mitford said, 'executed a brilliant charge of cavalry down an empty road'. But the Bizen men, though they could not aim, could certainly ride and were soon far away. Sulkily the foreign guards straggled back empty-handed, except for one poor old wounded pariah woman and impedimenta dropped by the fleeing Japanese – sandals, medicines, rain-hats and a writing-desk containing a passionate letter from a soldier's sweetheart.

The new Kobe Custom House was scarred by bullets, the flags on its roof shredded with shot, and the diplomats, when they had picked themselves up and brushed the mud from their clothes, were furious to the point of apoplexy. They were also alarmed, for they felt that future Japanese action was quite unpredictable. Nevertheless, most of them determined not to fly from Kobe as they had from Osaka, but to demonstrate their internationally-agreed right to remain in the settlements. So, the day after the Bizen attack, lines of sentries from the foreign vessels were posted round the settlement area and sand-bag breastworks, field-pieces and howitzers were made ready for action. In short, there was, as Mitford put it, 'all kinds of martial effervescence', and the whole business reminded him of a fox-hunt – 'it had all the excitement of war with only ten percent of the danger'.

It was a tense and uneasy time; every hour brought a fresh alarm. The French Consul was convinced that a steamer approaching the harbour was swarming with eight hundred armed-to-the-teeth *samurai*; an English merchant swore that the Mikado's main force was marching towards them and would throw every westerner's corpse into the sea that night; the Prussian Consul ran around waving his field-glasses through which, he said, he could spy at least three hundred men lurking in the hills behind the settlement. The foreign representatives, who were all cooped together in fractious fraternal proximity inside the two-storied Custom House, issued a memorandum which stated that, 'In the event of a night attack, all Foreigners who are provided with arms should rally together with the guard in the Main Street and be guided by the Officer in Command of the guard as to their future movements; those who have no arms should retire to the Concession Ground, by the beach.'

Ernest Satow, for one, was very cool about all this. He knew many of the Satsuma and Choshiu men quite well and was convinced from the beginning, as was Mitford, that the westerners were in no danger whatever. Both of them had been very reluctant to leave Osaka and continued to make semi-official forays to meet the advancing imperial forces. Soon their secret negotiations bore fruit and Parkes, wrote Satow, 'became the channel of communication between the Mikado and the other foreign ministers'. At Sir Harry's instigation the Consuls announced that 'a strict and impartial neutralism must be observed' by foreigners during any ensuing conflicts between the two Japanese armies; by the twenty-fifth of the month the British Minister was breakfasting with the brand-new Japanese Minister for Foreign Affairs in Kobe; it was painfully apparent that the western powers whose sympathies had been openly with the Shogun had made a costly mistake. A few days later, the French Minister suddenly packed his bags and returned alone to Yokohama; 'Roches', Parkes noted with quiet satisfaction, 'must be sensible of much mortification at the utter collapse of his policy.'

By this time Satow had become so friendly with his Satsuma acquaintances that he was allowed to accompany them everywhere he wished, and was thus given a rare opportunity of seeing the immediate aftermath of the national strife. He visited the ruins of Osaka castle less than two weeks after it had been sacked and burned and it was, he wrote, 'a wide scene of desolation. The white-plastered towers and wall of the inner moat were gone; all the barracks and towers of the outer wall to the south likewise; only the stones of the gateway to the right remained. We passed into the *hommaru* or keep, through the gateway constructed with huge blocks of stone. Nothing was left but the masonry, looking rather like the ancient Greek Cyclopean walls of Tiryns. The magnificent palace itself had disappeared; all that there was to show where it had once stood was a level surface covered with half-calcined tiles... Issuing again from the gate, we came upon a quantity of burnt armour and helmets piled up round a storehouse which the flames had spared; some had melted by the violent heat into an irregular mass of metal.' Behind the ruins, the British Legation, so recently occupied and more recently abandoned, was gutted beyond hope. Even Satow, in his prosaic way, was more than usually depressed and the Japanese were immensely uncomfortable and apologetic.

As further evidence of their cordial intentions towards the barbarians, the Princes of Satsuma and Choshiu ordered that the officer of the Bizen clan, one Taki Zenzaburo, who had barked the order to fire on the westerners in the settlement area, should 'perform *hara-kiri* in the presence of witnesses of the different nationalities'. Mitford, who, with Satow, had the unenviable job of being a witness, painstakingly describes the occasion, which took place in a Kobe temple that had become the Satsuma headquarters. The foreigners were conducted into the gilded, spacious temple-hall which was hung with jewelled ornaments and lit by tall candles. The dais in front of the high altar was covered with gleaming white mats over which was spread a deep rug of scarlet felt. There was a cold, nervous silence. Then Taki Zenzaburo, dressed in robes of blue hempen cloth, walked into the hall accompanied by two officers whose war-surcoats glinted with gold tissue facings. Behind came men dressed in filmy grey and black called *kaishaku*. The office of *kaishaku*, Mitford explains, has no western equivalent, 'in many cases it is performed by a kinsman or friend of the condemned and the relation between them is rather that of principal and second than that of victim and executioner'.

Slowly Zenzaburo mounted the dais, bowed to all the witnesses and then seated himself deliberately on the red felt in a position which would 'afford him the greatest convenience for falling forward'. One of the officers approached and, with further obeisances, presented to Zenzaburo a black lacquer tray on which lay the short, shining, infinitely sharp dirk. The condemned man took it, raised it reverently before his eyes and laid it on the cloth before him. In a distinct voice, which yet sounded small and broken in the large silent hall, the man acknowledged his guilt and added that 'for this crime I disembowel myself and I beg you who are present to do me the honour of witnessing the act'. Then, Mitford continues, 'the speaker allowed his upper garments to slip down to his girdle and remained naked to the waist. Carefully, according to custom, he tucked his sleeves under his knees to prevent his falling backwards; for a noble Japanese gentleman should die falling forwards. Deliberately, with a steady hand, he took the dirk that lay before him; he looked at it wistfully, almost affectionately; for a moment he seemed to collect his thoughts for the last time and then stabbing himself deeply below the waist on the left-hand side, he drew the dirk slowly across to the right side, and, turning it in the wound, gave a slight cut upwards. During this sickeningly painful operation he never moved a muscle of his face. When he drew out the dirk he leaned forward and stretched out his neck; an expression of pain for the first time crossed his face, but he uttered no sound. At that moment the *kaishaku*, who, still crouching by his side, had been keenly watching his every movement, sprang to his feet, poised his sword for a second in the air; there was a flash, a heavy, ugly thud, a crashing fall; with one blow the head had been severed from the body.' Quietly the witnesses left the hall, presumably satisfied that justice had been done.

However, the editor of *The Japan Times* in Yokohama, who reported the event a few days later, said it was disgraceful that Christian gentlemen should have attended such a disgusting ceremony and he added, rather gratuitously, that, if the Japanese were contemplating revenge for Zenzaburo's 'judicial murder', he hoped they 'would assassinate gentlemen of the foreign Legations rather than anyone else'. But to Satow, in particular, the occasion did not seem in the least disgusting; rather, he wrote, it was a 'most decent and decorous ceremony and far more respectable than what our own countrymen were in the habit of producing for the entertainment of the public in the front of Newgate prison'.

VI

So, to most of the foreign Representatives, the Bizen affair and its sequel was a satisfactory indication, not only of the cordial intentions of the Imperialist clans, but of these clans' confidence in their own authority. In the southern part of the country at least resistance to the Mikado's forces was almost over and the last, young, reluctant Shogun had, according to Parkes, 'thrown up the sponge and been banished'. And, now that the Mikado was growing into a ruler, Kyoto, his city, was gaining in importance. Those *daimyo* who had been loyal to the throne had taken over all the elegant residences near the royal palace and were enjoying the spoils of war at leisure.

One of these was Prince Yoda of the Tosa clan whose armoured guard wore demoniac masks and locks of black or white horsehair which hung down over their shoulders. The Prince was, according to Mitford, a very intelligent and alert statesman; he was also a rake whose first personal seal had been engraved 'The Drunken *Daimyo* of the Southern Seas'. Now, in his forty-seventh year, the Prince was sick unto death and in his terror begged that the famous British doctor should come to his aid. Thus it was that, in March, Algernon Mitford accompanied Doctor Willis to Kyoto and saw – what practically every western visitor to the place since must have wished to see – the Sacred City as it was before the world finally broke in on its three hundred years of seclusion. He saw the grey, quiet shrines sheltered by groves of ancient cryptomerias and pine, he saw, from a shaded hill, *Kinri* (literally, the 'forbidden place'), an austere slender building guarded by nine ornamental gates beyond which the Son of Heaven dwelt. He visited Gion, the entertainment quarter, where, in company with some Japanese gentlemen, he was privileged to see some of the city's most illustrious geisha – artists 'celebrated for their song and for the willow-like beauty of their thighs' – an expression, Mitford carefully adds, which implies 'no femoral revelations', but simply means gracefulness. 'In the middle of the feast,' he continues, 'the landlady, black-toothed and shaven-browed, came in armed with a murderous-looking chopper in one hand and in the other a small stand upon which was placed a bean-curd cake, the dish for which the house was famous. The cutting-up of the beancurd cake was a science and a ceremony, always taking place in the presence of guests. With a great assumption of dignity the old lady lifted her chopper and, bringing it with a crack upon the wooden stand, from the re-bound of the blow gave a dozen or so little raps that sounded almost like the roll of a drum, with which, as quick as thought, she had sliced the cake into as many little parts of almost mathematically equal size, which were carried off to be roasted on slender bamboo skewers. It was really a very pretty trick and received a loud tribute of applause, which the dear lady accepted with all the consciousness of merit of a prima donna after the execution of a brilliant *cavatina*.' Mitford dutifully swallowed his skewerful of roasted beancurd when it arrived, but confesses that he enjoyed the preliminaries of the cake's arrival better than its consumption.

Later that same month, the inner sanctuaries and seclusions of the Sacred City were invaded by the arrival of more barbarians – Sir Harry Parkes and several other Foreign Representatives who came to pay their respects to Japan's new ruler, the fifteen-year-old Mikado. The British Minister and his staff were housed in the magnificent temple of Chi-on-in which rested in the shadow of the eastern hills. Inside the temple's chaste halls hung precious silken scrolls, from the open screens one looked along wide avenues starred with cherry-blossom, above, the august bronze bell sent its rhythmical waves of sound rolling over the city.

At one o'clock on 23 March, Sir Harry set off from this lovely residence to meet, at long last, the Mikado himself. First rode the Legation's mounted escort, their long lances glinting in the spring sun, then came Sir Harry, very straight and firm in his gold-embroidered ambassadorial coat, then an infantry guard of the IXth 'red' Regiment with whom rode Dr Willis and Satow. Mitford, whose mare had gone lame the day before, reluctantly squatted in a *norimon*, and behind him came a troop of Japanese soldiers on foot.

As the procession meandered round the corner of Shimbashi Street – renowned for its *saké* shops and brothels – it was suddenly attacked by two armed men who sprang from cover, lunging and slashing at every foreigner in sight with a complete disregard of their own safety. In the narrow street with its overhanging eaves the high bright lances of the escort were useless. One of the desperadoes was felled by the two Japanese officials riding near Parkes; the other, 'crouching like a tiger',

Mitford wrote, swathed through the troops 'brandishing his sword like lightning'. Mitford, who had jumped like a jack-in-the-box from his vulnerable *norimon*, chased the assassin – 'a repulsive object covered with mud and clotted with gore so that his features were hardly human' – as he tried to escape over a wall. Several of the officers dragged him down and disarmed him before he had time to grant himself the boon of suicide.

Considering that there were but two attackers, the amount of havoc they caused was astounding: nine of the escort, one man of the IXth, a Japanese official, Sir Harry's groom and four horses were all wounded. The audience with the Mikado was, of course, immediately abandoned and the wounded carried back to the temple which was, Mitford remarked, 'turned into a hospital. Our wounded men, bleeding as if their life must ebb out, lay patiently on the verandah waiting their turn for the assistance of the surgeons... Everything one touched was sickening, wet and red. It was a nightmare.'

After doing what they could to help, Mitford and Satow interviewed the prisoner, a cowed and truculent priest who belonged to the Jo-i or anti-foreign party, a sect which was particularly active in Kyoto and whose members were fired by a fanaticism which was more religious than political. Founding father of the Jo-i was an eighteenth-century priest who taught that, while the children of Japan were offspring of the gods, the rest of the world was the issue of cats and dogs – an extremity of insularity that, perhaps, even the British never equalled. Though, in his last hours, the prisoner admitted that he had greatly underestimated the humanity of the westerners, such admission did not save his life, nor would he have wished it to. Three days after his wild attack he was, on the Imperial order, executed as a common felon; on the same day Sir Harry and his depleted procession again set out to see the Emperor.

This time all went off without a hitch. The British were guarded by two powerful *daimyo* whose hundred-strong retinue wore chain armour, fierce vizors and carried tasselled spears. Inside a spacious ante-room, Parkes, Satow and Mitford ate sponge-cakes and made small talk with some of the Emperor's minions, who were garbed in the ceremonial court dress: high lacquer hats which resembled a loaf of black bread tied on the head, wide hanging coats of dark silk, from the folds of which sheathed swords protruded tail-like, the baggy, clownish trousers and 'strangest part to our eyes', Mitford thought, 'huge black lacquer sabots worn in crossing the courtyards, but, of course, doffed on entering a room, so constructed that the wearer had to shuffle along in the most uncertain fashion, the very parody of walking'.

It was unhappily typical of the rigidity of royal prerogative at the time that only Sir Harry and Algernon Mitford were allowed to see the Mikado; poor Satow, who had done at least as much as they to promote the audience, had not been presented to Queen Victoria and therefore was not considered suitable company for a foreign potentate either. After an interminable half-hour, the two westerners were conducted to the Presence Chamber, a long, austere room in the centre of which rose a canopy of pure white silk supported by slim black pillars, the drapery gathered loosely aside with vivid red tassels. On either side of the canopy, stretching in a treble row to the far end of the hall stood the great princes of the Empire and their retainers, the men of Choshiu, Satsuma and Tosa – names that had been by-words of terror for foreigners during the last ten years. All were resplendent in their shining crested robes; all as utterly silent, as utterly immobile, as utterly expressionless as only rows of oriental gentlemen can be.

The Mikado was seated under the canopy; on either side of him stood a carved lion, one black, the other gilt, in front of him two Princes of the Blood knelt on a floor of shimmering green cloth. The Mikado rose as the foreigners entered, a supple young man wearing a white brocade coat and crimson trousers that trailed behind him on the dais floor. His eyebrows were shaved off and painted in a high arch on his forehead; his cheeks were rouged; his lips painted gold and red; his teeth shone black. There was a moment of awed stillness, then the Mikado delivered his speech – a short and ordinary enough little peroration on paper, but, in its way, remarkable and momentous. As Mitford afterwards put it, 'We were standing in the presence of a sovereign whose ancestors for centuries had been to their people demi-gods – to foreigners almost a myth. The sanctity of their seclusion had been inviolate, they had held no intercourse with a world of which they knew nothing. Now, suddenly, the veil of the temple had been rent and the Boy-God, in defence of whose Divinity myriads of his subjects were ready gladly to lay down their lives, had descended from the clouds to take his place among the children of men, and not only that, but he had actually allowed his sacred face to be seen by and had held communion with "The Beasts from Without".'

During the rest of the eventful year of 1868 and through part of 1869, bitter fighting between the two factions waged intermittently. For a while many of the ex-Tokugawa *samurai* remained in Yedo and, while ostensibly agreeing to keep the peace, became increasingly aggressive and obstreperous. During the summer these men formed rebel groups which became known as *shogitai* – a band which makes duty clear. The members of these bands, some of whom were not true *samurai* but merely dispossessed, swashbuckling riff-raff from many clans, soon became a menace to the city. They wore high clogs, ready swords and made a practice of blackmailing innocent citizens, and assaulting any lone soldier of the Imperial forces whom they happened to encounter. The Imperial soldiers were, indeed, easily recognisable because they wore on their left shoulders as a badge a loose piece of silk about six inches long – which earned them the name of *kingire*, literally 'shreds of brocade'. In June, things came to a head between the *shogitai* and the *kingire* when the former virtually seized the famous park and monastery at Ueno, on the outskirts of Yedo, from which commanding position they sneaked out at night to attack and plunder.

On 4 July at eight in the morning the Imperialist forces attacked the rebel stronghold. The battle of Ueno was hot, sharp and quick. The venerable monastery and its surrounding temples were razed to the ground; sparks, flying over the trees of the park, set fire to the sun-baked dwellings of the city for a mile around; hundreds of bodies riddled with the bullets from guns which both sides had learned only too well how to use, splattered the stony dust and the banks of the park-moat by evening. But by evening it was all over. The rebel chief fled to Nikko, his troops in disarray, and the wounded of both sides were carried to Yokohama to be tended by the skilled and over-worked foreign doctors.

After their victory, the *kingire* earned the respect of the Yedo citizens as they continued to press northwards in pursuit of the remaining rebels. The pattern of the war became increasingly clear and inevitable; as the historian, W. E. Griffis wrote, 'Victory everywhere perched upon the Mikado's brocade banner.' Yedo became a kind of garrison town with contingents of men constantly arriving from the southern provinces, billeting in the temples, buying sacks of rice and dried fish, collecting ammunition and then proceeding by foot or ship to the treacherous passes and rocky strongholds of the north, where every stony foot of ground was fought over and every strategic collection of peasants' huts became a fortress to be defended, assaulted and bloodily captured.

At the end of October there was another grim battle for the castle of Wakamatsu, headquarters of the Aidzu clan. The castle, lofty, remote among the autumn-stained mountains, withstood siege for seven days, at the end of which the two Aidzu princes, in robes of ceremony with their heads shaven and preceded by a retainer carrying a large banner inscribed with the dread word 'surrender', came slowly through the massive gates and gave themselves up to the besiegers. The Tokugawa leader, Otori Keisuke, however, whose name, wrote John Black, 'was looked upon as the equivalent of a host', escaped farther north to Sendai, where he joined the remnants of the rebel fleet. This fleet, oddly enough, included a battered, rusty and unpainted yacht, now called the *Banriyo*, the very vessel that, ten years before, had sailed proudly into Yedo Bay as the Queen of England's gift to the Shogun, presented by Lord Elgin himself. Her Majesty would not have been amused had she known that her bright offering was now being used as a weapon in the last desperate battles against the crowned Emperor of Japan. These 'pirate ships', as Satow called them, were still commanded by a few French officers who had thrown in their lot with the Tokugawa cause during the earlier skirmishes in the south – and very embarrassing it was too for the French Representative in Yedo to explain what his country-men were doing leading troops against a sovereign with whom France had recently established friendly diplomatic relations!

With the sort of imaginative, daring verve that one might expect from a Franco-Japanese alliance, the rebels next staged a landing at Hakodate in the hopes of capturing the whole island of Yezo and making it a Tokugawa colony. The foreign residents there were in a state of panic; as the British Consul put it, 'As the enemy approach we shall retire towards the hill, if he comes nearer, we shall go up the hill, and should it come to the last extremity we shall have no resource but to put our trust in an over-ruling Power.' The Consul's worst fears were realised insomuch as the rebels did indeed capture Hakodate and appointed their own Civil Governor, who gained an uneasy mastery over the port and the surrounding countryside. The rebel leaders then sent a message to the new Imperial Government in Yedo which explained their motives: 'Men who have the hearts of *samurai* cannot turn into farmers or merchants, so that it appeared that there was nothing for us but to starve. But, considering the uncultivated condition of the island of Yezo, we thought it better to remove thither, that, even under the endurance of every hardship, we might level steep mountains, cultivate the desert, and employ hitherto useless people in useful work and thus requite one millionth part of your benevolence. Accordingly, we formerly petitioned you with tears in our eyes that we might obtain such a grant; but, failing, it seemed that the three hundred thousand of our clansmen must surely starve. For this reason we sailed from Shinagawa Bay in the tenth month of last year and we have arrived here in order to emulate each other in the cultivation of the region; and to be the guard of the northern gate.'

This affecting plea was received with anger and some scepticism by the Mikado's counsellors, who did not wholly believe in the blossoming agrarian ambitions of the dispossessed clansmen; it also alarmed the Foreign Representatives, who wondered how their compatriots in the north had fared. A fortnight later, three British ships sailed up to survey the position and aboard one of them was Sir Harry's junior secretary, Francis Adams. He found that the foreign residents were safe – they had not been forced to resort to their last hill – but that Hakodate itself was in a state of some disorder, most of the shops shut, public buildings closed and streets teeming with rebel soldiers. Many of them, Adams wrote, 'were dressed out in baggy trousers with hair cut and combed after the European fashion; a number, said to be from Sendai, were clad in cherry-coloured trousers, others again had retained their Japanese dress or swaggered about covered from head to foot in red and green blankets'. Motley as the rebels were, they were unanimous on one point: it was no joy fighting for a deposed Shogun when they were never paid, there were no provisions for them and they were faced with the prospect of a freezing northern winter of fighting in the mountains.

There was not, indeed, much joy for either side during that last fierce winter of the war – nor for any unlucky foreigner who had the misfortune to be involved in it. Most westerners, wisely, kept clear of the conflict, especially now that it was as far away as Yezo. One of the few Englishmen, other than Francis Adams, to see something of the whole weary business was Doctor Willis of the British Legation, who, at Sir Harry's request, went north to give medical assistance to the Mikado's forces.

He travelled for about two months, during which he covered more than six hundred miles of mountain terrain, either on foot or – his huge frame distorted, joggled, cramped almost beyond endurance – stuffed inside an abominably small *noriman*. It was a harsh, lead-grey, desolate journey. Wintry winds surged continually over the empty landscape, bringing with them, for miles inland, booming echoes of breakers that thudded on the rocks of the wreck-strewn coastline. There were few beasts, except bears; few birds, except screeching gulls; few people, except poor peasants made poorer by their country's useless strife. The mountains themselves, piled black and high as far as the rheumy eye could see, possessed, wrote Willis, 'a sort of dreary grandeur' – an unremitting expanse of icy stone and scrubby thorn-bush which, on many a frigid night, would be blotted out under a new cover of blowing, hail-sharpened snow. There was no real respite: 'After a long day's work,' Willis wrote, 'the only refuge would be a house open to the blasts of the wind; the only comfort, rations of rice and stale fish, which we ate all huddling round the imperfect warmth of a charcoal brazier.'

And the day's work would, undoubtedly, have been gruesome – an almost single-handed fight to save the lives of some of the blood-splattered, bone-splintered soldiers who lay in quiet heaps on the filthy wet floors of village temples and farmhouses, where they had been left to recover or die. 'I attended six hundred wounded', Willis recorded, 'and gave directions for the treatment of a thousand others.' He performed thirty-eight amputations, 'varying in magnitude from removal of a finger to amputation of the thigh at the hip-joint'. Of these, Willis adds succinctly, 'about half recovered'.

The British doctor reached Wakamatsu some time after the siege had ended and found that about four-fifths of the town had been completely sacked by the Mikado's army. Skeletal sections of bullet-pitted walls, their plaster crumbled away, their wood supports fire-blackened, were the only indications of the former proud dimensions of the famous Aidzu castle.

Troops of soldiers were still quartered in the town; those of the Imperialist side had commandeered the temples, the scarce rations and sported three-hundred-year-old helmets taken from the Aidzu armoury; those of the defeated rebel clans were immured in small airless huts on the town's peripheries where they existed on a diet of cold rice or died in a state which even the hardened Willis termed 'indescribable filth and wretchedness'.

Grimly the doctor and his few assistants did what they could and Willis made several complaints to the Mikado's officers in an effort to get the conditions of the defeated men improved. At last, when Willis felt his own strength finally ebbing – and after that of most of his assistants had completely ebbed – he ordered a retreat, and made the infinitely long, icy journey back to Yedo. In due course, the good doctor was commended by the Earl of Clarendon for his endeavours and was presented by the Mikado with seven rolls of brocade – not, perhaps, an over-generous reward for services performed!

Considering their tenuous position and their low morale, it was strange that the rebels were not completely crushed earlier. It was not, however, until April 1869 that the armed Imperial Fleet sailed up to Hakodate and, within a few months, the last Tokugawa chieftain had sheathed his proud war-sword and surrendered to the inevitable. As a penance the rebel army, its *samurai* leaders working as navvies, were forced to construct a raised granite terrace and a noble shrine which was dedicated to the dead of the Imperial Army. But after this humiliation nearly all the ex-Shogun's men were freed, for the Mikado's counsellors understood that the best way of healing the wounds of civil war was to be clement in victory.

In any case, the Emperor could afford clemency, because he had thoroughly consolidated an authoritative leadership over the rest of the land long before the final rebel surrender in the north. In November 1868 it was announced that the new ruler of the Empire was coming to Yedo and soon after it was decided that the Imperial Court, which had, for centuries, been as fixed as a jewel in Kyoto, should remove itself to the erst-while centre of Tokugawa power. Yedo stirred into a rapture of activity: new bridges were built, streets re-paved, ward-gates given a lick of paint and, above all, the city received its brand new name – Tokyo, the Eastern Capital – within whose boundaries the Son of Heaven himself would henceforward dwell during his Meiji Era of 'The Enlightened Government or Brilliant Rule'.

On 26 November, Satow, Mitford and Charles Wirgman were three among several foreigners who watched the Emperor arrive in his new capital. It was, perhaps, one of the last great Japanese processions. After the escort came a black-lacquered palanquin about six feet square and with a domed roof. 'On the summit', wrote a spectator, 'is a splendid image, apparently of gold, of the *Ho-o* or phoenix, a fabulous bird with head and body of a peacock and spreading plume-like tail of the magnificent copper pheasant of Japan turned up over its head. From the four corners depend red silk ropes two inches thick, each held by three men. These and the bearers of the car, which is carried high upon their shoulders and on a frame which raises its base some six feet from the ground, were all dressed in bright yellow silk and wore a curious circular ornament of feathers at each ear like two outspread fan frames placed together. There were fully sixty of them immediately surrounding the Phoenix Car and the effect of the group with the brilliant sun lighting up the sheen of the silk and the glitter of the lacquer was very gorgeous and indescribably strange, comparable to nothing ever seen in any other part of the world.'

Already, however, the exotic pageantry of this oriental court was marred by the appearance of the troops who straggled behind the palanquin and who were, according to Satow, 'horribly untidy and with unkempt hair and clothing vilely imitated from the West'. And, by their very imitativeness, they did, of course, lay themselves open to the kind of scornful comment from westerners which was to become so damagingly widespread during the next forty years. As one Yokohama journalist reported the occasion in the local rag, 'The Japanese soldiers as compared with ours look insignificant, weak, mean and paltry. It is certain that the British Grenadier regards them with ineffable contempt; and it is probable that they are conscious of their inferiority.'

VII

And indeed the Japanese were suddenly very conscious, if not of an inferiority complex, certainly of a profound difference between their cloistered past and the turbulent dynamic past of the West, between their rigid, ordered social structure of the present and the flexible, liberated society of the West. The future, the Japanese had already decided, was to be another story.

And so, on 1 January 1869, Tokyo was opened for foreign trade and residence – five years later than the original agreement made with Townsend Harris. A few days after the opening all the foreign Representatives, with their various staffs and escorts trooping behind them, were granted audiences with the Mikado and entertained at a banquet by the Imperial Ministers. And the Imperial Ministers toasted the Queen of England and the King of Prussia and the Presidents of France and America and the Foreign Ministers all toasted the Son of Heaven.

From the Eastern Capital proclamations were issued which, in a few sentences, broke the patterns of centuries. The Mikado not only showed his Imperial Presence to the populace, he went aboard a Japanese man-of-war and inspected its crew; the nobles were not only free to live where they wished with their families, but the custom of clearing the road and ordering the people to bow down when they passed was abolished overnight; Princes who, but a year before, might have ordered the cutting down of any foreigner who dared to cross the path of their retinue, now visited Yokohama as the private guests of rich western merchants and thoroughly enjoyed bowling round Mississippi Bay with their hosts in a natty open carriage. One never knew what to expect in such a suddenly fluid society – as Satow remarked, when he saw one night the ex-governor of Yokohama himself riding along in a 'wretched cheap hackney *kago* without a single retainer'.

Not only was authority stripped from some, others gave it up voluntarily. A few months after the Mikado's entry into Tokyo, many of his loyal princes issued 'The Memorial of the *Daimyo* of the West' in which they surrendered their territories and their feudal rights to the Emperor. As they put it, 'Heaven and Earth [that is, Japan] are the Emperor's; there is no man who is not his retainer; this constitutes the Great Body. By the conferring of rank and property the Emperor governs his people: it is his to give and his to take away; of our own selves we cannot hold a foot of this land: of our own selves we cannot take a single man: this constitutes the Great Strength.' And, obviously, the Emperor would need all this proffered strength, for the *daimyo* go on to suggest 'that imperial orders be issued for altering and remodelling the territories of the various clans. Let the civil and penal codes, the military laws down to the rules for uniform and the construction of engines of war all proceed from the Emperor; let all the affairs of the Empire, great and small, be referred to him.' A formidable burden indeed for a young sheltered boy of sixteen, even if he was one day to grow into the great Emperor Meiji.

But perhaps the thorniest and most pressing question of all for the Emperor and his advisers to tackle during that hectic year of 1869 was how to treat the ever-increasing number of official foreign visitors to the court. Austrian barons, American admirals, Russian envoys all wanted to come and be presented to this secret unknown Mikado who had so suddenly revealed his presence to the world. And the rules that had governed behaviour towards the Son of Heaven for centuries had, now, to be drastically revised and modified. Should the Imperial Majesty actually be permitted to stand level on the same piece of ground and at close proximity to a barbarian, as if they two were equal? If the barbarian were not to come crawling in on his hands and knees, forehead to the floor, at least he should bow – and how many times and how profoundly should he do this? And was a barbarian to be allowed to actually drive in a carriage upon the sacred grounds of the Imperial Palace? And should the Emperor be expected to answer questions from the foreigner's lips, would he, even, be called upon to – chat?

Answers to these and other questions relating to the whole nation's new approach to foreigners were suggested in a sort of government handbook of civic duty which appeared that July and was entitled 'Seventeen Subjects of Inquiry as to the Means of Washing Away the Shame of our Country in regard to Foreign Relations'. And a fine chance to put all these cleansing processes into practice came just two months later, when it was announced that His Royal Highness, the Duke of Edinburgh, son of Queen Victoria, was coming to Japan on an official visit. The announcement stirred foreigners and Japanese alike into a fever of activity. Not even the new western edifices, apparently, were quite immaculate enough for the royal presence. And Sir Harry – writing to his wife who had returned to England because of poor health – complained that every room of the Legation 'was in the hands of paperers, painters, plasterers or carpenters. The mess is so great that it appals me from its gravity. I suppose it will come straight, but certainly not if the Duke comes in a moment before his time.' The Japanese in their turn, pleased with their new world-status, gave their innate sense of courtesy and hospitality full rein. The *Programme for the Reception of H.R.H. the Duke of Edinburgh* suggested that, even before he left England, prayers should be offered up for his safe voyage, that, on his arrival in Yokohama, 'the roads will be cleaned and repaired and prayers for his safe journey would then be offered to the god of the road' and that, when H.R.H. reaches the gate of his Tokyo residence, 'the ceremony called *Nuja* will be performed,' that is, 'the sweeping away of all evil influences with a sort of flapper attached to a hempen tassel'.

Eventually the Duke and his retinue were deposited, safely and virtuously, in the *Yen-Rio-kan* (place set aside for the reception of foreigners of distinction) and the Duke began the royal process of setting his seal of approval upon both foreign settlers and Japanese rulers. For the foreigners there were sought-after audiences, extra regattas and races and a Legation Ball for the select few, which Sir Harry describes to his wife with unaccustomed weariness: 'I faced the Prince with Mrs Norman, the second quadrille he danced with Madame Outrey and I with Lady Hornby. He only danced one waltz and that with Mrs Marshall, to the envy of many other ladies. He was unwell and left the room early. Mrs Norman made me dance her usual gallop and I had a turn with Mrs Berger also. So I think I danced enough. I omitted the Lancers with Mrs Walsh.' Clearly, Sir Harry's envy was reserved for the Duke, who was able to escape so early without fear of recrimination.

Most important in the Duke's programme, of course, were the meetings with the Emperor, the first of which took place in the quietly magnificent waterfall pavilion. While the suites escorting both dignitaries remained standing, the two men sat facing each other and the Emperor said how pleased he was to see the Duke and the Duke said how pleased he was to be there and how gratified Her Majesty would be to hear that Japan was now peaceful again, and would the Emperor accept a little trinket of a diamond-studded snuff-box from Her Majesty and the Emperor graciously consented – and that was the nearest the Mikado of Japan had come to a chat for many a century. As a final proof of the open-minded flexibility of the new order, the Duke carried away with him to England the Imperial Son of Heaven's very own autograph, an item which, heretofore, had been stored as a relic in the secret inner recesses of the holiest of temples.

Nothing was so sacred any more, nothing so mysterious or

impregnable. The spacious, dignified *yashiki* (nobles' residences) of Yedo which had always been concealed from the popular gaze by sturdy, guarded walls, were taken over by the government and became administrative offices for a new city called Tokyo. The nobles themselves, who were described in a propaganda pamphlet published that year as persons 'born and nurtured in the seclusion of the women's apartments, who have been cherished as tenderly as if they were delicate ornaments of jewels or pearls, who, even when they have grown up to man's estate, still exhibit all the traits of childhood', whose bodies, 'clad in gorgeous apparel, have felt not the winter's blast and know not that men pine of starvation and cold' – these rather ill-equipped men, feeling the cold for the first time, either loafed their lives away on small pensions or they actually began to work. The most active and intelligent of them became members of the first Japanese Parliament, which started off in a chaos of two hundred and seventy-six members, one for every clan. Others of them, with their retainers, became farmers, some, the most venturesome, actually became merchants and dabbled in the hitherto unspeakable business of buying and selling.

And these new men – the *daimyo* who sold cloth, the *samurai* who ploughed the fields, the lacquerers who painted twenty boxes a day instead of one in two months – were joined by the new men from the West. No longer was the foreign community made up almost exclusively of merchants, diplomats, soldiers and a sprinkling of missionaries; now was the chance for the technicians to come and make their fortunes. There was Mr Brunt from London who set about improving the harbours and laying water supplies; Mr Gilbert, the telegraph engineer from Liverpool; representatives from the firm of D. & T. Stevenson, Engineers to the Commissioners of Northern Lights, Edinburgh, who superintended the construction of lighthouses and lightships in Osaka and Tokyo bays, and a Mr Horatio Nelson Lay who tried to convince the Japanese that he was armed with a sufficient loan from the British Government to build a railway line from Yokohama to the new Eastern Capital. As it turned out, Mr Lay did not have so much credit as he said he had and he was quickly removed from the scene. But nothing could stop the railway. By the end of 1869 the iron lines were beginning to creep the whole way from Yokohama to Tokyo and above them soared the thinner, equally wonderful lines of the first telegraph. The miracles were now being made for the Japanese which, only fifteen years before, had been unknown magic controlled by Commodore Perry and his fellow barbarians.

Barbarians were they? Oh dear no; that was a very old-fashioned, insular and unsophisticated way of putting it. In a dispatch which reached the Foreign Secretary, Lord Clarendon, from Tokyo late in 1869, Sir Harry Parkes had noted, 'I lately took an opportunity to point out to the Prime Minister that I had noticed that members of the new Japanese Parliament made occasional use in their debates of the offensive word "barbarian" in allusion to foreigners, and I requested that this discourtesy might be discontinued by the Government. The Prime Minister assured me without hesitation that he had not noticed this practice until I had mentioned it, and that he would take prompt measures to ensure its discontinuance.'

Bibliography

Adams, F. O., *A History of Japan* (London, 1874)

Alcock, Sir Rutherford, *The Capital of the Tycoon* (London, 1863)

Barrows, E. M., *The Great Commodore* (Indianapolis, New York, 1935)

Batchelor, Rev. John, *The Ainu of Japan* (London, 1892)

Beasley, W. G., *Great Britain and the Opening of Japan* (London, 1951)

Black, John R., *Young Japan* (London: printed in Yokohama, 1880)

Blacker, Carmen, *The Japanese Enlightenment* (London, 1964)

Fortune, Robert, *Yedo and Peking* (London, 1863)

Griffis, W. E., *The Mikado's Empire* (New York, 1876)

Harris, Townsend, *The Complete Journal of Townsend Harris*, ed. M. Cosenza for the Japan Society of America (New York, 1930)

Hawks, F. L., *Narrative of the Expedition of an American Squadron to the China Seas and Japan* (U.S. House Executive Document. 33rd Congress, 2nd Session, Vol. 12. Washington, 1856)

Henderson, P. P., *The Life of Laurence Oliphant* (London, 1956)

Heusken, Henry, *Japan Journal*, trans. and ed. by J. Van der Corput and R. A. Wilson (New York, 1965)

Hodgson, C. P., *A Residence at Nagasaki and Hakodate in 1859–1860* (London, 1861)

Jephson, R. and Elmhirst, E., *Our Life in Japan* (London, 1869)

Mitchie, A., *The Englishman in China* (London, 1900)

Mitford, A. B. (Lord Redesdale), *Memories* (London, 1915)

Moss, Michael, *Seizure by the Japanese of Mr Moss and his Treatment by the Consul-General* (London, 1863)

Murdoch, J., *A History of Japan*. Revised and Edited Edition for the Asiatic Society of Japan (Yokohama, 1910)

Oliphant, L., *Narrative of Lord Elgin's Mission to China and Japan in 1857, 58, 59* (Edinburgh, 1859)

—— *Episodes in a Life of Adventure* (Edinburgh, 1887)

Preble, Lt. G. H., *The Opening of Japan*, ed. B. Szczesniak (New York, 1962)

Satow, Sir E. M., *A Diplomat in Japan* (London, 1921)

Smith, G., *Ten Weeks in Japan* (1861)

Tamba, Tsuneo, *Yokohama Ukiyoe (Reflections of the Cultures of Yokohama in the days of the Port Opening)* (Tokyo, 1962)

Weppner, M., *The Northern Star and the Southern Cross* (London, 1875)

Williams, H. S., *Tales of the Foreign Settlements in Japan* (Tokyo, 1958)

The Japan Herald (1861–1862)

The Nagasaki Shipping Register (1862–1870)

Index

FOR THE BEST IN PAPERBACKS, LOOK FOR THE 🐧

In every corner of the world, on every subject under the sun, Penguin represents quality and variety – the very best in publishing today.

For complete information about books available from Penguin – including Pelicans, Puffins, Peregrines and Penguin Classics – and how to order them, write to us at the appropriate address below. Please note that for copyright reasons the selection of books varies from country to country.

In the United Kingdom: For a complete list of books available from Penguin in the U.K., please write to *Dept E.P., Penguin Books Ltd, Harmondsworth, Middlesex, UB7 0DA*

In the United States: For a complete list of books available from Penguin in the U.S., please write to *Dept BA, Penguin, 299 Murray Hill Parkway, East Rutherford, New Jersey 07073*

In Canada: For a complete list of books available from Penguin in Canada, please write to *Penguin Books Canada Ltd, 2801 John Street, Markham, Ontario L3R 1B4*

In Australia: For a complete list of books available from Penguin in Australia, please write to the *Marketing Department, Penguin Books Australia Ltd, P.O. Box 257, Ringwood, Victoria 3134*

In New Zealand: For a complete list of books available from Penguin in New Zealand, please write to the *Marketing Department, Penguin Books (NZ) Ltd, Private Bag, Takapuna, Auckland 9*

In India: For a complete list of books available from Penguin, please write to *Penguin Overseas Ltd, 706 Eros Apartments, 56 Nehru Place, New Delhi, 110019*

In Holland: For a complete list of books available from Penguin in Holland, please write to *Penguin Books Nederland B.V., Postbus 195, NL–1380AD Weesp, Netherlands*

In Germany: For a complete list of books available from Penguin, please write to *Penguin Books Ltd, Friedrichstrasse 10 – 12, D–6000 Frankfurt Main 1, Federal Republic of Germany*

In Spain: For a complete list of books available from Penguin in Spain, please write to *Longman Penguin España, Calle San Nicolas 15, E–28013 Madrid, Spain*

FOR THE BEST IN PAPERBACKS, LOOK FOR THE 🐧

A CHOICE OF PENGUINS

An African Winter Preston King With an Introduction by Richard Leakey

This powerful and impassioned book offers a unique assessment of the interlocking factors which result in the famines of Africa and argues that there *are* solutions and we *can* learn from the mistakes of the past.

Jean Rhys: Letters 1931–66
Edited by Francis Wyndham and Diana Melly

'Eloquent and invaluable . . . her life emerges, and with it a portrait of an unexpectedly indomitable figure' – Marina Warner in the *Sunday Times*

Among the Russians Colin Thubron

One man's solitary journey by car across Russia provides an enthralling and revealing account of the habits and idiosyncrasies of a fascinating people. 'He sees things with the freshness of an innocent and the erudition of a scholar' – *Daily Telegraph*

The Amateur Naturalist Gerald Durrell with Lee Durrell

'Delight . . . on every page . . . packed with authoritative writing, learning without pomposity . . . it represents a real bargain' – *The Times Educational Supplement*. 'What treats are in store for the average British household' – *Books and Bookmen*

The Democratic Economy Geoff Hodgson

Today, the political arena is divided as seldom before. In this exciting and original study, Geoff Hodgson carefully examines the claims of the rival doctrines and exposes some crucial flaws.

They Went to Portugal Rose Macaulay

An exotic and entertaining account of travellers to Portugal from the pirate-crusaders, through poets, aesthetes and ambassadors, to the new wave of romantic travellers. A wonderful mixture of literature, history and adventure, by one of our most stylish and seductive writers.

A CHOICE OF PENGUINS

Adieux: A Farewell to Sartre Simone de Beauvoir

A devastatingly frank account of the last years of Sartre's life, and his death, by the woman who for more than half a century shared that life. 'A true labour of love, there is about it a touching sadness, a mingling of the personal with the impersonal and timeless which Sartre himself would surely have liked and understood' – *Listener*

Business Wargames James Barrie

How did BMW overtake Mercedes? Why did Laker crash? How did McDonalds grab the hamburger market? Drawing on the tragic mistakes and brilliant victories of military history, this remarkable book draws countless fascinating parallels with case histories from industry world-wide.

Metamagical Themas Douglas R. Hofstadter

This astonishing sequel to the best-selling, Pulitzer Prize-winning *Gödel, Escher, Bach* swarms with 'extraordinary ideas, brilliant fables, deep philosophical questions and Carrollian word play' – Martin Gardner

Into the Heart of Borneo Redmond O'Hanlon

'Perceptive, hilarious and at the same time a serious natural-history journey into one of the last remaining unspoilt paradises' – *New Statesman*. 'Consistently exciting, often funny and erudite without ever being overwhelming' – *Punch*

A Better Class of Person John Osborne

The playwright's autobiography, 1929–56. 'Splendidly enjoyable' – John Mortimer. 'One of the best, richest and most bitterly truthful autobiographies that I have ever read' – Melvyn Bragg

The Secrets of a Woman's Heart Hilary Spurling

The later life of Ivy Compton-Burnett, 1920–69. 'A biographical triumph . . . elegant, stylish, witty, tender, immensely acute – dazzles and exhilarates . . . a great achievement' – Kay Dick in the *Literary Review*. 'One of the most important literary biographies of the century' – *New Statesman*

A SELECTION OF PEREGRINES

The Uses of Enchantment Bruno Bettelheim

Dr Bettelheim has written this book to help adults become aware of the irreplaceable importance of fairy tales. Taking the best-known stories in turn, he demonstrates how they work, consciously or unconsciously, to support and free the child.

The Rise of the Novel Ian Watt

Studies in Defoe, Richardson and Fielding. 'This book is altogether satisfying within the wide framework of its scheme . . . Every page of Dr Watt's admirably written book repays study, as enlivening and enriching the works the purport of which we are too often inclined to take for granted' – *The Times*

Orientalism Edward W. Said

In *Orientalism*, his acclaimed and now famous challenge to established Western attitudes towards the East, Edward Said has given us one of the most brilliant cultural studies of the decade. 'A stimulating, elegant yet pugnacious essay which is going to set the cat among the pigeons' – *Observer*

The Selected Melanie Klein

This major collection of Melanie Klein's writings, brilliantly edited by Juliet Mitchell, shows how much Melanie Klein has to offer in understanding and treating psychotics, in revising Freud's ideas about female sexuality, and in showing how phantasy operates in everyday life.

The Raw and the Cooked Claude Levi-Strauss

Deliberately, brilliantly and inimitably challenging, *The Raw and the Cooked* is a seminal work of structural anthropology that cuts wide and deep into the mind of mankind. Examining the myths of the South American Indians it demonstrates, with dazzling insight, how these can be reduced to a comprehensible psychological pattern.